BROTHERS

JUSTICE
CORRUPTION
AND THE MICKELBERGS

First published in 2011 by
Fremantle Press
25 Quarry Street, Fremantle, Western Australia 6160
(PO Box 158, North Fremantle, Western Australia 6159)
www.fremantlepress.com.au

Editor Janet Blagg
Designer Allyson Crimp
Printed by Everbest Printing Co Ltd, China

National Library of Australia Cataloguing-in-Publication entry

Buti, Antonio.
Brothers : justice, corruption and the Mickelbergs / Antonio
    Buti.
9781921888472 (pbk.)
Notes: Includes bibliographical references and index.
Subjects: Mickelberg, Brian.
    Mickelberg, Peter.
    Mickelberg, Raymond.
    Swindlers and swindling--Western Australia.
    Judicial error--Western Australia.
    Police corruption--Western Australia.
    Trials (Larceny)--Western Australia.
Dewey Number: 364.16309941

ANTONIO BUTI
BROTHERS
JUSTICE
CORRUPTION
AND THE MICKELBERGS

FREMANTLE PRESS
fine independent publishing

ABOUT THE AUTHOR

Dr Antonio Buti was educated at the University of Western Australia, Australian National University, Oxford University and Yale Law School. He is a member of the Western Australian Parliament and Honorary Senior Fellow at the Law Faculty, University of Western Australia. Dr Buti's biography on Sir Ronald Wilson, *A Matter of Conscience*, won the 2007 Western Australian Premier's Book Award for non-fiction and the Premier's Prize.

BY THE SAME AUTHOR

A. Buti, *Separated: Aboriginal Childhood Separations and Guardianship Law* (Sydney: Sydney Institute of Criminology, Sydney, 2004).

A. Buti, *A Matter of Conscience: Sir Ronald Wilson* (Crawley: University of Western Australia Press, 2007).

Co-authored:

A. Buti and S. Fridman, *Drugs, Sport and the Law* (Mudgeeraba: Scribblers Publishing, 2001).

D. Thorpe, A. Buti, C. Davies, S. Fridman and P. Jonson, *Sports and the Law* (Melbourne: Oxford University Press, 2009).

If the law represents an expression of moral sentiment, then police officers stand as instruments of that morality.

Chief Bob Harrison
Vacaville (California) Police Department
68(8) *FBI Law Enforcement Bulletin*
August 1999

Dedicated to Oxford

CONTENTS

PREFACE

A few years back I was asked by a supporter of the Mickelbergs to write a book about their twenty-five year campaign to have their conviction overturned. The supporter and the brothers, Ray and Peter, were keen for a book to be written. While a tough challenge, I thought it worth writing a book which analytically scrutinised the various legal issues in play and chronicled in detail the Perth Mint swindle and the Mickelbergs' confrontation with the criminal justice system.

The brothers have always maintained that they served time in gaol only because some of the police officers investigating the case had behaved corruptly, fabricating evidence. Ray and Peter Mickelberg wanted to make these officers pay. Their court saga spans twenty-five years; it involves seven unsuccessful appeals before the eighth and final appeal in 2004. Whether they embarked on their journey from a sense of outraged innocence or from a personal need for retribution is for others to decide. But whatever motivated them to engage in it, their long struggle has had a socially valuable outcome.

There are two possible consequences of police corruption in a case like this. First, if the corrupt police get away with it, an innocent person might go to gaol. Second, if a court uncovers behaviour that corrupts the judicial process to the extent that a jury does not have before it all the evidence, or it has before it evidence that police officers have corrupted in their zeal to get the job done, a guilty person might go free. In each instance, the public has been let down and the integrity of the police force has been tarnished.

While the courts have a significant role to play in maintaining the integrity of the justice system, the police must also play their role; they must look within to uncover, remove, and punish corrupt officers. Invocation of mateship is neither warranted nor defensible when corruption rears its ugly head. True esprit de corps results not from sticking by your colleagues come what may, but from expecting and demanding that those who want to share in the proud tradition of the police force behave in a manner that reflects and enshrines the normal, decent standards of the community. This is the moral I draw from the Mickelberg story.

The Mickelberg story is part of a larger narrative about the temptation to take a furtive step outside the moral boundaries for a cause one thinks is noble, or, in some cases, in spite of the fact that it is not. That is why I have included accounts of corporate cowboys who were taking such steps over the period that the Mickelbergs were pursuing their personal cause. There are stories, too, of those who lived in the shadows, but often could not avoid the glare of the media spotlights, never referred to as crooks or criminals but by the titillating euphemism 'well-known identity'. Nor were politicians immune to the opportunities that the rambunctious 80s threw up. The Mickelberg saga was regularly upstaged by disclosures of the deeds of errant politicians, such as Western Australian premiers Ray O'Connor and — later and more spectacularly — Brian Burke.

And then came more bombshells; two revelations of police corruption that preceded by many years the Mickelberg case, and one that emerged at the very time that the Mickelbergs were approaching the end of their long journey. These were three separate instances of wrongful convictions for murder for which three innocent men went to gaol, and each the result of corruption by police officers to whom no noble cause can be attributed.

I have included accounts of these other instances of corruption because they added grist to the Mickelberg mill; over twenty-five years they were able to point to each new revelation as support for their claim that corruption was endemic. And in the process they became adept at enlisting media to make their feeling known to the public.

Their twenty-five year war of attrition against the police force had a dramatic finale. The case was over, the appeal court had quashed their conviction, but, in an impassioned address to the media, the Assistant Commissioner of Police still declared them guilty. Such were the passions of this extraordinary battle. I have recounted the verdict and its consequences in chapter seventeen.

I spent approximately twenty months writing this book, and more than three years doing the research on which the writing is based. I interviewed many people and spoke informally with others, including Ray and Peter Mickelberg. Some of those with whom I spoke would only do so off the record, and thus unfortunately I have not been able to record their views and opinions here. I trawled through court transcripts and documents, legal judgments, legislation, inquiry reports, Hansard speeches and media reports. I have also referred to several books and journal articles dealing with various aspects of rules of evidence, criminal law, police conduct and corruption. Two books by Avon Lovell, *The Mickelberg Stitch* and *Split Image*, were a valuable resource. I do not claim that my chronicle and analysis is the only one possible. But it is my honest and detailed assessment. I can do no more.

A note about courtroom dialogue

In chapters one, two, three and sixteen, I have taken counsel and witness dialogue from the official court transcripts. In presenting the case for the Crown I have attempted, in my reconstruction of the courtroom dialogue, to present the oral evidence in the way the jury would have heard it. You, the reader, can react to the dialogue in your own way, making up your mind as you read whether or not the jury would believe what the witnesses were telling them. I have adopted the same approach with defence counsel rebuttal of the Crown's case. This, I think, allows you better to appreciate the nature of the jury's task in teasing out the truth from the often self-serving evidence of witnesses from either side.

Endnotes

It is unavoidable that, in recounting the court process, many terms common to legal practitioners, but not so well known to those outside the legal system, will appear. Unless they are vital to understanding the unfolding narrative, I have consigned these terms to endnotes. There they are available to you if you wish to know more, but, in the meantime, they do not interfere with the narrative flow of events.

Antonio Buti

ACKNOWLEDGEMENTS

I wish to thank first my dear friend Eric Fisher, without whose help, advice and encouragement over the years, I could not have completed this book. You are a most special individual and I am privileged to have your friendship and counsel. Thanks also to my dear family of Mandy, Alkira, Paris and Tennessee for your continuing love and support. You are all very precious to me, as is our new puppy, Sophie. And to my beautiful mum, Mimma, thanks for your delicious scones, which provided much needed sustenance for the early morning writing sessions.

I spoke to many people in researching this book, some in person, some by phone and some by email. I deeply appreciate the useful and valuable information generously provided by: Carol Adams, David Baxendale, Mike Dean, Jamie Edelman, Alison Fan, Rod Hatcher, Rex Haw, Hal Jackson, Bob Jennings, Bob Kucera, Peter Mickelberg, Ray Mickelberg, Jim McGinty, Graham Pidco, Robert Radley, Harold Tuthill and (the late) Henry Wallwork. Thank you all. Others of you to whom I spoke wish to remain anonymous, and I am respecting your wishes. But that does not lessen my gratitude for your contribution.

To Joe Freeman, thanks for your research efforts, which made the daunting task of researching and writing this book a little bit more manageable. I also thank Bevan Eakins, a cool dude with a fine mind (even if he does support the Pies) and excellent editorial pen — great work and thanks for referring me to Jane Fraser at Fremantle Press. A nicer and more helpful publisher would be difficult to find. Jane, you have made the 'torture' of the publishing process that much more bearable through your sensitivity and understanding. I am deeply grateful to my editor Janet Blagg for her skills and pushing me that bit harder to make this project as good as we could possibly make it. To the whole team at Fremantle Press, thanks for being such a talented and supportive bunch.

To my former employers, Murdoch University and the University of Western Australia, my appreciation for providing the ideal environment in which to undertake this project.

Finally, I sincerely thank a certain person for his outstanding generosity over so many years. I have not named the individual here but his support will never be forgotten by me.

PROLOGUE

Police divers mostly love their job — work that takes them under the temperate waters of the Indian Ocean or the Swan River where, for at least six months of the year, the diving weather is ideal.

But on an otherwise perfect day in 1983, they were not a happy lot, despite the welcoming waters off the coast of Kalbarri. A favoured tourist destination 800 kilometres north of Perth, this was where Raymond and Peter Mickelberg had made a very good living diving for abalone, which was why the police divers were there.

They were frustrated. For months they had painstakingly crawled across the same area of seabed, every centimetre of it, searching for gold. This was not some long-lost treasure trove. This was gold bullion, worth then just in excess of $650,000 (though commonly reported by the press to be worth more than one million dollars), that had been swindled the year before out of the Perth Mint on Hay Street, situated within the spiritual shadow of nearby St Mary's Cathedral.

Perhaps some Mint officials found solace in this architectural symbol of West Australian Catholicism, but divine intervention was not to spare them embarrassment. The Mint, this emblematic fortress of material wealth, had been breached, and not by professional robbers but by a bold team of swindlers armed with nothing more than a few pieces of worthless paper.

Nor had they stolen cash; that would have been embarrassment enough. This lot had stolen gold — a precious metal treated almost with reverence in Perth. Gold was more than just money and power. Gold was at the core of Western Australia's history.

In 1885, the first discovery of gold in the remote Kimberley region of the north brought an early rush of eager diggers. It was a hard life, and rewards were meagre, except for the few who struck it rich. Those that did not simply folded their tents and moved to the next field, their hopes fuelled often by nothing more than embellished stories, told by diggers, of the fortunes others had already made there. However, it was in the goldfields of Coolgardie and Kalgoorlie where, in the last decade of the nineteenth century, the romance of gold blossomed, after three Irish prospectors discovered enough gold to change the course of Western Australia's history. This newfound source of wealth was a watershed for the newly self-governing colony. Gold revenues and related income flowed into the Colonial Treasury and Perth prospered.

Although the fortunes of gold waxed and waned throughout the twentieth century, the precious metal never lost its iconic status; nor did the Perth Mint lose its lustre as the shrine at which fortune hunters worshipped. Little wonder then, that when someone violated the shrine, people reacted with shock.

The public expected the police to act quickly and decisively to bring the culprits to account. What they did not expect were the revelations of police corruption that would result. Nor could anyone have imagined that two highly respected police officers would come to violent and tragic ends because they believed their role was to get the job done, no matter what it took. After all, theirs was a noble cause.

Which brings us back to the police divers and their exhaustive but fruitless expedition off the coast at Kalbarri, where two of the leading protagonists in the story of the Perth Mint swindle used to camp and go diving for that other treasure: abalone. As it turned out, it would be a long time before Ray and Peter Mickelberg would again have an opportunity to dive for that seafood gem, because someone had decided they were going to gaol — with or without evidence.

The Perth Mint swindle is a story of intrigue and 'noble cause' corruption that would wreck the lives and reputations of many who played a part in it.

CHAPTER I
IF THE CROWN PLEASES

On a typically hot February morning in Perth, Chief Crown Prosecutor[1] Ron Davies QC[2] rose to his feet before the Chairman of the District Court,[3] Judge Desmond Heenan, to begin his opening address to the jury.[4]

A criminal trial before a judge and jury follows a set procedure. It begins with the prosecutor outlining to the court the nature of the case it will present. Counsel for the accused then has the opportunity to tell the court how it intends to present its defence to the court. After prosecutor and defence counsel have finished these opening addresses, the prosecutor calls and questions all its witnesses, each of whom the defence is entitled to (but does not have to) cross-examine. The sum of all the evidence that the prosecution adduces from its witnesses is the prosecution evidence-in-chief. When the prosecutor has finished, the court invites the defence to do the same thing with its witnesses. In simple terms, counsel thoughtfully and benignly guide their friendly witnesses through the oral examination process to attempt to present the evidence in the most favourable light. It goes without saying that the cross-examiner does their best to extinguish that light.

'Mr Foreman, ladies and gentlemen, the story you are about to spend certainly the next few days if not weeks on involves a tale of a very clever, but not quite clever enough, planned scheme to obtain gold bullion from the obvious place, the Mint.'

So began the Perth Mint swindle trial on 7 February 1983.

Three men stood accused of the crime. They were brothers Raymond Mickelberg, aged thirty-seven, a former SAS soldier and Vietnam veteran who operated a successful abalone fishing business in Kalbarri, 800 kilometres north of Perth; Brian, thirty-five, a helicopter pilot operating from Perth's second airport, Jandakot; and the baby of the family, twenty-three year old Peter who worked with Ray as an abalone diver.

On 7 December 1982, the three brothers were indicted[5] on eight counts.[6] The first was the general count of conspiracy to defraud the Mint.[7] It was alleged that, between 1 April 1982 and 23 June 1982, Ray, Brian and Peter conspired to defraud the director of the Perth Mint by inducing him to part with a quantity of gold without being paid for it. The other seven offences were said to have been committed to further the conspiracy. The second was the burglary[8] offence committed on 7 April 1982 and the stealing of WA Building Society (WABS) cheque forms from the building of Conti Sheffield Estate Agency Pty Ltd. The third count was arson,[9] committed at the same time, allegedly to cover up the identity of the offenders.

Counts 4 and 5 were charges respectively of burglary and the theft of Perth Building Society (PBS) cheque forms from a Bull Creek real estate agency on 13 May 1982, again with an accompanying offence of arson. Finally, counts 6, 7 and 8 on the indictment alleged that on 22 June 1982 each of the three men falsely claimed to an employee of the director of the Perth Mint that three cheques presented in payment for the bullion were genuine.[10] The two PBS cheques were to the value of $104,492.50 and $298,550 and the WABS cheque was for $249,932.74.

Over ten engrossing days, Davies, a hard-nosed and uncompromising prosecutor, led circumstantial and scientific evidence[11] to present a story that might have come from the pages of a crime novel. Crucial to the Crown's case were alleged admissions and statements made by Ray, Brian and Peter to the police that pointed to their involvement in the swindle. Davies was relying on police evidence regarding these admissions to convince the jury that the three accused were guilty as charged. Davies also asserted that 'there are certainly strong hints of other involvement than three persons.' But, he said, all that would mean is that someone had yet to be caught.

Day after day, the Crown introduced its witnesses[12] — more than a hundred in total. Included in their number were many of the police officers and Criminal Investigation Bureau (CIB) detectives who had been involved in the Mint swindle inquiry. The star witness was head of the inquiry, Detective Sergeant Don Hancock, known as the 'Silver Fox' because of his silver grey hair and cunning.

It was apt that Hancock should head an inquiry into missing gold; he came from three generations of gold prospectors. Born at Boulder City in 1937, Hancock worked in the family goldmine at Grants Patch before joining the police force in 1959 aged twenty-two. He spent some time with the Gold Stealing Detection staff and later rose to the head of the CIB and assistant commissioner. In 1988 he was awarded an Australian Police Medal.

Hancock and his partner in the Mint swindle investigation, Detective Sergeant Tony Lewandowski, were the perfect Crown witnesses. They withstood cross-examinations from three defence lawyers,[13] one for each accused brother. Ron Cannon represented Ray. He had been a brilliant law student at the University of Western Australia in the late 1940s and practised law in Africa and Hong Kong before returning to Perth where he specialised in criminal law. Brian Singleton QC represented young Peter, and Cannon's nephew, the relatively inexperienced Michael Bowden, represented Brian.

But Hancock and Lewandowski were unflappable. Cannon tried to force Hancock to admit that without the police interviews they had little evidence against Ray. And the notes from those interviews, he accused, were concocted 'because you were convinced that Ray Mickelberg was guilty and this was the only way to bring him to justice, by admissions?'[14] Cool as a cucumber, Hancock replied, 'I'm telling you, the interview was not concocted.' Hancock's loyal offsider Lewandowski followed him to the witness box, and equally calmly supported Hancock's evidence.

With their multitude of witnesses, Davies and his assistant, Senior Assistant Crown Counsel John McKechnie, methodically developed the Crown case.

The court heard that in the two years leading up to the swindle, Raymond and Peter made purchases of gold bullion from the Perth Mint, paying for them with building society cheques. In the several months before the swindle, using the false identities of Bob Fryer and Mr Blackwood, Ray and Peter regularly phoned the Mint to buy up to $250,000 of gold when the price dropped below $300 an ounce. Though the identities were false, the cheque accounts did have the necessary funds to pay for the gold.

The Mint made no effort to check the identity of people buying gold or silver. Its usual practice was to take an order over the phone and assign an order number. The purchaser, or someone acting on their behalf, would attend the Mint, quote the order number, and hand over a cheque in exchange for the gold. As far as the Mint was concerned that was the end of the matter. It seems no one gave any thought to the potential money laundering and tax evasion opportunities this practice created.

On 5 March 1982, Peter signed a six-month lease for a residential unit at 112 Rupert Street, Subiaco. He paid the whole rent in advance. For one referee, Peter offered the name Otto Kleiger, which was in fact one of Ray's many aliases.

The Crown alleged the brothers' next step was to obtain blank building society cheques. On Wednesday 7 April 1982, the premises of Conti Sheffield Estate Agency in North Perth, which was an agency of WABS, were broken into and a bundle of blank WABS cheque forms were stolen. The burglars set fire to the building to cover the theft. Called to the scene, the managing director of the agency saw a small burnt-orange car, which he believed to be either a Mazda or a Toyota, slow down, change lanes and pause outside the building. He noticed three men inside. Suspicious, he attempted to note down the car's registration number. He wrote down the letters XAK and noted that two of the digits were the same. Brian Mickelberg owned an orange Porsche, registration number XRK 500.

The mysterious Bob Fryer re-entered the story on 27 or 28 April 1982. By phone, he rented business premises at Suite 3, Barker House, Hay Street, Subiaco, without any prior inspection, paying the rent and the bond by untraceable bank cheque. A courier delivered the key to 'Fryer'. Less than a month later, a man calling himself Frank Harrison rented the nearby Suite 15, also without prior inspection, and had a telephone service connected in that name.

On 13 May 1982, burglars broke into a real estate agency in Bull Creek, a southern suburb of Perth. They stole a bundle of blank

PBS cheques and set fire to the building to cover their traces.

Twelve days later, on Tuesday 25 May 1982, a man calling himself Robert Talbot purchased a 1965 white-coloured Ford Falcon car from a Mr Allen in the outer south-east suburb of Armadale. The Crown alleged Talbot was Peter, dressed in disguise, wearing a wig and dark-rimmed glasses. He gave Mr Allen a slip of paper on which he had printed the words 'Robert Talbot C/o Meekatharra Post Office, Meekatharra' as the address at which he wished to receive the disposal notice.

On Thursday 27 May 1982, PBS issued a cheque for $20, drawn on a savings account which Ray had opened on 10 March 1976 in the name of Peter Gulley. The cheque was payable to C. Wilson, but never presented. Only two transactions had been processed through that account since 1979. The first was a $10 cash withdrawal made on 22 April 1982, and the second was the C. Wilson payment. The Crown case was that the building society cheque, drawn on the account Ray had opened in the name of Peter Gulley and made payable to the mysterious C. Wilson, was to serve as a model when the time came to fraudulently fill in details on the stolen blank PBS cheques.

Wilson's name comes up again. A Colin Wilson operated an account with PBS which, unlike the Gulley account, had been very active over the period March 1982 to June 1982. Withdrawals from it were reasonably proximate in time and amounts to the rentals paid for Suite 3, Barker House. The cheque for $20 withdrawn from the Gulley account had not been deposited into the Wilson account.

On 8 or 9 June 1982, a man using the name Fryer telephoned Peter Duvnjak and engaged him through an employment agency as a temporary driver. He was told to drive a vehicle, fitted with a citizen band (CB) radio, to move geological core samples from Barker House to Jandakot Airport and to other offices in Subiaco.

From 15 June 1982 onwards, security guards from three different firms were hired by phone. They were instructed to collect bank cheques from Suite 3 in Barker House on 22 June and then transport bullion from the Mint to that suite. A young secretary, Jo Armstrong, was also hired, by phone, to be in attendance at the suite.

On 20 June 1982, Duvnjak spoke by phone to a man calling

himself Frank, from Fryer Investments. Duvnjak agreed to use his own car for the work he was to do. His car was fitted with a CB radio. Frank instructed Duvnjak to park his car in Churchill Avenue, a street running parallel to Hay Street in Subiaco. He was told to wait for radio instructions to enter Barker House, pick up mining equipment, transport it to Jandakot Airport and leave it at a designated point.

The Crown alleged that on the morning of the swindle, Peter, in disguise, parked the white Ford Falcon off a laneway near Barker House. He entered Suite 3 before the young secretary Jo Armstrong arrived and he left three fraudulently completed building society cheques there. One of the cheques was a WABS cheque form stolen from Conti Sheffield. The other two were PBS cheque forms stolen from the Bull Creek agency.

The old Falcon, fitted with a CB radio, was parked at the rear of 31–33 Hay Street in a parking bay belonging to the sales manager of City Business Brokers, Mr Henry. He saw a man step out from the driver's seat of the Falcon, open the boot, take out a lightweight white plastic shopping bag and, with a white glove on his right hand, wipe the lock of the boot as he closed it. Henry also observed the man wiping the driver's and passengers' door handles.

His suspicions aroused, Henry telephoned the police. When Constable Buchanan arrived at the scene, the driver had disappeared but the driver's door was unlocked and the driver's window half down.

Some two hours later, Henry returned to the car park with a work colleague, Mr McCracken. The Falcon's engine was running and the driver was bending under the dashboard. McCracken told the man that he shouldn't be parking on private property. The young man told Henry that the car had been difficult to start. (During the trial, McCracken said that the man looked similar to Peter but his hair was shorter.) Henry, the amateur detective, noted the registration number of the Falcon, which matched that of the car sold by Mr Allen.

On the afternoon of 22 June 1982, the hired security guards from Transurety, Armaguard and ASAP headed to the Mint with the cheques and boxes collected from Barker House. The Mint had earlier received three telephone orders to buy large quantities of gold bullion. One purchase was in the name of Blackwood, a second in the name of York and a third in the name of Fryer.

The guards handed over the cheques to the Mint in exchange for $650,000 of gold bullion. In what the police argued was a major mistake by Ray, who they were confident was the mastermind behind the swindle, the cheques used for the Blackwood and York purchases bore the account number of the PBS savings account kept by Ray in the name of Peter Gulley. The details on the cheques and the application for the telephone service in Suite 15 had been written on the one typewriter and the WABS cheque bore Ray's fingerprint. On it, the word 'forty' was spelled 'fourty'.

The hired guards drove out of the iron gates of the Mint and returned to Barker House where Jo Armstrong took delivery of the boxes, unaware of their contents. A security officer from Arpad (a security firm made up of serving and former SAS soldiers) guarded the gold bullion at Barker House. After receiving instructions over the CB radio, allegedly from the white Falcon (which was later found abandoned and burnt), Duvnjak collected the boxes and drove to Jandakot Airport. Duvnjak, who had no idea he was carrying a fortune in gold, believed he was followed to the airport.

What happened to the gold bullion after Duvnjak left it at Jandakot Airport has remained a mystery until this day.

In a hangar near where Duvnjak deposited the boxes, airline Captain Graham Hewitt was working on an old Auster aeroplane. Hewitt told police that some time before the arrival of Duvnjak, two young men in their twenties started their powerful car nearby and sped off towards the main part of the airport.

The next day, Mint executives finally became concerned about the size of the previous day's transactions. When the bank cheques bounced, red-faced Mint executives notified the police. Soon, detectives from the CIB were running in all directions, following up leads.

A few days later, courier Duvnjak appeared on local Perth radio station 6PR with well-known radio personality Howard Sattler, talking about his role as a courier. He had gone to the radio station because he was concerned he wasn't going to be paid for his services. On air, he told Sattler he observed an unidentified man taking photographs of people entering and leaving Barker House during the time the swindle was taking place. Apparently, the police did not follow up this information, and never provided a reason why not.

Their break finally came with the Peter Gulley account. Australia-wide inquiries had revealed Peter Gulley did not exist and the address that the non-existent Peter Gulley had given when opening the account in 1976 was now a vacant block. Detective Sergeant Round checked council and State Energy Commission records, which revealed the last SEC account for the address, 144 Barker Road in Subiaco, was for the period 1976 to 1979 in the name of P. Macjelberg. Further digging turned up a similar name, Meckelberg, who lived at Unit 7, 112 Rupert Street, Subiaco. This was in fact Peter Mickelberg, who had terminated the lease in July 1982. Detective Round next discovered that an R. Mickleberg lived at 1 Leach Street, Marmion. This was Ray's home.

On 9 July 1982, Round and Detective Sergeant Dennis Henley visited Ray's home at Marmion. Ray was not there, he was in Penang, Malaysia, with his family, and Peter was looking after the house. Round asked Peter to ask Ray to telephone the Perth CIB on his return. Meanwhile, the detectives took the opportunity to question Peter.[15] He confirmed that his mother had run a boarding house at the Barker Road address but said he could not otherwise help with the inquiry about the cheques used by Gulley.

The police interviewed Ray twice on his return from Malaysia on 15 July 1982. Round and Detective Sergeant Henry Hooft conducted the first interview at Ray's home in Marmion as police searched the premises. Initially, Ray denied any knowledge of Gulley or that he had operated the PBS account in that name. However, when confronted with the fact that the handwriting on the application forms for the opening of that account had been identified as his, and that it could be proven that he had operated the account since 1976, Ray admitted the account was his. He claimed he had operated it for tax purposes. (At trial, he also admitted operating the Wilson account.) According to Round, Ray said he would make a phone call to see if he could retrieve the passbook.

Round and Hancock conducted the second interview at police headquarters in East Perth. Ray told them he did not have the Gulley passbook. He said it had been in a black clipboard folder which he had lost, most likely at the Karrinyup PBS office. The detectives asked him to explain how two of the cheques used in the Mint swindle had the Peter Gulley account number on them. Ray said someone could have found the passbook and used that number.

Round and Hancock also questioned Ray about some burnt papers police found while searching his Marmion home earlier that day. Ray confirmed he had burnt a number of papers 'in the last day or so.'

During one of the interviews, Ray was asked to write $49.19 in words and he wrote 'fourty', which corresponded to the misspelling on one of the cheques.

At around 3 p.m. on Thursday 15 July 1982, Hooft, Henley and Detective Porter went to Brian Mickelberg's house in Jandakot with a search warrant.[16] While the police were searching the house, Brian telephoned his lawyer, with whom Hooft had also spoken. Brian asked the detectives whether Ray was at police headquarters and when they said yes, he agreed to accompany them.[17]

At police headquarters, Hooft told Brian he was investigating the fraud of the Mint as well as two arsons and breaking and entering offences. Brian said he could not help Hooft with his inquiries, but Hooft continued the interrogation. He asked Brian where he was on the night of 7 April when the Conti real estate office was broken into and set on fire. Brian replied, 'In Port Hedland,' and gave the same answer in relation to his whereabouts on 13 May, the time of the Bull Creek real estate office fire. Hooft then said, 'There were a number of cheques stolen from these premises. Three of the cheques were used to obtain gold from the Mint on 22 June. Where were you on that day?'

Brian replied, 'On 22 June, I would have been in Hong Kong.'

'When did you go to Hong Kong?'

Brian replied, 'I wouldn't have a clue.' Hooft thought the answer strange and said to Brian that surely he would know when he went to Hong Kong and when he returned, as it was recent. Brian replied, 'You're making the inquiries. You probably already know.' Hooft then asked whether Brian had ever made a gold transaction with the Perth Mint. Brian replied, 'No.'

Hancock then had his turn with Brian. When Hancock asked what he knew about Ray using the name Peter Gulley, Brian said, 'Nothing.' He also repeated the answer he gave to Hooft as to his whereabouts on 22 June. 'I have already explained that. I was in Hong Kong.'

Hancock handed Brian a piece of foolscap paper and asked him to write $49.19 in words. Brian correctly wrote 'forty'.

Hancock then asked Brian when he had arrived in Perth from Port Hedland. Brian told him he came down on 9 July 1982. He wasn't actually due until Tuesday but came down early because Ray had telephoned to tell him their father was sick. When Hancock asked Brian what he thought about the likelihood of Ray being involved in the Mint swindle, Brian responded, 'It's got nothing to do with me.'

Meanwhile, on 16 July 1982, detectives Hooft and Henley searched the garage at the Mullaloo home of Peggy and Malcolm Mickelberg, the parents. Peter was present during the search, having accompanied the police from Ray's home. Peter told the detectives that on the day of the Mint swindle he was positive that he and his two brothers were erecting a fence at his parents' home. He then agreed to accompany Hooft and Henley to Subiaco.

The police parked their car at the rear of the premises of City Business Brokers at Hay Street, hoping Henry would be able to identify Peter.

Unfortunately for the police, Henry couldn't identify Peter as the man he had seen on the morning of the Mint swindle. He said Peter was taller and his hair was shorter. But he did tell Hooft 'the face was familiar' and that the man he had seen had had a wig on.

Then Henry and Hooft walked away. Peter got back into the police car and started to cry, saying, according to Henley, he thought Henry had recognised him. Henley said, 'I think he did too, because it was you in the white Falcon. Is that not right?'

Peter responded, distraught, 'Christ, if he recognises me I'm gone. Shit. Why this?'

Shortly after, Hooft returned to the police car. He turned to

Peter and said, 'What's wrong with you?'

Henley interjected before Peter could answer. 'He's very worried that he was recognised.'

Peter said, 'Did he recognise me?'

'Calm down, Peter. What are you worried about?' Hooft said.

'What's happening to this family? Ray'll kill me for this. Can I see Ray first? I've got to see Ray.'

'What's the matter?'

'Did he recognise me?'

'He may have,' Hooft responded. 'It was you in the car parked here on the morning of 22nd June, wasn't it?'

'If I see Ray first I'll tell you what you want to know. If Ray says it's all right, I'll tell you. I'll tell you everything.'

The Crown's case seems very compelling. Especially because, at the time, there was nothing to suggest that the notes from which evidence was allegedly drawn were not genuine, even if at times the comments attributed to Peter might otherwise have seemed implausible at best.

Hooft's evidence continued.

'Can you tell us where the vehicle is now?'

Peter insisted that he had to see Ray. 'I've got to see Ray. I can't say anything until I see Ray. He'll kill me if I tell you.'

Hooft then said, 'All right. We'll leave that for the moment. Just calm down. You had a flat in Rupert Street, Subiaco. Is that right?'

'Yes.'

'I'd like you to come with us while we search those premises. Is that all right with you?'

Peter agreed but he added that he had to be at his lawyer's office by 'nine o'clock.' His lawyer was Ron Cannon, who at that stage was the lawyer for all three brothers. Only at the trial was each brother represented by a different lawyer.

Later that day, detectives Andrew Tovey and Ljiljana Cvijic interviewed Peter at Unit 7, 112 Rupert Street, Subiaco. Tovey asked Peter what the weekly rent was. Peter said $95. Tovey thought that was pretty high, but Peter said he shared the rent with a mate who had returned to his girlfriend not long after they moved into the flat. When Tovey pressed Peter for the name of his mate, Peter said, 'Otto.'

Tovey asked for Otto's full name. Peter replied, 'Otto Kleiger, but he has gone up north.' He couldn't say exactly where. The reason Peter had moved out of the Rupert Street unit and back to his parents' home was because his father was sick.

On 26 July 1982, Peter was questioned further, this time by Hancock and Detective Sergeant Tony Lewandowski. Initially, the interview took place at the Belmont CIB office, about a ten-minute drive from Perth. Peter was driven to Belmont by Tovey and Detective Russell August.

At the start of the interview, Peter produced a letter from his lawyer stating that Peter was not going to make any statement to the police. This was a standard letter that Cannon gave most of his clients. It was well known around the police force, who derisorily referred to it as 'Cannon's Joke'. Also on Cannon's advice, Peter had obtained a medical certificate testifying that he was in good physical condition. Cannon thought this prudent in case the police assaulted his client. Despite 'Cannon's Joke' the police continued with the interview.

At the trial, the Crown attack was relentless as they led still more evidence from Hancock and Lewandowski's unsigned notes of what they said occurred at the interviews. The two detectives claimed they asked Peter about the 'Talbot note' which, they said, police handwriting experts[18] had concluded was in Peter's handwriting.

'So what if I bought the car?' responded Peter.

Hancock asked Peter, 'Did you buy the car?'

'I can't say.'

'Why?'

'I know. But we made an agreement that we wouldn't say anything.'

Hancock said, 'On the morning that the gold was obtained from the Mint, that car was parked at the back of Barker House from about quarter past eight till about half past ten. A man from a nearby business actually spoke to the driver as he was leaving and I have reason to suspect that that driver was you.'

Peter replied, 'I know him. You took me up there last time. Did he recognise me or not?'

'When he saw your photo with a wig on, he recognised you.'

'I thought so.'

Hancock continued. 'Peter, we would like to know where that

vehicle is now.'

Peter replied, 'I would tell you, but I promised not to say anything about it. If Ray says it's all right, I'll tell you where it is.'

'We have searched everywhere for it, even up at Kalbarri. Is it up there somewhere?'

'No. It's not up there. It's not far away really.'

'Is it hidden in a garage somewhere?'

'No. It's been dumped. You will find it eventually but you mightn't recognise it.'

Hancock asked if it had been burnt and again Peter remained silent. Hancock then asked where the car had been dumped.

Peter replied, 'I can't tell you until I talk to Ray. If he says it's all right I'll show you.'

Hancock then moved onto Otto Kleiger. 'When you made the application for the lease of that unit [in Rupert Street, Subiaco] you gave the name of Otto Kleiger as a referee. Who is Otto Kleiger?'

Peter remained silent.

'Who is Otto Kleiger, Peter?' Hancock repeated.

'I can't say anything about that.'

'You told Detective Tovey that Otto Kleiger was your flatmate and he had gone up north.'

Peter again refused to answer.

'Otto Kleiger is Ray, isn't he?'

'How do you know that?'

'Never mind that. Why did you use one of Ray's false identities when you leased the unit?'

'That was Ray's idea.'

'We suspect that that unit was leased purely as a headquarters for the job on the Mint.'

'That was Ray's idea, too.'

'Is that where the phone calls were made to the Mint and where the cheques were typed out?'

Peter said he couldn't say anything about that.

Hancock showed Peter a Mint voucher and receipt for the purchase of bullion in the name of Rodgers. Peter said he had never seen it before but the Crown led evidence at trial from a police handwriting expert which opined that Rodgers' signature had been written by Peter.

Hancock then moved onto the whereabouts of the Mickelberg brothers on 22 June 1982, the day of the Mint swindle. Peter repeated what he had previously told Hooft, that on 22 June the brothers were erecting a fence at their parents' home. But Peter did change his story in one respect. He remembered that Ray was not at the home but rather at an abalone divers' meeting.

Hancock wanted to know how it was possible for Peter to be at his parents' home all day building the fence and at Subiaco in the morning. Peter replied, 'I didn't say I was at Subiaco. You'll have to prove that. He mightn't have recognised me.'

Hancock said, 'We are extremely anxious to recover the gold from the Mint. If it is recovered, half the problems are over. Are you prepared to tell us where it is?'

'I can't tell you, sergeant; you'll have to talk to Ray,' replied Peter. 'I know that if you get the gold back all this will stop but I can't tell you unless he says so.'

Hancock then turned to the issue of Brian's knowledge of the whereabouts of the missing gold. He asked Peter, 'What about Brian? Does he know where the gold is?'

'Look, sergeant, we can't tell you anything without Ray's say-so. I would like to tell you where it is and get this over with. If I can talk to Ray and he says yes I'll tell you everything.'

Peter refused to answer questions about the building society fires, saying the brothers had agreed they would not talk about them.

When Hancock raised the issue of Brian's orange Porsche, Peter confirmed that he and Ray sometimes drove the Porsche. Hancock then asked whether he or Ray were in the Porsche seen at the fire site in North Perth on 7 April 1982. Peter responded, 'I don't want to answer that. You'll have to talk to Raymond. If he says it's all right I'll tell you the whole story.'

Hancock then said to Peter, 'After we have interviewed Ray I will make arrangements for you to have a talk to him. If he agrees, will you be prepared to tell us the full story and help us get the gold back?'

'Yes,' said Peter.

When the interview was over, Hancock asked Peter if he was prepared to make a statement. Peter declined. Lewandowski said at the trial that he made notes during the interview. He claimed to have read these notes back to Peter who agreed they were accurate but would not sign them.[19]

Round then drove Peter to central police headquarters, where he and Detective John Gillespie continued the interview.

Round asked Peter what he had told Hancock. Peter said, 'I haven't told him where the gold is but I have certainly told him a lot more than I intended to. Ray won't be very happy about it.' When Round asked Peter to tell him where the gold was, Peter replied, 'Look, I can't. I have to talk to Ray. If Ray says it's all right, I'll tell you. You know what it's like being brothers and that. I can't say anything.'

'Did you tell them where the car is?'

'Not exactly. I told them it had been burnt and dumped but I didn't tell them where.' Round urged him to tell them more but Peter refused to give further details.

Round moved on to the all-important Peter Gulley. 'Why did you tell me the other day you didn't know the name Peter Gulley?'

'That's obvious now, isn't it? I knew you were looking for Ray and I knew it was Ray and I knew why you were looking for him.'

'You told Detective Tovey that Otto Kleiger was your flatmate.'

'Yes, that was a bit silly, wasn't it? That was the only name I could think of at the time. You know that's just a tax dodge.'

Round then said, 'Did you ever live at the unit with anybody?'

'No.'

'The neighbours said you were hardly ever there but the lights used to be on at the place.'

'Yes. Ray gave me one of those time switches that put the lights on and off so it would look like someone was living there.'

'Don't you think you should tell us the full story, Peter, and help us get the gold back?'

Once again, Peter said he couldn't talk without Ray's approval.

'Peter, you talk a lot about Ray. What about Brian?'

'Ray's been like a father to me. Dad's been sick and Ray's been the head of the family to all of us. What he says goes.'

'I can understand you looking up to Ray but what about Brian? He is older than you.'

'Brian goes along with the rest of us.'

On that same day, 26 July 1982, detectives also interviewed Ray on three separate occasions. By that time, his fingerprint had been identified on the back of the WABS cheque.

Round, Gillespie and Detective Trevor Porter carried out the first interview at the local Whitford Shopping Centre car park. Ray's wife Sheryl was also there.

Round asked Ray whether he used the name Otto Kleiger. Sheryl spoke before Ray could give an answer, saying, 'You're a bloody joke. That's not Ray. Otto used to live with us for a while, didn't he, Ray?' Ray told Sheryl to keep quiet. Round repeated the question to Ray, who replied, 'All right.'

But Sheryl didn't want to be quiet. She asked, 'Who were the two detectives who went to Penang, anyway?' Gillespie said that Penang had not previously been mentioned in the conversation. Ray once again told his wife to keep quiet. As the two detectives, Hancock and Billing, did not go to Penang until 11 August 1982, it seems unlikely that Sheryl could have asked the question at that particular interview. By raising it in his evidence, however, it would suggest to the jury that Sheryl might have something to hide, because Ray and she had visited Malaysia earlier in July.

From the Whitford Shopping Centre car park, the detectives drove Ray to police headquarters in East Perth and, from there, to the Belmont CIB office where Hancock and Lewandowski had interviewed Peter. During the journey from East Perth to Belmont, Round told Ray that things did not look too good for him. He told the court that Ray responded, 'I know everything does look bad but like I said the other day, last time, I can't say anything. There's too much involved.'

Round did not give up. He moved on to the various names that Ray had been using, like Otto Kleiger and Peter Gulley. Ray responded, 'They are nothing really. I really shouldn't talk to you but it doesn't matter. They were just to dodge tax.'

At the Belmont CIB, Hancock and Lewandowski interviewed Ray. Again, the only record of the interview was the handwritten notes allegedly made at the time. They told him about their interview with Peter earlier that day. Hancock said, 'Peter has told us that he knows where the gold is and he is prepared to tell us if you agree. What do you say about that?'

Ray replied, 'Peter is just a kid. He can't tell you where it is.'

Hancock asked Ray, as he had Peter, whether the gold could be returned. Ray replied, 'I can't say.'

'Can it be recovered? Is it possible to recover it?' Ray shook his head.

'Where is it?'

'You already know where it is.'

'What do you mean, we already know?'

'Someone opened their big mouth this morning.'

'I don't know what you are talking about.'

'Don't worry about it then.'

'Ray, if we can get that gold back, half the problems are over.'

'I can't say anything.'

'Why can't you tell us?'

'There's too much involved.'

'Are there other people involved that we don't know about?'

'I can't say.'

On the same day, Hooft, Henley and other police officers, armed with a search warrant, paid Brian another visit at his Jandakot home and asked him to accompany them to police headquarters. Brian asked if Peter was there and Hooft replied he thought so. After speaking to his wife and then to his parents by phone, Brian went to police headquarters.[20]

Once there, Hooft did most of the questioning. He asked, 'Do you remember the last time I spoke to you? You told me you were in Port Hedland on 7 April when the building society in North Perth was broken into and cheques stolen.'

'Yes.'

'Well, we checked that and you were not in Port Hedland at that time. You also told us that on 13 May, when the building society in Bull Creek was broken into and the Perth Building Society cheques were stolen you were in Port Hedland. Is that right?'

'I don't remember.'

'That's what you said and we've checked that and you were in Perth at that time. What have you got to say about that?'

'I wouldn't know.'

Hooft continued, 'You also told me that on 22 June you were in Hong Kong and we now know that you returned on 17 June.'

'I know that now. Since the last time I spoke to you, I checked with Ray and we were doing the fence at Mullaloo.'

At some stage during the interview, Hooft left the room to

speak to Hancock. When he returned, he said, 'It appears that Ray and Peter are both going to be charged with these offences. There is also a lot that tends to show you are involved also.'

Brian said, 'Are they both being charged?'

'Yes.'

'I never thought it would come to this.'

'What do you mean by that?' Hooft asked.

'I'm not supposed to be here. Ray thinks he's so smart.'

Hooft went on to tell Brian that they had evidence to show that he was involved. Henley then said, 'Brian, did you pick up the gold when it was delivered to Jandakot on 22 June?'

Brian replied, 'I've got nothing to say about that.'

Henley repeated the question. 'Brian, did you pick up the gold when it was delivered to Jandakot on 22 June?'

'I got nothing to say about that.'

'Why not?'

Brian remained silent and Henley said, 'The office of Mayne Bristow [Brian's employer] is 100 yards from where the bullion was dropped and you live within a mile of the airport.'

Brian said, 'It looks bad, doesn't it?'

Henley continued, 'We can also show that you and your brothers have all done gold transactions with the Perth Mint.'

Brian wanted to see Ray. 'Where's Ray?'

'He's here. The main thing now is, can we recover the gold?'

'I'm the little man. You see Ray about that.'

'Why see Ray? Can't you tell me?'

'I can but if Ray hasn't told you, I won't.'

Some time later, Hancock took over the interview. He referred to Brian's earlier interview that day. 'Sergeant Hooft tells me you know where the gold is from the Mint. Are you prepared to tell us?'

Brian replied, 'Are Ray and young Peter going to be charged?'

'Yes. They are obviously involved and I have reason to suspect that you are involved with them.'

'I'm not supposed to be here.'

'I gathered that. Ray has described you as a safe house, a person who is involved but who is kept out of sight to look after the others if something goes wrong.'

'That's Ray all over.'

'Are you involved?'

'It's pretty obvious isn't it? If you're going to charge them you'll have to charge me, too.'

'Are you prepared to tell me the part that you played?'

'Not unless Ray has told you the whole thing and he hasn't if you're still asking about the gold.'

'What about the gold? Are you prepared to tell us where it is?'

'That's up to Ray.'

Hancock turned to what Brian was doing on 22 June 1982. 'That business about the fence at your parents' house on the day the gold was obtained from the Mint?'

Brian replied, 'That was another one of Ray's brilliant ideas.'

'Where were you on that day?'

'No, I can't tell you.'

'Did you pick the gold up from Jandakot?'

'I can't say.'

Hancock then asked Brian about the transfer of his matrimonial home into his wife's name, mentioning that Ray had transferred his home to his wife, Sheryl. (In fact, though Ray had intended to transfer the house to Sheryl, he had not done so. Nor had Brian's transfer gone through.) Brian's home had been in the joint names of Brian and his wife Faye, and on 21 June 1982, a transfer was executed to his wife. However an accountant advised Brian that it would be better if the disposition went to a unit trust, and the transfer was not finalised. Brian said the transfer was for business reasons. When Hancock asked him about it, Brian said, 'Ray tries to cover all the angles,' and 'it looks like a pretty good idea now.'

Hancock said, 'We have checked with your employer in Port Hedland and you were rostered to have your two weeks off in Perth on 8 June to 22 June, that is the day of the Mint job. You were due to start back in Port Hedland that day. However, you applied for an extra week off because you were going to Hong Kong. Is that right?'

'Yes.'

'According to the Immigration Department you left Perth on 9 June and got back on the 17th so you had plenty of time to be back in Port Hedland on the 22nd if you had wanted to.'

Brian said, 'We all know what happened now, don't we?'

Hancock asked Brian if he had an account at the Conti Sheffield

Agency in North Perth. Brian said he hadn't and added that he didn't light the fire. Hancock said, 'We know that but if you were part of the whole plan and knew about it, then under the law you are equally guilty.'[21]

Brian replied, 'There's no way out then. If they're going to be charged I'll have to be charged, too.'

'Are you saying that you took part in the gold fraud on the Mint?'

'I've already told you. If you are going to charge Ray and Peter, you'll have to charge me too. I'm not going to say any more about it. That's up to Ray.'

'Are you prepared to talk to Ray about us getting the gold back?'

'I'll talk to him but it won't do any good. He's made up his mind.'

Later that evening, Ray, Brian and Peter were given an opportunity to speak to each other. Soon after, they were subjected to more questioning by Hancock, Lewandowski and Round, this time with the three brothers together, but still without lawyers present. Hancock asked whether, having had a chance to talk together, they were prepared to tell the police where the gold was. Ray spoke for all of them.

'We made our decision a week ago, and we'll stick by it. You will just have to charge us and we will see what happens.'

Two weeks later, on 12 August 1982, the burnt-out Falcon with a CB bracket but no radio was found north of the city, on a bush track in Joondalup. Inside the car were the charred remains of the *West Australian* newspaper, dated 22 June 1982.

On 23 September 1982, a few weeks after the discovery of the Falcon, detectives again interviewed Peter. This time Tovey and Detective Sergeant James Allen conducted the interview at Warwick police station.

'I want to talk to you about the gold from the Perth Mint,' Tovey said.

Peter replied, 'I've already spoken to Sergeant Hancock and Sergeant Lewandowski.'

'Things have changed now though and we still want to get the gold back.' He did not elaborate on how things had changed.

Using Tovey's first name, Peter said, 'Andrew, you don't really expect me to tell you where it is, do you?'

'Do you realise that it would be better for everyone concerned if the gold from the Mint can be recovered?'

'Andrew, if I tell you where it is, Ray will kill me.'

'Why are you so scared of Ray?'

'You don't know what he's like.'

'What are you going to do? Sit on the gold forever?'

Peter replied, 'We're prepared to get twenty years.'

'Who told you that?'

'Cannon,' said Peter, referring to his lawyer.

Tovey then questioned Peter about the night of Friday 17 September 1982. 'Peter, at about 10.30 p.m. last Friday the 17th two men were seen with a Landrover in the bush off Glendale Crescent, Jandakot.'

'Oh, yeah, about that. I was with my girlfriend all night.'

'Was the gold buried out there?'

'Andrew, I can't tell you that.'

Tovey persevered, 'Peter, if you tell us where the gold is, Ray doesn't have to know you told us.'

Later on, Peter raised the issue of his father's ill health. 'What about Dad? What can you do for him? He's pretty sick.'

'Would you like me to talk to Sergeant Hancock about that?'

'Yes I would.'

Tovey left the interview room to talk to Hancock. On returning, he said, 'I have just spoken to Sergeant Hancock. He is prepared to approach the Crown Law Department on behalf of your parents, provided the gold from the Mint can be recovered.'

Peter said, 'Andrew, it's a hard decision.'

'It's up to you.'

'Do you mind if I think about it for a while?'

'Sure.'

Tovey allowed Peter a small break. Then it was back on. 'Well, Peter, are you going to tell us where the gold is?'

'No, Andrew, I can't. Ray would kill me. I won't waste any more of your time.'

'Just tell me one thing,' Tovey asked, 'is the gold overseas?'

'No, it's not.'

'Are you sure you won't tell me where it is?'

'Nothing personal, Andrew, but I can't.'

On the same day, 23 September 1982, Hancock and Detective

Sergeant Francis Bower interviewed Ray. Hancock did not beat about the bush. 'You know that we still badly want to recover the gold from the Mint. If you tell us where it can be recovered, I'm prepared to approach the Crown Law Department on behalf of your parents.'

Ray provided him no joy. 'I know what you're getting at, but you're wasting your time and mine ... we've made our decision.'

'You're not going to tell me where the gold is?'

'I think you know me, Don. I'll take a bullet in the head before I tell you where that is.'

'Even if it means the whole family being locked up?'

'We can handle it; we'll do it on our ear.'

'What about Mum and Dad?'

'They can hack it.'

The jury might have been puzzled about where this was leading. At no time had the prosecutor alleged or implied that the Mickelbergs' parents were involved. Nor had they been charged in connection with this matter. Was it just an implied threat to put more pressure on the brothers? Or was there something the jury was yet to learn? If that were the case, they would have to wait.

On 18 February 1983, Chief Crown Prosecutor Davies turned to face Judge Desmond Heenan. 'If your Honour pleases, that is the case for the Crown.'

CHAPTER 2
THE YELLOW ROSE OF TEXAS: 'IT LIKE TO BROKE MY HEART'

Legend has it that the Yellow Rose of Texas was a free Black American woman named Emily D. West. Seized by the Mexican forces during the Texas War of Independence, she is credited with having seduced General Antonio López de Santa Anna, president of Mexico and commander of the Mexican forces. So preoccupied with her charms was Antonio, that the whole Mexican army was caught unawares, thereby allowing General Sam Houston to win the 1836 battle of San Jacinto in literally only a few minutes, while Emily 'was helping' Antonio with his siesta. The story was immortalised in a song, written in 1853, that became a favourite of the Confederate army during the civil war and, later, the US Cavalry. In 1955, it became an international hit for Mitch Miller.

If Ron Cannon, opening the case for the defence, was hoping for a similar triumph of seduction with a contemporary Yellow Rose of Texas, he was to be bitterly disappointed. But, before getting to the cause of his disappointment, we need to go back two years, to the morning of 24 July 1980.

Peggy, the Mickelberg matriarch, received a phone call from Ray while she was visiting the fourth son in the family, Graeme, in Brisbane. Ray asked her to fly home for a media stunt in which she would have to hold up a gold nugget for the cameras. She arrived back at Perth Airport at midnight to be met by Brian and his wife Faye, who drove her to their house near Jandakot Airport.

The following morning Peggy boarded a single-engine Cessna-185 aircraft piloted by Brian. Also on board was Brian

Pozzi, an acquaintance of Ray's. Brian took off, flew just a short distance and returned to Jandakot. Pozzi had earlier invited a handpicked group of media representatives to meet the plane, which, he said, had flown in from some isolated area rich in gold in outback Western Australia. He claimed they were keeping the actual location quiet to protect the interests of the lucky prospector who had discovered the large gold nugget.

Peggy, wearing wig and glasses, stepped out of the aircraft holding a gold nugget so heavy she nearly lost her balance. The wig and glasses, Peggy said later, were an attempt to make her look more appealing to the cameras, an appeal considerably diminished by the fact that she was missing her false teeth. She claimed to have taken them out in the plane because she was feeling sick and didn't have time to put them back in before the nugget was thrust into her hands. The prosecution argued, perhaps reasonably in the circumstances, that her fashion makeover was an attempt to hide the identity of the bogus prospector.

Peggy was not supposed to talk to the media. However, under the insistent gaze of the cameras and the relentless questioning of reporters, she blurted out that she had found the nugget while prospecting. One of the reporters was Alison Fan from Channel Seven in Perth, who was to figure prominently in the recounting of the Mickelberg saga as it unfolded over the ensuing years.

The supposed find quickly attracted local and international attention as Pozzi ran a competition to name the nugget, offering a prize of $200. It was won by a US seaman, who suggested the Yellow Rose of Texas. Offers for the nugget came from all over the world, the best coming from local tycoon Alan Bond, who paid $350,000 for what he, and others, saw as a good buy based on the Perth Mint's authentication. The flamboyant Bond, who later rode a roller coaster of notoriety from national hero (after heading the historic 1983 America's Cup victory) to corporate villain when he was gaoled for corporate fraud in the 1990s,[22] planned to display the nugget in the foyer of his Palace Tower office block in the Perth CBD.

Selling the nugget caused tension between Ray and Brian. Brian, who had lent Ray $60,000 to help buy the $250,000 of gold that went into the manufacturing of the nugget, disliked Pozzi and was strongly opposed to selling it to anyone but the Mint. He only relented when Bond offered $350,000 for it.

We pick up the story again two years later.

In early September 1982, Hancock and other CIB detectives went to the Tuart Hill home of Brian Pozzi to investigate a matter that had nothing to do with the Mint swindle. While searching the house, the detectives came across photographs and negatives recording the manufacture of a 419 ounce gold nugget. Pozzi confessed that the nugget had been manufactured in the garage of Ray's Marmion home, and was not, as the Perth Mint had mistakenly authenticated two years earlier, the second largest alluvial nugget ever found in Western Australia. When interviewed by Hancock on 23 September 1982, Ray also confessed. He and Pozzi, along with Brian, Peter and their feisty mother Peggy, were charged with fraud in that they had manufactured the nugget with the intention of deceiving prospective buyers.[23]

The Mickelbergs and Pozzi argued they had merely manufactured the nugget to generate publicity for a gold prospecting safari business Ray and Brian were establishing. They claimed they planned eventually to sell the nugget back to the Perth Mint to recoup their original outlay of $250,000 for the gold used to make it.

Arguably, it was irrelevant what their initial purpose was. The facts are that the Mickelbergs were involved in deceiving the media and the public, and in selling the nugget to Bond by representing it as something it was not. They had engaged in criminal activity and gold was central to the fraud. It seems self-evident that knowledge of this alleged earlier fraud would adversely influence a jury's perceptions of the defendants in the Perth Mint swindle trial.

Surely then the Mickelberg defence counsel would have wanted to keep the Yellow Rose of Texas charges well away from the jury, especially as the matter would not go to trial until 1984. Under normal rules of evidence, past adverse or criminal activity cannot be used to argue propensity to commit the crime for which the defendant is being tried. An accused should only be found guilty if they have done the deed they are on trial for, not for what they did previously or because of their reputations, notorious or otherwise. Since the accused's history will almost inevitably influence a jury's perception of whether or not they are guilty, prior criminal activity, or other prejudicial evidence, normally cannot be admitted in evidence. However, it may be admissible in questioning the truthfulness of the defendant's evidence given on oath. That is, as a matter of law, prosecutors can use the witness's past activity to attack their credibility as a truthful witness, especially when the accused makes allegations of police abuse. Whether or not potentially adverse prior activity will be admitted is a matter determined by the judge, but normally it is not allowed.[24]

Crown prosecutor Davies certainly didn't think it would be admissible. 'In a criminal trial judges (and) all counsel, including the Crown, move heaven and earth to avoid letting juries know that accused persons have been involved in any other fraudulent or criminal-type activity,' he told the jury. 'No way could the Crown have told you about the Yellow Rose matter.'

But it was Ron Cannon, Ray's counsel, who let the cat out of the bag.[25]

As an experienced criminal lawyer his knowledge of procedure and the rules of evidence was as good as that of anyone plying their trade on St Georges Terrace, the top end of town where the corporate and legal money resided. Weighing up the pros and cons, he nevertheless decided to raise the Yellow Rose of Texas in the Perth Mint trial when conducting his examination in chief of Ray. Davies and McKechnie couldn't believe their collective luck and, as the evidence unfolded during the prosecutor's cross-examination, Ray may well have been reflecting on a line from the old song: 'It like to broke my heart!'[26]

Cannon used the Yellow Rose of Texas charge to explain why the brothers were concerned about being questioned by the police. He told the jury the brothers had medical certificates (attesting to their good health) in their possession when picked up by the police for questioning over the Perth Mint swindle because they were anticipating police interrogation over the Yellow Rose of Texas affair (although they had not yet been charged with any offence relating to the Yellow Rose of Texas).

Before the jury, Cannon asked Ray, 'When the publicity about the Mint swindle first arose were you concerned in any way?' Ray replied that he was because he thought that as the gold had been left at Jandakot Airport, all commercial pilots would eventually be checked. In response to Cannon's question, Ray admitted he was involved in the manufacture of the nugget. He thought it likely someone at the airport would mention to the police that Brian had been involved in transporting the Yellow Rose of Texas and he feared that because both incidents involved gold fraud, the police would target them as likely suspects in the Perth Mint swindle.

Cannon's gamble did not pay off. Davies commenced his cross-examination by asking Ray whether his long hair at the time of the Yellow Rose of Texas airport scam was an attempt to disguise himself. He played Channel Seven's film of the arrival of the nugget at Jandakot Airport to the jury and Judge Heenan. However, the judge was not impressed, saying that nothing in the film resembled Ray and that Davies' eyesight must be better than his if he thought otherwise. But, the jury, the arbiter of fact[27] and thus of guilt or innocence, had seen a film, no matter how poor the vision, apparently of Ray taking part in another crime. Not just any crime but a crime involving gold.

Ray's case was also not helped by his answers to questions relating to his mother's involvement in the Yellow Rose of Texas crime. It was understandable Ray would seek to minimise his mother's involvement in the whole affair. When Davies asked who came out of the aircraft with the nugget, who else got out of the plane and what was expected of Peggy, Ray's answers were evasive. This would not have impressed the jury. While some jury members may have understood a son's attempt to protect his mother, Ray's evasiveness damaged his credibility as a truthful witness.[28]

Issues of credibility and truthfulness were central to the defence as the Mickelbergs vigorously denied any involvement in the Mint swindle. They denied making the police statements attributed to them by the prosecution. Moreover, they alleged major and serious police misconduct, the most serious allegations being that the fingerprint evidence on the fraudulent cheque was fabricated; that Peter, then only twenty-two, had been subject to significant and outrageous treatment by the police; and that the records of interviews of the three brothers were fabricated.

Cannon set out to convince the jury.

He began by arguing that Ray's fingerprint on the Western Australian Building Society (WABS) cheque for $249,932.74 was not on the cheque on 23 June 1982, the day the police obtained possession of it. He told the court that on 15 July when Ray was in police custody being questioned, they handed him the WABS cheque to inspect, at which point he left his fingerprint on it. Sometime later, he was taken away and fingerprinted.[29] The defence claimed that the police later fabricated the fingerprint evidence by using the print placed on the cheque on 15 July to link Ray to the crime.

The drama of that winter day had started early for Ray when, at six o'clock, loud and repeated banging on the door of the family home woke Sheryl and their three children, Lynda, Ross and Kelly. Not completely awake, Ray answered the door and before he knew it, the police had entered his house, verbally identifying themselves but refusing to present documented identification or a search warrant.[30] They went through the house and collected documents from Ray's office. They told Ray they wanted him to accompany them to Warwick police station for questioning. But the police car set off in a different direction, towards police headquarters in East Perth.

Hancock and Round kept Ray at headquarters for around twelve hours. For a small part of his interview, Noel De Grussa, a police officer with whom Ray had served in Vietnam, was present. Round had instructed De Grussa to attend. The court was told that a few days later Ray contacted De Grussa, who said, 'I do not know what is going on but there will be no way out for you if they have decided to hit you. I suggest you get a medical certificate today. If you don't you will regret it.'

Unaware that Ray had been taken away by the police, Peter went to his house to collect him to go diving. Sheryl greeted him in tears. Over the course of the day, the police undertook three searches of Ray's home. During one search, Peter showed the police some gold and silver bars that belonged to Ray. That night, Peter stayed at Ray's home to keep Sheryl and the children company. He slept with the bars. He didn't trust the police officers 'as far as [he] could kick them.'

Detective Tovey, one of the search officers, said to Peter, 'We want you to come to police headquarters to talk to your brother because he is incoherent.' Peter, who knew his brother well, didn't believe it. He replied, 'Why do you want to talk to me?' Tovey said they wanted to have a yarn. Peter telephoned Cannon who informed Peter that he didn't need to go unless they charged him.[31] When Peter relayed that advice to him, Tovey telephoned Hancock to tell him 'the bastard' had spoken to Cannon who advised Peter against going to police headquarters.

Next morning, 16 July 1982, Ray was still at police headquarters. Hooft and Henley came to Ray's home and told Peter they were investigating the Perth Mint swindle. The officers wanted to search his parents' home and asked Peter if he would go with them. Peter agreed as he wanted to be there to support his parents during the search.

At Peggy and Malcolm Mickelberg's home, Hooft and Henley undertook a thorough search, although they had no search warrant.[32] They collected some photographs of Peter, his girlfriend and her family.[33] They then told Peter they would be taking him to an identification parade,[34] as they believed he was involved in the Mint swindle. Peter refused, saying that he wanted to make a phone call. He told the court Henley threatened to break Peter's arm if he moved anywhere and Peter thought he had no choice but to go with the detectives.

They drove him first to the laneway behind Barker House in Subiaco where they told him he was to be in an identification parade. He was pulled out of the car and stood in front of a man he did not know. It was Mr Henry. Henry moved closer to Peter and said to the detectives, 'No I think he is too tall and the hair is wrong.' Hooft then pushed Peter into a pothole and said to Henry, 'He might have been standing in a hole. Does he look the right height now?' Henry again said, 'No.' The detectives were not happy. They led Peter back into the car. Peter was amused. He said to Henley, 'If that was your identification parade, it is a big joke.' Henley did not respond. He turned to Hooft and asked, 'Did he pick him?'

Hooft said, 'No, he didn't.'

Hooft and Henley then drove Peter to Barrack Street in the city. They parked their car and radioed another CIB car. When it arrived, there was an exchange between the officers in the two cars about whether Peter had been identified. He was then driven to his residence at Unit 7, 112 Rupert Street, Subiaco, where Hooft and Henley and others, including Tovey and Cvijic, searched his premises, again without a warrant. They did not take anything away. At the end of the search, they drove Peter to St Georges Terrace so he could see Cannon.

On 26 July 1982, Peter was at Whitford City Shopping Centre, although his mother, who was scared for him, had not wanted him to leave the house. He said he would be okay. At Whitford City, he purchased a newspaper and some medication for a cold. As he was driving his blue Fiat 131 Sedan along Dampier Road heading back to his parents' home, an unmarked V8 XD Falcon drove up alongside him, then abruptly pulled in front of him, forcing Peter off the road. Two of the three occupants, Detective John Gillespie and Detective Russell August, got out of the car while Detective Tovey remained in the driver's seat. Gillespie and August pulled Peter out of his car and threw him across the bonnet. Then Gillespie pushed Peter into the back seat of the unmarked police car and drove Peter's car away. Tovey took charge of the police car, with August and Peter in the back seat. All the car doors were open. Tovey planted his foot on the accelerator as he executed a U-turn. The doors closed as the car accelerated away.

Peter asked where he was being taken. Tovey shouted, 'Shut the fuck up; you will be talking pretty soon.' Peter told them about his lawyer's letter, which said he didn't need to answer any questions. Peter thought they were probably taking him to police headquarters in East Perth, where they had taken him ten days earlier, so he was surprised when he realised he was on his way to Belmont CIB.

Peter was marched into the police station by Tovey, who grabbed him by the back of his trousers, pulling them up his backside. Once inside, Tovey yelled, 'Everyone out of here.' Peter was thrown into a small room in which there was a desk up against a wall and two chairs. He was left there alone. Peter felt 'sick as a dog.' He placed his head on the table and dozed off.

Sometime later, Tovey entered the room. He asked Peter to describe all the clothes he was wearing. Peter wondered why but he obliged. Tovey left the room and Peter went back to sleep, but not for long.

What happened next answered his unspoken question — why Belmont and not police headquarters? Suddenly, he was gasping for air as a hand squeezed his windpipe. It belonged to Detective Anthony Lewandowski. The burly detective, only inches away from Peter's face said, 'This is where you die, you little fucker.' Only Lewandowski and Peter were in the room. Peter was terrified.

Lewandowski grabbed Peter by the shirt and pushed him into another room, a long room with a bricked-in fireplace, a blue chair and two or three desks. Another man, grey haired and dressed in a black pinstripe suit said, 'Do you know who I am?' Peter responded, 'No.' It was Hancock, who he would soon get to know very well.

Hancock grabbed Peter by the hair, smacked his head back into a windowsill and chopped him twice in the throat. Not full-blooded chops but half chops. Peter was again gasping for air. It was difficult to speak. Hancock didn't stop there. He threw Peter back onto the chair and punched him three or four times in the solar plexus, winding him. Then Hancock picked Peter up and barked, 'Strip.' Peter stripped, terrified of what might happen next.

Peter stood there naked as Lewandowski roughly slapped handcuffs on him, squeezing them tightly around his wrists, and pushed him down into the chair. He then turned to Peter's clothes and began rummaging through them.

It was Hancock's turn again. He slapped Peter around the head. Peter was scared. Lewandowski yelled, 'For Christ's sake Don, stop hitting him.'

'Why?'

'The bastard has a medical certificate.' Lewandowski had found the medical certificate that Peter had got on the advice of Ray's police friend, De Grussa. It was only a couple of days old, verifying that Peter was in good health and had no marks, abrasions or bruises on his body.

The revelation of the medical certificate made Hancock angrier. He stopped hitting Peter, but that was not the end of the abuse. Now he repeatedly kicked Peter off the blue chair, then grabbed and pushed him back onto it. He and Lewandowski took a few turns in punching Peter in the stomach and threatened to kick him in the ribs.

Peter said he did not intend to answer any questions. He showed them the letter from Cannon. They laughed, calling it 'Cannon's Joke,' saying he gave that to every client and the police thought it is a big laugh. The questioning continued for about three hours.[35] Occasionally Hancock tried the soft line. 'We know that you and your brothers did it; if you confess you can go to Wooroloo [a minimum security farm prison on the outskirts of the city].'[36] Peter repeatedly denied involvement in the Perth Mint swindle. 'As far as I am concerned I had nothing to do with it; I do not wish to answer any questions and here you are beating the hell out of me.'

At one stage, Hancock said, 'We need a handwriting sample from you, please sign your name at the bottom of this page.' Peter refused. Hancock tried again. 'If you sign your name and write in your name and address, you can go home.' Finally, Peter signed his name at the top of the page and wrote that he was doing so because the police demanded it. He was not admitting to any guilt.

After the interview, Peter complained to Detective Sergeant Bob Kucera, officer in charge at Belmont CIB, that Hancock and Lewandowski had physically assaulted him. He told the court Kucera said, 'It's got nothing to do with me. I can't help you at all.'

Ray was also taken in for questioning late afternoon on 26 July 1982. After being questioned in the car park at Whitford City Shopping Centre by Round, he was forcefully led to the police car and driven to Belmont CIB. Gillespie and Detective Trevor Porter were also in the car. Round and Gillespie then drove Peter to police headquarters in East Perth.

An eerie atmosphere pervaded the Belmont station. There was no one in sight apart from the detectives who had escorted Ray there. He was thrown into a room. He heard a vehicle pull up, then slamming doors, and shortly Hancock and Lewandowski appeared in the room. Ray told the court that Hancock said, 'We have been questioning Peter. We now require you to confess to the crime.' Ray had a medical certificate, as well as Cannon's letter. They again refused to take it seriously and renewed their questioning. After Ray refused their request to confess, Hancock and Lewandowski threatened Ray that Peter would be raped in prison. They said they would arrange for Peter to be in a cell with a prisoner 'who will fuck him.' At the time, Ray did not know who the prisoner they named was (he was a homosexual prisoner doing time for murder and drug trafficking).

Hancock also raised the threat of the 'toe-cutter', something he had also mentioned to Peter. He said the toe-cutters were an eastern states gang that went after criminals who had stowed away the products of their criminal labour. Hancock said to Ray that the toe-cutters and Abe Saffron, the Sydney-based owner of the Raffles Hotel on the banks of the Swan River, could do heinous things to him and his family, including the children. He also said they would ensure Sheryl and his parents ended up in gaol too. Still Ray refused to give them what they wanted.

From Belmont CIB, Ray was driven to police headquarters in the city. It was around 7.30 p.m. when he arrived. Brian was already there, having been questioned earlier by Hooft and Henley and later by Hancock.

Ray and Brian were both asked to write 'forty'. After they both spelled it correctly, they were asked to spell it with a 'u' as in 'fourty'. Only Ray did so.

Peter, meanwhile, had been led up a side stairwell into the building by Detective Ljiljana Cvijic. Once settled in the interviewing room, Gillespie and Round entered. Gillespie took his jacket off, stared at Peter and said, 'I am going to beat the shit out of you.' Peter, already traumatised from the treatment by Hancock and Lewandowski at Belmont, trembled with fear. The room was mirrored and soundproofed, and he noticed marks on the soundproofing brown walls where chairs had cannoned into them. To Peter's great relief, Gillespie did not touch him and left with Round. Peter thought the medical certificate might have saved him from further physical abuse.

Cvijic re-entered the room. Pointing to his chest, Peter said, 'Look at this.' He undid his shirt buttons. The skin on his chest, on the sternum, was peeled off. During Hancock and Lewandowski's rough handling, the chain around Peter's neck had dug into his skin and ripped some flesh off. Cvijic said, 'You must have fallen down the stairs.' Clearly, she was not going to provide support to Peter's allegation of police abuse and misconduct.

Cvijic then led Peter out of the room and down narrow corridors between partitioned offices. The corridors were lined with detectives, and Peter was pushed from one to another like a beach ball at a pool party. His destination was a room where Ray and Brian were being held. On seeing Peter, Ray could tell he had been physically abused. After further questioning by Hancock, the three brothers were charged[37] with the Perth Mint swindle.

They spent the night together in the women's section of the police lockup, the night silence punctuated by screams from female prisoners.

In the morning, a prison 'trustee' (a prisoner who has the 'privilege' of working at the lockup rather than being in the main prison system) brought them breakfast. The trustee knew Brian and said, 'You guys have been kept away from everyone.'

It was still early morning when Round and Gillespie reappeared. Peter was worried he was to be taken away again to 'get another flogging.' He was taken away but Round and Gillespie did not harm him. They told him he could go home if he signed a confession. Peter refused but was bailed and allowed to go, as were Ray and Brian.[38]

For a little while, life regained some normalcy. Then at 6 a.m. on 23 September 1982, loud banging on the front door again disturbed Ray's family. This time the police didn't wait for Ray to answer the door. Led by Hancock and Detective Sergeants Taylor and Bower they forced their way into the house. Ray and his wife jumped out of bed. Bower and Taylor took Ray into another room of the house and said, 'We are taking the wife and kids and you.'[39]

'What for? What am I charged with?'

'Hancock has ordered that we take the lot of you.'

Ray argued with them that they should leave Sheryl and the three kids out of the matter. Bower responded, 'I am sorry about this.'

Ray believed Bower and Taylor were genuinely unhappy about involving Sheryl and the children. They also said, 'We do not like doing this sort of thing but we have been ordered.' They added that if Ray and the family did not agree to go to police headquarters they would 'be dragged out of here screaming, take it or leave it.'

Ray replied, 'Give me a couple of minutes to talk to my wife.'

Hancock observed proceedings, directing traffic and wandering around the house.

Ray told Sheryl he was afraid that if she did not agree to come to police headquarters they would take her by force. After what Peter had experienced, Ray was in no doubt the police were willing to use force if they deemed it necessary.

Sheryl agreed to go with the police but insisted on having a shower first. Bower and Taylor were not happy to wait, and Ray was thrown into one of the police cars, which left the house at high speed. He wondered what fate awaited his family.

His oldest child, who had just begun school, was allowed to stay with a neighbour, who took her to school. Sheryl and the two youngest children, still in their pyjamas, were driven to police headquarters.

Ray wasn't allowed to see Sheryl or the children but he could hear them because they kept the door of the room he was in ajar. He could hear the children crying and Sheryl trying to calm them; no doubt the police were hoping this would weaken his resolve.

He was not alone in the holding room. Inspector Mulvey and two other police officers were there, all staring at Ray. Then Hancock stormed into the room. He threatened Ray but the former SAS man stood up to him. Ray said, 'If you want to play it that way, we will do it right here and now — if you want to be physical.' This made Hancock even angrier. Ray told the court that Mulvey stepped in between the two, diffusing the threat of a physical confrontation between Hancock and Ray, at least for the time being. However, Hancock still pressed. 'I am going to make you confess.' This amused Ray, considering he and his brothers had allegedly confessed in July.

Mulvey and the other officers left the room, leaving Hancock alone with Ray. Hancock shouted that unless Ray signed a confession Sheryl would be charged and the children would be made wards of state.[40] Ray said, 'Look, you do what you have to do but I have not committed this crime and I will not sign any confession.' Hancock added an ultimatum to his demand that Ray sign a confession. 'We will just tell your missus you are screwing the bird down the street.'

Ray demanded to ring his lawyer Ron Cannon, then, to his amazement, spotted Cannon on the bitumen outside. Someone in the family must have called him. He said, 'I can see Cannon,' but his lawyer was clearly unaware he was in such close proximity to his client.

Later on Mulvey re-entered the room. Ray said, 'You have a woman and two children in their nightgowns here. It is an outrage and against everything that we stand for in this country.' Ray believed in his country but couldn't believe what was happening to him and his family. 'You are gone for all money,' he said to Mulvey.

Mulvey turned to Hancock. 'He is right, you'd better get rid of her,' referring to Sheryl and the children. Hancock left the room. Ray could no longer hear the children crying. It was nearly 11 a.m.

During questioning on 23 September 1982, Ray was also charged over the Yellow Rose of Texas fraud. Soon afterwards he was allowed to go home where he was greeted by a distraught wife.

When Sheryl was allowed to leave police headquarters, she found herself on the street with two children in their nightclothes and no money. She hailed a taxi and told the driver, 'I have no money, but if you take me home I promise to pay you.' Fortunately, the taxi driver agreed.

Others too suffered collateral damage. On 12 November 1982, Andrew Foster, the brother of Peter's girlfriend, was on his way to work when a police vehicle in Jandakot ran him off the road. They left Foster's car in the ditch and drove him to central headquarters where they kept him for four hours, pressing him to admit that Ray and Brian had been involved in the Mint swindle. They offered him money and women. But Foster, who was just seventeen years old, would not give ground. They bashed him and held a knife to his throat. They rang his workplace to tell his employer he was not there because he was at police headquarters. When the police let him go and Foster went to work, he was told he was finished because the police had said he was a nasty character.

This was the case put to the jury by the Mickelberg defence. This was the core of the Mickelberg defence. They denied they had confessed to any crimes or that the police made contemporaneous notes of the interviews. And they denied that they had made the statements attributed to them at the interviews. The evidence of the three accused was central to the defence. Other defence witnesses were, in the main, only called to give alibis[41] to the whereabouts of the defendants on the day of the Perth Mint swindle and on the nights of the two arson attacks.

In addition, there was the evidence of salesman Douglas Walsh and of Rosemary Knight, who ran a bakery in the Warwick Grove Shopping Centre. They both confirmed Ray coming to see them about his lost black file containing the Gulley bank passbook — significant evidence for Ray who had told the police someone else must have found the passbook and used it for the swindle.

CHAPTER 3
CAUGHT AT GULLEY

Sergeant Hancock believed Gulley had caught out Ray. Michael Bowden, coming on as first change for the defence, was hoping a slip would similarly catch out Detective Sergeant Hooft. As the defence rebuttal continued, Bowden was there to get Brian off the hook.

To continue the cricket metaphor, Bowden was very much on the front foot as he set out to blunt Crown Prosecutor Davies' attack. He reminded the jury that only the alleged confessions — which Brian had vigorously denied making, and certainly had not signed — implicated him. He asked the jury to contemplate why a police officer of Hooft's experience would wait until after a suspect had confessed before bringing in a tape recorder. And why it would then slip his mind to ask the suspect to repeat his confession so he might record it. Helpfully, Bowden offered an answer. 'Brian Mickelberg did not make the alleged admissions.'

Bowden was quick to assure the jury he was not accusing Hooft of deliberately seeking to frame an innocent man. Nevertheless, this apparently conciliatory concession must have sown seeds of doubt in the minds of the jurors. Moreover, those seeds may have started to germinate when, in a less mollifying manner, he suggested Hooft and his colleagues believed all the rules favoured the accused, thus frustrating their attempts 'to investigate to the best of their ability.' He suggested that, feeling their cause was noble, the police might have been prepared to adopt inappropriate or even corrupt behaviour to nail those who they believed were guilty — a case of 'noble corruption.'[42] To make sure they got the point, he reminded the jury that 'this is a very dangerous state of affairs.'

He finished his summing up by reproving the Crown for

having conducted a 'trial by innuendo'. Because Brian had been part of the Yellow Rose of Texas sting; because he had bought gold — legitimately — from the Perth Mint; because he was a pilot and lived near Jandakot Airport, the Crown pointed the finger of suspicion at Brian as a participant in the Perth Mint swindle. However, suspicion is not enough. The Crown had not met its burden of proof that his client was guilty of the charges beyond reasonable doubt.[43] Bowden thanked the jury and sat down. It was early Friday afternoon, 25 February 1983.

Judge Heenan adjourned[44] the trial until Monday and expressed the hope that Brian, who had been feeling ill through either stress or some physical ailment, would be feeling better by then. Prison staff took Brian from the court to Royal Perth Hospital for observation and treatment before returning him to Canning Vale Remand Prison on Sunday. He appeared to have recovered by Monday morning when the court shifted its focus to Brian Singleton QC, appearing for Peter.

Clearly, Singleton did not want the seeds of doubt that Bowden had sown to languish for lack of cultivation. Subtly, he urged the jury not to allow prejudice and preconception to cloud their judgement.[45] He was well aware of how much discussion the case was generating in newspapers and on television and radio, at dinner parties, in bars and around backyard barbecues.

This was more than a crime against property; it was a crime against that most iconic of properties — gold. Singleton knew how unlikely it was that any juror would not have read or heard much about the swindle before they were sworn in. He wanted to minimise the likelihood of jury deliberations being swayed by smear and innuendo. 'We are, as humans, very susceptible to accepting adverse comments about somebody. Smear is the easiest thing to lay on somebody and almost impossible to disprove.' He invoked the example of smear in political campaigns, which he noted was 'quite relevant at the moment.' Western Australians were in the midst of two elections, federal and state, in both of which controversy abounded.

Singleton argued that the Crown's case 'commences at the end and works backwards.' He said the Crown had no evidence that the Mickelbergs had broken and entered the real estate agencies to steal the cheques that were subsequently used to buy gold from the Mint. Furthermore, the fact that the cheques presented to the Mint were endorsed with Peter Gulley's account number was only circumstantial evidence — a long way short of what was needed to incriminate his client. Singleton mocked the investigation. 'The police of course, putting two and two together come up with five. I can say it clearly, because it is a comment and I do not wish to denigrate them. I do not have to do that. They do it themselves.'

Resorting to the jargon of the racecourse, where as an owner of thoroughbreds he was very much at home, Singleton lampooned the evidence of Conti, the real estate proprietor, to emphasise what he called a 'leap in logic'. He recounted how Conti, naturally suspicious when he saw an orange vehicle pass by his burnt premises, 'wrote down the number, he says, XA or XR, or whatever it was and cannot remember the rest.' Singleton asked the question, 'How in the blue blazes he cannot remember the rest, if it is Brian Mickelberg's car, you may well ask because you will see the photograph of it and you will see its licence plate loud and clear. The number is 500. You might be excused for forgetting the prefix — the letters — but you could not forget the number, 500. That stands out like the proverbial dunny.' As, apparently, did Singleton's use of colloquial speech to Judge Heenan who cut in to ask, 'Mr Singleton, I hesitate to interrupt but please will you reduce your use of colloquialisms?'

Singleton was in full flight. He told the jury Conti said the car was a Japanese make, a Mazda or Toyota, but it suited the police to say Conti said it was a Porsche, because Brian owned one. In misrepresenting what Conti said, the police behaviour was 'fundamentally wrong because it was a lie.'

Singleton acknowledged that the Mickelbergs bought gold from the Mint using false names like 'Wilson and Bloggs and so on.' But, he added, so do a lot of other people, especially those who need to launder 'black money', such as those who are paid cash for work. He said men convert their black money from cash to gold to keep it away from their wives. 'They do not want the cash lying about; no doubt their wives will get their hands on it so they have to turn it into something their wives cannot get their hands on and is going to increase in value, hopefully gold and silver. If they ring up the Mint and buy the gold and silver, they are not fools, they are awake to the fellow down there at No. 1 St Georges Terrace [the tax office] who has got a bad habit of inquiring who has been buying gold, so they use false names.'

Singleton poured scorn on the identikit picture of Peter composed from information from the Allens and the alleged identification of Peter in the car park at Barker House by witnesses Henry, McCracken and Hondros. He highlighted the discrepancies between witnesses' evidence on the length of hair, whether it was curly or not, and the difference in height of the young man who purchased a car from the Allens and the man who parked at Barker House. He was amazed that neither the Allens, Henry nor McCracken mentioned Peter's prominent front teeth, or 'that when he talks ... he has a habit ... of licking his lips.'

It was, he said, a classic stitch of the three accused. Singleton reiterated Peter's allegations that he was 'touched up — struck — not bashed, not beaten, softened if you like,' by the police and was made to strip naked at Belmont CIB. He reminded the jury Peter had denied making the so-called confessions or admissions of his involvement in, and knowledge of, the conspiracy to defraud the Perth Mint.

Singleton asked the jury to accept that 'on the evidence and on the Crown's case itself ... it could not have been Peter Mickelberg who purchased the vehicle' or who Henry, McCracken or Hondros spotted or spoke to on the day in question. If that is the case, Singleton asked, 'why then would he make all these so-called semi-type confessions?'

There was a lack of evidence to connect Peter with any agreement with his brothers to swindle the Mint, Singleton said. While jury members may have some suspicions against Peter, that was not evidence of his guilt. He concluded by asking the jury to 'leave your prejudices at home, which I am sure you will do.'

At the end of Singleton's summing up, the court adjourned for the day. It reconvened the next day, Friday the first day of March, to listen to Ron Cannon, counsel for Ray. For the police and Crown, Ray the 'mastermind' was the primary target.

Cannon agreed with his learned friend, Crown Prosecutor Davies, that the plan was 'the product of a mastermind' with a genius for organisation. But it was not Ray. This mastermind — identity unknown — would have been aware of the police modus operandi; would have anticipated the media sensation the swindle would create; would have predicted 'that the whole majesty of the police force is going to be devoted to tracking' the culprit down. This unknown genius for organisation would have foreseen that the police would be under enormous pressure and 'would never rest until they caught the perpetrators of this crime.' They would know that the police would watch the gold market for years to see if the stolen bullion ever showed up.

'So what does this genius do? He takes his lesson from the movies. "What will I do to put the police off my trail? I will point them in the opposite direction," and this is precisely what I submit happened.' He knew how the Mint operated. He knew they did not require bank account numbers to be endorsed on the cheques they received for gold. Yet this mastermind wrote somebody else's account number on the cheque. Why? To point the police in the wrong direction when the Mint discovered the swindle. No one capable of planning and organising a fraud of this magnitude would be so stupid as to write their own account number on cheques they were going to use to perpetrate the fraud.

Cannon noted that the WABS cheque — one of the three used to buy the gold — had no account number that could be linked back to Ray. Some other connection was needed and how convenient that the cheque had a fingerprint on it, apparently belonging to Ray. But, according to Cannon, that fingerprint was manufactured. 'They had shown him the WABS cheque. He had handled it. He was then taken up and fingerprinted and they were happy now because they had his prints — or a print — on the cheque and his own fingerprints.' To emphasise the point, Cannon drew the jury's attention to Ray's evidence that Detective Round — whom Ray thought was more friendly and decent than the others — had confided in him, saying, 'I might have to go along with certain things later on that I don't particularly agree with.' Cannon contended that the 'certain things' included the manufacture of Ray's fingerprint on the WABS cheque.

He then tried to steer the jury towards an alternative scenario by pointing the finger at the SAS, Ray's former regiment. Ray said in evidence that he lost the building society passbook on or about 27 May 1982. On that day, he also visited the headquarters of the SAS at Campbell Barracks in the beachside suburb of Swanbourne. Cannon argued, 'It is not improbable that that book was lost at Campbell Barracks and the mastermind behind this activity was associated with Mickelberg at the barracks and when he found that book with a number, knowing Mickelberg's past activities in respect of dealing in gold and false names, said to himself, "I have devised a simple plan which will get the gold out of the Mint but, ah, fate has given me a chance of putting the police in the wrong direction. If I use this number ... on two of the cheques it will point to Peter Gulley; it will point to 144 Barker Road, the premises of Peggy Mickelberg's boarding house, the premises of Otto Kleiger who purchased the property," and we know in fact that Otto Kleiger is Raymond Mickelberg.'

It seems that in trying to finger a member of the SAS, without specifying anyone, Cannon was running his own race. Ray had never suggested that possibility.[46] And it certainly runs contrary to the code of mateship of the tight-knit brotherhood of elite SAS soldiers — past and present — that he would finger one of his own.

Cannon again brought up the Yellow Rose of Texas to explain why Ray started to tell lies when the Mint swindle investigations started. He could not tell them about the fake bank accounts because 'who knows where it would stop and, of course, it did not stop. Eventually, on 23 September, they [Ray, Brian and Peter] were arrested, together with Mum and Dad — the complete family, together with another gentleman — for the Yellow Rose of Texas.'

Taking his lead from Singleton, Cannon rejected the police explanation for the tape-recording debacle and accused the police of fabricating their notes after the interview because, without the 'admissions there is no proof whatsoever ... against Ray Mickelberg.' He also described Ray as 'a pretty prickly sort of bear to get into a cage with,' who people would think twice about laying a hand on. Moreover, it was unlikely that a man who, police claimed, was prepared to see his parents go to gaol because they could 'hack' it, would break down under police questioning.

Cannon also raised the issue of noble corruption. The pressure was on the police. 'Somebody had knocked off the Mint; no wonder Detective-Sergeant Hancock had pressure on him. Our sacred institution penetrated, not by a General Sherman tank, not by a helicopter, but by three pieces of paper and dud pieces of paper at that. Even the word "forty" is spelt wrong. That is what penetrated the Mint and that is why the pressure was put on them to solve it.' There was insufficient evidence for a jury to find them guilty beyond reasonable doubt, he said. But when you have a family of brothers comprising a former SAS soldier, a pilot and a young abalone diver it's enough to make a policeman salivate. And, of course, there was the Peter Gulley account. All that was missing was evidence. So, Cannon charged, they decided to invent evidence to convict men who they were convinced were guilty.

Cannon did grant the police a concession; that Western Australia does have a good police force. But, he added, sometimes, as in any job, they were over-enthusiastic and this sometimes led to jumping to conclusions and doing things to support that conclusion. 'I suggest the key to this particular case is the fact that the police started off with preconceived notions. It had to be a military operation. Once they got the sniff of Raymond Mickelberg SAS, Brian Mickelberg helicopter pilot, the coincidence of the lost passbook, they lost all sense of exploring other directions but pursued what they thought was the correct direction and, failing to find evidence which they knew would stand up in a court of law, deliberately went out of their way to manufacture evidence, believing in their hearts that in the long run they were doing justice by having guilty men convicted by a jury. They themselves are guilty, in our submission, of usurping your role of evaluating the evidence, starting off with the principle that all men are presumed innocent until they are found guilty.'[47]

Cannon thanked the jury and Judge Heenan called lunch.

Taking up the attack after lunch, Crown Prosecutor Ron Davies settled in for a marathon spell that was to last two days. He started with a bouncer to the Mickelbergs' counsel, calling the defence 'a rather well organised attempt perhaps to swindle the jury that is trying to get to the bottom of it [the Mint swindle].'

Davies did not miss the chance to remind the jury again of the Yellow Rose of Texas, although he almost seemed to suggest he was doing so more in sorrow than in anger because, had the defence not introduced it, he would not have been able to raise the matter. But now that the videotape of the Yellow Rose of

Texas incident was in play, he thought that perhaps it 'may assist you with the credit, the believability of some of the witnesses that you have to consider — some of the members of the family you have to consider — in coming to your decision on this case.'

The Crown vehemently rejected the defence accusation of noble corruption. Davies scoffed at Bowden's and Cannon's claims that Western Australia's 'good police force' would attempt to frame only those they thought were guilty, which is only a bit less derogatory than suggesting the police would frame someone even if they didn't think they were guilty. The defence were asking the jury to accept that 'there has been disgusting, vile, outrageous, concerted behaviour on the part of a large group of police officers who in a bald-faced way present themselves before you and brave it out — perjury, a concoction of evidence, fabrication of evidence, cheating with documents, cheating with fingerprints, cheating with the word 'forty', terrorising wives and kids, bashing people — and they try to make it sound as if it is not all that bad because they only did it because they thought they had the right people.'

Shamelessly flattering the jury, Davies suggested they were too smart to swallow that concoction, even when the defence tried to 'sugar the pill'. Derisively, he challenged the logic of the good-but-misguided-police-force argument that his adversary expected the jurors to buy. 'Mr Cannon would have to be joking to stand up there in a bald-faced way and say to you, "We have a very good police force" after what the defence has been saying about these fellows for days, but they do not want you to quite realise what it is you are being asked to accept.'

He gave equally short shrift to the defence version of how the Gulley account number came to be on the PBS cheques, simply repeating the words of Hancock. 'Just in case they [the Mint] rang up to see if it was a genuine account number.' Davies argued the Mint would only be concerned to see if it were a genuine account; they would, he said, assume there was enough money to meet the cheque. This argument seems as porous as that of the defence. Surely, if the Mint was suspicious about the genuineness of the account, they would be also curious to know whether the account held sufficient funds to cover the cheque, even though it was a building society cheque.

He was just as scathing of the defence claim that Ray held the Gulley account to avoid tax; the account only ever had $66 in it at any relevant time, an amount hardly likely to excite even the most insatiable taxman.

Davies contemptuously dismantled the SAS 'mastermind' defence Cannon had proposed. It was fanciful, he sneered, to propose that 'these cunning SAS fellows' had, from the stroke of luck of Ray losing his passbook at the barracks, concocted a fantastic scheme to swindle the Mint. 'How hopeless a proposition is that? It is a pure fluke that the CIB officers, assisted by Sergeant Billing, even traced it. If they [the Mickelbergs] had stuck with their answer "it's a boarding house, he must have lived there, we didn't keep any records," it would never have been positively sheeted home to him.'

Furthermore, 'According to Mr Cannon's fanciful solution ... the SAS ... knew that Gulley was Mickelberg and they knew that the police would find out that Gulley was Mickelberg. How?' Davies maintained there was no sensible answer to this 'wild nonsense-type proposition.'

Davies argued that to corroborate his story that he lost the black folder with the Gulley passbook in it, Ray fabricated evidence by revisiting a couple of premises he had been in on 27 May, inquiring if a black folder had been found. He also wrote a note to himself in his diary to remind him to look for the black folder. However, that note was in different ink to other writing on the diary page and he wrote it at the top of the diary.

Contemptuously, Davies dismissed the defence SAS conspiracy theory, arguing that what made the suggestion so nonsensical was that the planning for the swindle must have been in train at least as early as April when the mastermind stole the cheques. Yet the defence wanted the jury to believe that the chance loss of the Gulley passbook on 27 May was the trigger for the whole diabolically clever SAS plot. It just didn't add up.

As his marathon spell continued into day ten, Davies sought to persuade the jury the police confessions were not concocted, nor was any prosecutorial evidence, including incriminating scientific evidence such as Ray's fingerprint on the WABS cheque. He concluded his summing up by defending the integrity of detectives against the defence claim they were engaged in 'a vile, rotten conspiracy to pervert the course of justice, to fabricate evidence, to put fingerprints onto documents, to make confessional material, to come forward one after another in a carefully orchestrated, well planned, well worked out, well documented, rotten conspiracy to try and persuade you to convict innocent people.'

Davies was disdainful of the defence right to the end. Not only would the defence have the jury believe the detectives were reprehensible, they also painted them as lacking the skill and cunning to fabricate evidence successfully. That was nonsense, said Davies. Had they concocted evidence, they would have made it more definitively damning so that the statements would shout unequivocally, 'We are guilty.'

Finally, Davies was ready to put the ultimate question to the jury. 'Do you have a clever, although hampered, investigation by experienced police officers who after all are ordinary family men and women, going about their duty, doing the best with the evidence that was available, asking the questions ... in a way which did its best to put legitimate pressure on the accused to bring about such answers as they got and the Mickelberg family trying to swindle you, or is it the other way around? It is all a great fabrication; we should have been after the SAS and there is something vile and rotten in the whole of this group of officers who paraded themselves before you in such a brazen fashion and carried it off so well.'

Now it was the turn of Judge Heenan, a foundation judge of the District Court (1970)[48] and a member of a prominent Perth legal family, to sum up for the jury matters of law.[49] He would also need to touch on matters of fact. However, while they had to accept what he said on matters of law, anything his Honour said about facts did not bind the jury; they were the final arbiter of facts and on them rested the ultimate decision: guilty or innocent.[50]

He emphasised the golden principle of criminal law in the common law system: that the burden or onus of proof of proving the charges against the three accused rested with the Crown. There is a presumption of innocence. There is no onus on the accused to prove that he is innocent. Unless the Crown can convince the jury of guilt, the accused remains innocent according to the law. In addition, the standard of proof required in criminal cases is proof beyond reasonable doubt because 'it is better that ten guilty persons escape than that one innocent suffers' — widely known in legal circles as the 'ten-to-one rule'[51] and founded on the belief that greater social harm is caused by an innocent person going to gaol than a guilty person being set free. 'So,' Judge Heenan said, 'before you are entitled to find any of the accused men guilty on any one of the counts in the indictment, you must be satisfied beyond reasonable doubt, not only that the offence was committed but also that the accused person in question committed the offence. If you have a reasonable doubt as to either of those matters then the appropriate verdict is not guilty in relation to that person in respect of that count.'

Judge Heenan traversed each of the eight charges, which each jury member had on a copy of the indictment sheet in front of them. Charges 2 to 8 flowed from the first charge, which was the conspiracy to defraud[52] the director of the Perth Mint. The judge told the jury that '[a] conspiracy is an agreement by two or more persons to do an unlawful act or to do a lawful act by unlawful means. The agreement does not have to be in writing. It does not have to be formal in any way at all. It does not have to be expressed orally or even in explicit terms.' But there does need to be a 'meeting of minds so as to make an agreement to carry out a particular form of action and there must be not only a meeting of minds but an intention formed in the minds of conspirators, to carry it out. In other words, a common purpose must be formed.'

He pointed out that any oral or written statement made by one of the accused could not be admissible against the other accused 'unless confirmed or adopted from the witness box by the maker of the statement.'[53] This means that if one of the accused claims during his oral evidence that another of the accused had made a statement, the jury cannot accept that claim as evidence unless the person who is alleged to have made the statement himself confirms it from the witness box. The judge then moved on to the evidence and facts of the case.

He drew the jury's attention to the large volume of evidence presented to the court in relation to the other activities of the brothers, including transactions under false names to buy bullion from the Mint. But the judge warned the jury such evidence could not be used to show a propensity to commit the crimes they were being trialled for but only as showing 'some familiarity with the procedures that applied at the Mint when bullion was sold.'[54]

The Yellow Rose of Texas again reared its head. By now the brothers, particularly Ray, would be wondering 'why in blue blazes' (to borrow Singleton's vernacular) their defence counsels had raised the incident. While the judge prefaced his comments with the observation that the Yellow Rose of Texas 'seems to have no great relevance to' the Mint swindle case, its unintended consequence — on which Judge Heenan now ruminated — was that it provided the Crown with 'an opportunity of testing the credibility, in particular, of Raymond Mickelberg and his mother, Mrs Mickelberg.' One must also wonder what influence it had on the jury as it floated the notion of Ray's lack of candour.

In weighing up the evidence, Judge Heenan told the jury; in determining the truthfulness of that evidence, jury members 'will have to be influenced in some cases, at least, by the impression that particular witness left upon you when giving evidence in the witness box.'[55] Ray's reluctance to answer questions in relation to his mother's foreknowledge of the Yellow Rose of Texas drama more likely than not compromised his credibility as a witness of truth.

Judge Heenan reminded the jury of the oath they each took at the beginning of the trial to 'return a true verdict according to the evidence.' They would comply with their oath if they applied the law as directed by the judge to the facts according to the evidence presented in court. Evidence consisted of testimony of witnesses under oath in the witness box and of exhibits — so-called direct evidence. Jury members could also evaluate the witnesses themselves, draw inferences, and reach conclusions from the evidence presented. Then there was the circumstantial evidence, on which, as Judge Heenan noted, the Crown placed a heavy weight. 'It is clear that in this case the Crown relies a good deal upon proof of facts or circumstances from which it asks you to infer that the accused are guilty of the offence in question. In other words, the Crown asks you to act upon circumstantial evidence.'

He reminded them that, in relying on circumstantial evidence, they had to exercise care. 'The test really is one for your understanding and for your conscience and you have to look at the picture as a whole using what I think is a most satisfactory way of putting it: I direct that you are not entitled to find any of the accused guilty on the basis of circumstantial evidence alone unless the circumstances are such that you may reasonably draw an inference of his guilt and can reasonably draw no other inference.' In other words, there is no other reasonable alternative. As the judge put it, 'You are not entitled to find a person guilty on the basis of circumstantial evidence alone if there might be a reasonable explanation for the proven circumstances which is consistent with innocence on his part.'[56]

The judge thought that some of counsels' attacks on the police, such as comments about 'Hancock and his merry men', while maybe harmless, were unfortunate. He was more forthright about the more serious allegations against the police. 'Clearly ... attacks have been made upon the police by the accused in the course of their evidence and from counsel from the bar table. They have charged the police with misconduct of a very serious nature, misconduct which I think each of the counsel for the accused ascribed to excessive zeal on the part of the police, suggesting to you that the police believe that the accused were guilty and that they were short of evidence and, as I understand the allegations, that the police then set about concocting further evidence to implicate the accused.'

But, he emphasised, the police were not on trial. The jury's decision must not be a determination on whether the police or the accused were telling the truth. Because even if the jury did not believe one of the accused but still had reasonable doubt as to his guilt, they must return a not guilty verdict. But, he asked them, if the jury found that 'the accused have told lies about the police in relation to such an important matter, what weight can you give to the evidence of the accused in relation to other matters?'[57] While the judge had previously mentioned the credibility of the police testimony, he did not reiterate it here as he did with the Mickelbergs' evidence.

On the face of it, failing to give the same emphasis to the need to test police credibility works against the accused. If police witnesses had lied, this would affect the weight that the jury could give to their evidence. However, it is not surprising that Judge Heenan did not say this to the jury. When it is only the word of the police against the word of an accused — with no compelling evidence one way or the other — courts generally are loath to question the veracity of police evidence. Persons accused of criminal offences are generally less credible witnesses than well practised and presentable police officers who will often have colleagues to corroborate their evidence. Police officers will also often have the benefit of holding most if not all evidence and information concerning the offence.[58]

Judge Heenan then moved on to the indictable charges and laid out the chronology of the police investigations and the evidence against the three brothers. He reminded the jury that it was the Gulley account number on two of the cheques that led the police to the Mickelberg family.

He said the Crown's case could be divided into two parts. First, that someone committed the offence. It would seem that 'there is no real challenge made to that aspect of the Crown case,' although that was for the jury to decide. Second, that the three accused committed the offences. This was the crux of the matter, the essence of issue in dispute.

The case against Brian, the judge said, was not as strong as that against his brothers. 'As Mr Davies has so clearly acknowledged, the case against Brian Mickelberg is not as lengthy, at least, as the case against either of the other two.'

Crucial to the Crown's case was Hancock's evidence that, when he accused Brian of being part of the whole Mint swindle plan, he replied, 'There's no way out then — if they are charged, I will have to be charged.' Judge Heenan directed the jury that, if they accepted that evidence, the Crown says 'that you are entitled to find, that you would be justified in finding, that in that exchange the accused Brian Mickelberg admitted that he was part of the whole plan, and ... that he was involved from the beginning; at least ... before the breaking and entering of the Conti Sheffield Estate Agency and the setting fire to that premise.' Apart from the police evidence, the judge said, there was nothing to connect Brian with the Mint swindle or with any of the alleged offences leading up to it.

The judge then turned to the case against the youngest of the family, Peter. He said, 'The most significant physical evidence ... which tends to implicate him is the white Ford Falcon motor car.' There were, he said, two main groups of evidence. The first revolved around the descriptions of the eyewitnesses, particularly the Allens and Mr Henry. The second group was the handwriting of the 'Talbot note', which was written at the Allens' Armadale home on 25 May 1982.

Judge Heenan warned the jury that they must treat eyewitness identification evidence carefully; frequently it is wrong and often has resulted in miscarriages of justices.[59] It is common for a number of eyewitnesses to give contradictory descriptions of the same person. In any case, there was no positive identification of Peter. Probably, the most that could be made of the eyewitness evidence 'is that you may think they were saying the accused Peter Mickelberg could have been the young man involved with the car.'

He warned of a 'lurking danger' that the jury 'might treat the evidence of each as not being sufficient by itself but when put together as amounting to convincing evidence.' This would be treating the identification evidence in the same way as circumstantial evidence, but due to the unreliability of identification evidence, this cannot be done.[60] Judge Heenan could not have been clearer on this point. 'So I direct you in the end that the evidence of Mr and Mrs Allen and Mr Henry and Mr Hondros and Mr McCracken cannot be accepted as identification of Peter Mickelberg as the young man in question.' Likewise, the identikit composed by the police from information provided by the Allens could not 'be accepted as evidence tying in the accused Mickelberg with the young man.'

Judge Heenan considered the Talbot note the main evidence of identification. He asked the jury to take into account the exhibits the Crown had produced and to compare the Talbot note with other handwriting from various documents Sergeant Billing used in forming his conclusion the handwriting on the Talbot note was Peter's. If the jury needed assistance in reaching a conclusion, he said, they should weigh up Billing's testimony. Was it reliable? Did Billing impress them as being honest and competent? Could they accept his conclusions beyond reasonable doubt? If so 'then it would seem quite clear that the accused Peter Mickelberg was the young man who bought the car at Armadale on 25 May. If he bought the car you may well conclude that he was involved in the Mint swindle.'

The Talbot note was an important test for Peter. If his credibility on this issue was weighed in the balance and found wanting, the jury might be reluctant to give credence to his allegations of police maltreatment. Judge Heenan said, 'If his evidence in that regard is true then the police officers behaved in disgraceful fashion — there are no two ways about it — and their evidence should be rejected out of hand.' But, he reminded them, 'even if you are not convinced that it is true, in the end the final question is not whether the police are telling the truth or whether the accused is telling the truth but rather whether the Crown have established beyond reasonable doubt in relation to each offence that he is guilty.' Of course, if the jury did accept what the police officers said, it was 'very persuasive evidence to put into the scales' against Peter.

He urged the jury to gauge each police officer individually, to how they presented themselves in the witness box. 'Think back as to each of them as a human being. What did you think of him at the time? What did you think of her? What impression did you get as to the honesty, the reliability and the fairness of that particular man or woman? Did you find that that person was a person upon whom you could rely? Did you find that what that person said was convincing? It is important, members of the jury, I suggest to you, that you should not bundle them all together as it were and say "that's the evidence of the detectives." Try to separate in your mind the individual detective. Try to separate in your mind the role that that particular detective played in the investigation.'

Then it was time for the alleged 'mastermind'. The most direct evidence against Ray, the judge said, was the fingerprint on the WABS cheque. And, because no one had challenged Sergeant Ken Henning's evidence on the point, the jury 'may safely accept that a fingerprint is, in effect, an unforgeable signature.'[61] Therefore, the critical question was whether the print was on the cheque when the Mint received it or whether, as Ray alleged, the police placed it there after he handled the cheque during an interview with Hancock on 15 July 1982. If it was there when the Mint received the cheque, the jury could draw an inference that Ray was involved in the Mint swindle.

The judge did not give much weight to the defence counsel argument that independent evidence was not available to show the print was on the cheque prior to 15 July. Nor did he attach significance to Cannon's assertion 'that if the fingerprint was there before 15 July it should have been identified before then, before Raymond Mickelberg was interviewed at all, because he has told you his fingerprints had been taken in 1975 or 1976 and therefore were on file and available to the police officers.' He reminded the jury that no one else had corroborated Ray's claim. 'There is no evidence that his fingerprint from that time was available to the police officers and you would have expected, if it were, that when Sergeant Henning found the fingerprint, as he has told you, on 24 June that it would have been compared with Raymond John Mickelberg's fingerprint if it were in the records.'

Judge Heenan next turned to the Gulley account. He explained the issues, particularly the question of how the account number came to be on the two PBS cheques, and reminded the jury of Ray's explanation that he initially denied knowledge of the account because 'he did not want to be charged with using yet another false name.'

His Honour referred briefly to the police evidence that Ray said he knew where the gold was but could not say anything more, because 'there was more involved than Hancock realised.' On this point he left the jury with the enigmatic statement that Ray could not say whether it was possible to recover the gold 'because he was a soldier.'

As he was obliged to, the judge reminded the jury that Ray had denied under oath any involvement in the Perth Mint swindle. He alluded to the Cannon hypothesis of a mastermind at work and his claim 'that the three accused are here because the police have been led to them by a false trail and in following that trail the police have fabricated admissions, they did not have sufficient evidence and so they made it up.' The judge added, 'You have heard comments from each side of the bar table in relation to those matters and I shall say no more about them.'

As he did with the case against Peter, Judge Heenan said it was convenient to consider it in two parts. First, there was the circumstantial evidence. Second, there were the interviews with the police officers. He suggested that it might be best for the jury to commence their deliberations by looking separately at each part. Further, he said, 'Look at the picture presented by the evidence as to the fingerprint on the Western Australian Building Society cheque, look at the association between the other two cheques and the Gulley account, look at this explanation in relation to those matters.

'I remind you also to look at the evidence relating to the operations on his bank accounts — for example, on the opening of the bank account in the name of Wilson on 17 March 1982 and the various withdrawals from it; look at the evidence as to what he was doing on some of the key dates that you have heard, 7 April, 22 June; look at the evidence as to his interviews with the police; try, if you can, to decide where the truth lies; and finally, look again at the overall picture presented by the evidence. Then, members of the jury, in relation to him, as in relation to the other two accused, you go back and approach your final deliberations in those three stages.'

Acknowledging that this was a long process, the judge added, 'I hope that this is not too tedious but I think it is important that I stress in relation to each of the accused, you look at them separately, you look at the offences separately, you examine the case against each.' He emphasised again, that in considering each charge against each of the accused, they had to be satisfied beyond reasonable doubt before they could return a guilty verdict on any charge.

If judge and counsel were tired but happy that their ordeal was over, the jurors' heads were probably swimming as they contemplated the magnitude of the task that lay ahead as Judge Heenan invited them to 'retire and consider your verdict.'

The trial had commenced on 7 February 1983. It was 4 March 1983.

In the event, it did not take long for the jury to reach a verdict. After two and a half hours, the ten men and two women filed into court and resumed their seats. The Clerk of Arraigns said in a voice audible to all, 'Members of the jury, are you agreed upon your verdicts?'[62] The foreman, the spokesman for the twelve-member jury, replied, 'We are.' The atmosphere in the court was hushed and tense. All eyes were on the Clerk of Arraigns.

'As to the first count on the indictment, how say you? Is the accused Raymond John Mickelberg guilty or not guilty?'

The foreman replied, 'Guilty.' Raymond showed no trace of emotion.

'Is that the verdict of you all?'

'It is,' the foreman replied.

This process was repeated for Brian and Peter on the first count and for all three accused on the other seven indictable charges. Ray and Peter were found guilty of all eight charges; Brian found guilty of four — the conspiracy charge and each count of obtaining gold by false pretences with intent to defraud. The jury found him not guilty on the breaking and entering counts, and each charge of arson.

Judge Heenan thanked the jury for having discharged their civic duty on behalf of the community, for their attention and for their efforts in this 'long' and 'difficult' trial.

After the jury was discharged, the judge asked each accused if they had 'anything to say why sentence should not be passed upon you accordance to law?' Neither the three accused nor their counsel took up this offer. Perhaps they were already thinking about an appeal. The brothers were remanded in custody to 18 March 1983.

The sentences imposed were long: Ray was sentenced to twenty years with a twelve-year minimum before being eligible for parole; Peter was given sixteen years with a nine-year minimum; and Brian was sentenced to twelve years with a seven-year minimum.[63]

As journalist Jim Odgers reported in the *West Australian* a week later, some legal and social observers considered the length of sentencing to be excessive. The paper reported that the assistant director of the Australian Institute of Criminology, Colin Bevan, said, 'When thirteen years is the average time served for capital crimes then twelve years for a million dollars seems a little cockeyed.' Bevan added that sentencing for property crimes seemed to still be guided by a feudal mindset in that 'we regard property to be of such paramount importance.'

The president of the Australian Women Against Rape said her executive discussed the question of sentencing for rape offences following the Mickelberg case. She said judges needed to sentence rapists to terms that reflect 'public outrage' about the crime. She added, 'If sentencing appears to attribute more value to property than to people then people will lose confidence in the judicial system ... judges need to change their feudal attitudes and show that they regard human life as more important than property.'

But law reform campaigner Brian Tennant supported the sentencing principles in the Mickelberg case. 'The court has a duty to see that crime does not pay and that justice is seen to be done,' he said. Not surprisingly, Hancock agreed, reportedly saying, 'Burglary, the use of false cheques and, for two of the brothers, arson, had been used. Had those fires got away lives may have been endangered.'

Odgers concluded his article with a comparison of early 1983 sentences in Western Australia for crimes against people: maximum sentences ranged from twelve years to sixteen, and minimum sentences from six years to nine. The crimes all involved multiple rapes against women. For example, in February 1983, twenty-seven year old Craig Herron was sentenced to sixteen years with a minimum of eight for a 'horrendous' list of crimes including 'three counts of depriving women of their liberty and three counts of rape and one of indecent assault.'[64]

The Mickelberg sentences reflected how severely the law viewed property crimes. All the more so, perhaps, because the property was gold from the Perth Mint. And as prosecutor Davies had been at pains to remind the court, the police still had not recovered the gold, a fact he urged Judge Heenan to consider when handing down the sentences. The judge agreed, making it clear that he would have imposed lighter sentences if the Mickelbergs had revealed where the missing gold bullion was.[65] Which has a Kafkaesque quality about it if, as the brothers insist, they didn't steal it.

CHAPTER 4
BRIAN'S RELEASE

The convicted Mickelbergs were no shrinking violets, but even Ray, the tough former SAS Vietnam veteran, who loathed weakness[66] was shocked by the conditions inside Fremantle Prison. In November 1983 he wrote in his prison diary, 'Peter and I have now decided that one cannot remain silent in respect of the shocking conditions in [this] barbaric establishment. Of course, if one speaks out one can "expect special treatment". This has never deterred us nor shall it now.'[67] They did not remain silent, and informed the social and welfare workers who worked at or visited the prisons of the mistreatment of prisoners.

Built by convicts in 1850, Fremantle Prison had a reputation as one of the toughest prisons in the country. Solitary confinement and corporal and capital punishment were all part of its infamous history; it was the site of the last execution in Western Australia when serial killer Eric Edgar Cooke was hanged there at eight o'clock on the morning of 26 October 1964. Living conditions were appalling and violence was a constant. Prisoners spent fifteen hours of each day in small limestone cells with only a metal bucket for a toilet. They endured century-plus heat in summer, when the afternoon sea breeze — the Fremantle Doctor — provided a temporary respite if they were lucky. In winter they shivered through long, cold nights as howling westerlies blasted the prison.[68]

The Mickelberg brothers weren't the first to complain about the atrocious conditions: the gaol was condemned as a health risk just a few years after it was built in 1850. Yet in 1983 it still held more than 800 prisoners, crammed two to a small cell. Many desperate men sought release in suicide; others reacted to the subhuman conditions by perpetrating violence on their fellow inmates. Prison officers rarely intervened. Rape of younger and weaker inmates was common.

During the few hours each day when prison officers allowed them to leave their limestone cells, more than 150 men crowded together in an exercise area about one-and-a-half times the size of a tennis court. They shared one working toilet. There were open sewers into which, each morning, they poured the contents of the metal toilet buckets. In winter the sewers overflowed, further reducing the size of the recreation area where the prisoners prowled like caged animals. Their only release from the fear, tension and boredom was one forty-minute a week visit for those lucky enough to have someone on the outside who was able, or cared enough, to come.

The shameful history of Fremantle gaol came to a merciful end in 1991 when the last prisoner left and the building became a tourist site for those with a penchant for penal history or a macabre interest in this monument to human misery.

Brian was lucky. He spent only three days at Fremantle Prison, serving the rest of his term at Canning Vale Remand Centre. Ray and Peter had a longer time at Fremantle: from 18 to 21 March 1983 and from 4 November 1983 to 17 September 1986. In between these two stays they were inmates of Canning Vale Remand Centre, and after their second stint at Fremantle they were transferred to Canning Vale Prison.

Like most prisoners, Peter and Ray were alert to the dangers of prison life. They stood with their backs to the wall when brushing their teeth, afraid even to bend to spit for fear of having their head bashed into the basin. Prisoners showered quickly, their backs to the taps ready to defend themselves, ever aware they were especially vulnerable when soap and water got into their eyes and blurred their vision.

But avoiding violence was not that easy. One day, a prisoner lunged at Peter with a splintered broomstick, cutting open his right eye. Shortly after that, another prisoner attacked Peter, and Ray rushed over to help. It was a trap. Known police informer and former champion boxer Ron Smith was waiting for Ray, confident that he would come to the aid of his younger brother.

Smith attacked Ray with a metal bucket, opening up a deep gash on his head. Ray and Smith wrestled each other until Smith broke loose and lunged again at Ray, biting hard and deep into Ray's fourth finger on his left hand until the finger tore away at the second joint. With blood pulsing from Ray's severed finger, more than a dozen assailants encircled the brothers. Eventually, the prisoners allowed Peter to drag a protesting Ray out into the prison yard. In spite of his injury, Ray still wanted to take on his attacker. But by now, Smith and his 'assistants' were more interested in kicking the severed finger around like a soccer ball until, tiring of this game, they flushed it down the toilet. None of the prisoners involved in setting the trap ever told Ray or Peter why they did it. Was it simply because they were the Mickelbergs?

On 28 August 1984, Ray and Peter witnessed a struggle between guards and twenty-five year old Aboriginal prisoner, Robert Walker. After the guards calmed Walker with an injection of largactil, they carried him to an observation cell. His breathing was shallow and his pulse weak. Prison officers summoned a doctor, but Walker died within moments of his arrival. The official cause of death was asphyxia resulting from compression of the chest which Walker suffered during the struggle with prison officers. At the Royal Commission into Aboriginal Deaths in Custody six years later, the Mickelbergs alleged that a number of officers had severely beaten Walker. However, the Counsel Assisting the Royal Commission discounted the Mickelbergs' version of the episode, without giving any adequate explanation for doing so.[69]

Even within the relative comfort of Canning Vale Prison, danger and violence were still constant companions. Just one wrong word was sometimes all it took, as Peter found out when he offered the opinion that the TV program *Neighbours* was 'crap'. A fellow prisoner disagreed and pulled a knife on him.

Unsettling as this confrontation was, Peter was to stumble upon a scene more sickening than he could have imagined. Entering the back of the cookhouse he saw four inmates holding another prisoner, who would have been no more than twenty. They slashed his pants down the back, squirted mayonnaise into his anus then took turns raping him. Peter rushed off to find Ray. Accompanied by another prisoner, they ran to the cookhouse yelling to the rapists to 'fuck off.' After threatening Ray and Peter, the assailants fled, leaving their young victim crying on the floor.

Ray reported the rape to the authorities, whose only response was to move the Mickelbergs away from kitchen duties.

In early 1984, Ray wrote in his diary, 'Peter has just said to me, "Ray, we must get out of here fast." I concur fully. No one can live here and remain sane or human.' The brothers were already doing everything they could to escape this dehumanising environment. Ray had written to WA Attorney-General Joe Berinson seeking answers to his allegations of police misconduct and access to some of the trial exhibits. Berinson did not reply. So the brothers took matters into their own hands. Lacking the money for high-priced legal representation, they immersed themselves in legal textbooks, most provided by visitors, readying themselves to storm the court as their own advocates. They had no other alternative.

Ray and Peter had already commenced private prosecutions against several police officers involved in the Mint swindle investigation.[70] In October 1983 they alleged that several officers committed perjury, conspiracy to pervert the course of justice, deprivation of liberty and assault. In particular they alleged that Hancock and Lewandowski assaulted Peter and deprived him of his liberty and that they committed perjury when recounting in court their recollections of the 26 July 1982 interviews at Belmont CIB.

But these actions would fail. Allegations against police misconduct and corruption were nothing new in the WA police force; they had preceded the Mint swindle and the Mickelbergs. A case in point is the mysterious death of Shirley Finn and police control of the prostitution industry.

On 23 June 1975 well-known brothel madam Shirley Finn was shot dead in her car near the South Perth foreshore. The murder is still unsolved and from the early stages there were speculations of police involvement. The murder made huge headlines and conspiracy theories and speculation resurfaced in the media every few years since. It has developed into one of Perth's most intriguing and enduring murder mysteries.

At the time of her death, Shirley Finn was a leading Perth socialite and the wealthiest madam in Western Australia. She held lavish parties at her South Perth foreshore mansion attended by many of Perth's wealthiest and best-known people. She once entertained Elton John on a visit to Perth. A $3000 diamond set in one tooth was testament to her distinctive, if slightly idiosyncratic, style.[71]

Lack of evidence and apparent motive has ensured that public interest in her murder has never waned. All that is known is that she went out to meet an unknown person or persons. She dressed well, wearing her favourite ball gown, which suggests it was a meeting of importance in which she wanted to impress. The most popular and persevering theory is that she was killed by corrupt police officers for an unknown reason. Another theory is that interstate crime groups, wanting to move into the Perth vice industry, murdered her, perhaps because she was resisting their entry into Western Australia. A third, and highly speculative rumour, is that the murder was organised by a prominent member of society, perhaps a politician or businessman, in order to silence Finn. As Perth's queen of vice, Finn knew secrets that could have been very damaging if released into the public domain.

A year before Finn's murder, a bomb blasted the facade of one of her massage parlours, suggesting she had enemies willing to act violently against her. Perhaps the bomb was a threat or warning. Just who her enemies were and why she had to be murdered is still unknown.

On 14 October 1975, just four months after Finn's death, a Royal Commission[72] inquired into allegations of police impropriety in regulating the prostitution industry. The Royal Commission briefly touched on the subject of Shirley Finn, without suggesting police or political connection to her death.

The 1975 Royal Commission, titled The Royal Commission into Matters Surrounding the Administration of the Law Relating to Prostitution,[73] arose from the persistent actions of Police Superintendent Harold Daniels (known as 'Spike' Daniels), who became fixated on what he believed was the rampant spread of prostitution in Perth. He claimed the existence of a renegade police system of prostitution 'protection' as distinct from mere 'toleration.'[74]

The 1975 Royal Commission did not make any findings of impropriety against the police. Moreover, in accepting the generally held view that prostitution could not be eradicated, Commissioner John Norris found that the current system of tolerance and containment was the only practical path for police to follow. Police allowed brothels to operate provided no men were involved in their running and the girls complied with age, health and behavioural requirements. The police did not allow working girls with criminal records and strictly enforced the rule that excluded men or criminal syndicates from the industry.[75]

The Royal Commission also found Daniels' claims of police impropriety were unjustified,[76] that he was suffering a nervous breakdown and that most of his ideas and beliefs arose through extreme stress and paranoia. Only his high rank had enabled him to persist with his claims all the way to calling for a royal commission.

The Royal Commission made no findings as to the Shirley Finn murder and only touched on it briefly — hardly surprising given the murder had only occurred four months earlier and police were still investigating. Several witnesses did provide hearsay evidence of Shirley Finn's close association with police and claimed that several detectives regularly received protection money. However, the Commissioner was sceptical and made no adverse findings about the police.[77]

Compared to the 2004 Police Royal Commission report,[78] the 1975 Royal Commission report suggests a too-ready willingness by the commission to regard the integrity of the police force and the behaviour of its officers as above reproach. Given that the 2004 Royal Commission report found that corruption was widespread after 1985, it is possible pockets of corruption existed within the force well before then.

On 4 February 1982, not six years after the release of the 1975 Royal Commission report, claims similar to those that led to the 1975 hearings prompted the Minister for Police to announce another investigation (not a royal commission) into recent allegations of graft and corruption in relation to prostitution. The 1982 report, by former WA Ombudsman (1972–1980) Oliver Dixon, focused on what action the police took following the recent allegations of corruption and whether they dealt with them appropriately and in the correct manner.[79]

A front-page article in the *Western Mail* on 24 December 1981 precipitated the 1982 investigation. Headlined 'Police Quit After Claims of Payoffs', the article reported that 'two senior policemen have resigned after inquiries into allegations of protection payments by prostitutes.'[80] The two officers were Detective Sergeant Kerry Tangney and Detective Laurie Butler. The men had faced questions from the Police Commissioner about whether they had taken bribes from brothel keepers. They denied the allegation, and the investigation could find no conclusive evidence to support it. But the Commissioner was satisfied that the two detectives had formed an 'association' with brothel keepers. In what the Dixon report was later to describe as a 'significant' act, both men resigned immediately.[81] In total, seven police officers were dismissed or resigned. The Dixon report found that the Police Commissioner had fully investigated all allegations and had dealt with them appropriately.

In all, the Dixon inquiry investigated eleven allegations of police corruption, including two made by Tangney and Butler.[82] The pair claimed that brothel madams and illegal casino operators regularly made massive cash payments to police officers. Senior police officers organised the payments and then distributed the proceeds amongst other officers, they said. However, the Dixon report noted that there was no evidence to support these allegations. Furthermore, it formed an unfavourable view of the two men because they refused to cooperate with the investigation and would not elaborate on their claims.[83]

That the two detectives refused to cooperate is not surprising. They had already been charged and tried for conspiracy and other offences.[84] Although acquitted, they were exhausted after the long trial and very bitter about the way former friends and colleagues had treated them.[85] What was in it for them to cooperate with Dixon?

During the investigation into their conduct, Tangney and Butler had also reprised Shirley Finn. They alleged a police link to her murder because the site of her death was a regular meeting place between police and informants. The pair also claimed evidence disappeared from police headquarters, a claim the report dismissed after Dixon investigated and saw the allegedly missing evidence in the police safe.[86]

In summary, the Dixon report found no conclusive evidence of bribes and, because many of the allegations lacked credibility, it could not reach any positive conclusion about corruption.[87] It concluded that the Police Commissioner had investigated each matter in a thorough and appropriate way and had not attempted to 'cover up' anything.[88] Therefore, another royal commission was not justified. However, the sheer volume of hearsay evidence, when added to the concrete information, ensured that speculation about the vice squad dealing corruptly with the prostitution industry would continue.

In 2005 the police announced they would reopen the Shirley Finn case.[89] They said they were confident of finding the killer and would investigate police officers if necessary. But serious doubt remains about whether the case will ever be solved.

The inquiry into police corruption was grist for the Mickelbergs' mill as they pursued their own corruption suit against the investigating police officers. At the same time, they were also grinding out material to support other matters they were pursuing, namely, the validity of their convictions and the length of their sentences.

Over three days, 12, 13 and 14 September 1983, the Full Court of the Court of Criminal Appeal (CCA) of the Supreme Court of Western Australia heard Peter's appeal against his convictions on counts 2, 3, 4 and 5. These counts dealt with the offences against the Conti Sheffield Estate Agency in North Perth and the Bull Creek premises of another estate agency. Brian Singleton acted for Peter, while Ron Davies and Mary Ann Yeats appeared for the Crown.

Chief Justice Francis Burt, along with Justices Peter Brinsden and Charles Smith, presided over the appeal. Colloquially referred to as 'Red' Burt, Chief Justice Francis Burt was an icon of the judiciary and of the WA legal fraternity. He had vast experience as an appellant counsel, including clients challenging the basis of their criminal convictions. He was the great-grandson of Sir Archibald Burt, the first chief justice of the Supreme Court of Western Australia, and became Governor of Western Australia in 1990. Francis Burt and John Wickham were the pioneers of the independent bar in Perth in the early 1960s. Burt[90] and Sir Ronald Wilson,[91] who in 1979 was to become the first Western Australian justice of the High Court of Australia, were considered the leading advocates appearing in WA courts in the 1960s.

Chief Justice Francis Burt and Justices Peter Brinsden and Charles Smith delivered their judgments on 4 November 1983.[92]

In a unanimous decision, the convictions stood. In a brief written judgment, Chief Justice Burt (Justices Brinsden and Smith concurring) held that there was sufficient evidence to convict Peter on all counts and that the sentences imposed in respect to arson and conspiracy were not excessive (if anything the sentence for arson was lenient).

However, he agreed with the appellant's argument that 'prosecutions for conspiracy and for a substantive offence ought not result in a duplication of penalty.'[93] Thus, in the opinion of the Chief Justice, 'the sentences on the false pretences counts, made cumulative as they were upon the conspiracy count, does result in a duplication of penalty and in my opinion all those sentences ought, as among themselves, be ordered to be served concurrently.'

This resulted in an effective sentence of fourteen years instead of sixteen, which the Chief Justice did not view as 'excessive having regard to the totality of the applicant's criminal behaviour, and with reference to that total effective sentence I would fix seven years as being the minimum term during which the applicant is not eligible to be released on parole.'[94]

Ray did not even get to first base, having lodged his appeal against his conviction out of time.[95] The CCA did hear his appeal against the length of his sentence at the same time as they heard Peter's but, in contrast to his brother, he was unsuccessful.[96]

Ray sought an extension of time to lodge his appeal against his conviction. The CCA heard his application on 4 February 1984, before Justices Alkin Wallace, Peter Brinsden and Geoffrey Kennedy. The substance of his appeal was that the fingerprint found on the back of the WABS cheque was a forgery. His claim was that there were two possible ways the forgery could have been committed. It could have been made from the silicone casts of Ray's hands, which he had made as an experiment in his spare time and which, he alleged, the police had taken from his home. Or, he could have placed his finger on the back of the cheque when the police handed it to him to inspect while they were interviewing him on 15 July 1982.

Ray's counsel also contended that the appellant had obtained new evidence to support his claim that the police fabricated notes of the record of interview conducted on 26 July 1982.

Ray was surprised and angry when the CCA refused to grant an extension of time. He reckoned he had prepared a strong, persuasive argument. He could not believe the court would deny him the same opportunity to present his case as it had given Peter. In fact, in his more optimistic moments, he had even thought he might pull off the same result as Brian had done.

The court heard Brian's appeal against his convictions at the same time as Peter's appeal, before the same justices. Once again, Davies and Yeats appeared for the Crown, and Hugh McLernon for the appellant. Brian's basic contention was that there was insufficient evidence to prove he had been a party to the alleged conspiracy. In a two-one decision,[97] with Justice Brinsden dissenting, the court found for Brian.[98]

Although the majority justices wrote separate judgments, their general approach did not differ. Chief Justice Burt said it was dangerous to allow the guilty verdict to stand 'if this court is of the opinion that although it is a verdict which can in a general way and in logic be supported by the evidence, it is a verdict which cannot by the same process be sustained to the necessary standard of persuasion.' While the majority commented there was direct evidence linking Ray and Peter to the conspiracy and other charges, that was not the case for Brian. All the evidence the Crown had submitted 'was evidence of statements made by him which are said to be severally or in combination an admission of guilt.'

The majority noted Brian's initial lie to the police that he was in Hong Kong on the day of the Mint swindle and his later admission that he was in Western Australia but was helping Ray and Peter erect a fence on their parents' property on that day. Chief Justice Burt drew on the decision of Lord McDermott of the Privy Council in *Tumahole Bereng v R*[99] that the giving of false evidence or out-of-court lies may become important and assist in convicting an accused 'when there is other evidence in the case, either direct or circumstantial and including confessional evidence, "sufficient to sustain a verdict".' But without such evidence, a lie proves nothing. The Chief Justice added that even if he lied to provide an alibi for Peter it did not mean he was part of the conspiracy to swindle the Mint. And even if Ray asked him to lie and Peter told the same lie, it didn't prove he was part of the conspiracy.

The judges also held that the other out-of-court lies Brian told — denying he had ever purchased gold from the Mint or had knowledge of the Gulley account — did not prove anything. They could not severally or in combination with the alibi lie, raise 'an inference that the appellant had committed the offences of which he was convicted.'

Equally, the fact that Brian had initiated a transfer of his interest in the family home to his wife on 21 June 1982, the day before the Mint swindle, on its own proved nothing. Although signed, the transfer was never registered. This means that, under the *Transfer of Land Act 1893* (WA), Brian's interest in the family home had not legally transferred to his wife.[100] Therefore, the unregistered document was of doubtful value as evidence that Brian was involved in the swindle.

Even though Chief Justice Burt acknowledged it could be inferred that Brian knew where the stolen gold bullion was, one could not 'in the circumstances of this case' make 'any inference that he was a party to the conspiracy which had led to its acquisition.' Furthermore, the conclusion from the Hooft and Hancock interviews that he was 'involved' was ambiguous. Burt rhetorically asked, 'Involved in what?'

Chief Justice Burt also questioned the trial judge's directions to the jury. Even though Judge Heenan instructed the jury that there was no evidence directly connecting Brian 'with the Mint swindle or with any of the activities involved in it,' the Chief Justice did not think the trial judge's directions went far enough. He held that the jury may have 'been allowed and encouraged to act upon views of the evidence which were unsafe.' He added that the trial judge should have told the jury 'in the clearest of terms that they could not convict the appellant on the count of conspiracy' and false pretences unless the evidence from Brian's confessions allowed a jury to make a finding of guilt beyond reasonable doubt.[101] Therefore, because the trial judge's directions were inadequate, the Chief Justice allowed the appeal and quashed the conviction.[102]

In his concurring judgment, Justice Smith also expressed his concern at the absence of any unqualified admissions of guilt. He concluded, 'At the end of the whole case, in my opinion, no primary facts directly admissible against the appellant have been established from which it was open to the jury to draw the inference that the appellant had joined in the membership of the conspiracy which had led to the acquisition of the gold at a time after such conspiracy had commenced. The proposition that he had become a member of the conspiracy during its continuance was not put to the appellant by the investigating officers and there was no admission made by the appellant to them as to his involvement in the making of the false pretences whereby the gold was obtained on 22 June 1982 — lies told by him as to his movements on that day, standing alone, can prove nothing and no particular inference can be drawn from them.'

In a dissenting judgment,[103] Justice Brinsden followed Justice Menzies' reasoning in *Plomp v R*[104] that the question before the court was not whether it 'thinks the only rational hypothesis open upon the evidence was that Brian was guilty of conspiracy but rather whether this court thinks that upon the evidence it was open to the jury to be satisfied beyond reasonable doubt that he was guilty.' On that rationale, Justice Brinsden decided that, from the evidence available 'it was open to the jury to be satisfied beyond reasonable doubt of Brian's guilt of the conspiracy charge' and the false pretences charges.

Unlike the majority justices, Justice Brinsden believed Brian's out-of-court lies went towards guilt. He also thought there was other evidence implicating Brian. First, there was Brian's statement to the police that he would only tell them his role in the Mint swindle if Ray told them the whole thing. Second, Brian's reaction to police questions about why Ray and he transferred ownership of their homes to their wives, to which Brian replied that Ray attempted to cover all angles and it did seem a good idea. Justice Brinsden also remarked that Brian's lies in and out of court were of 'such quality and nature' as to lead the jury to inferring that he had joined the conspiracy.

Brian had mixed feelings after the court handed down its judgment on 4 November 1983. He was disappointed that he did not win his appeal unanimously, but was more upset that Peter and Ray remained behind bars, and that the judiciary still did not believe the brothers' allegations of police corruption and misconduct. Still, it was good finally to be free. Well, almost ...

Six hours after the court's decision, Brian was still at the

Canning Vale Remand Centre dealing with a mass of paperwork, including an arrangement for his parents to stand surety for $25,000 bail, using their house as security. The bail was necessary because Brian, along with his mother and incarcerated brothers, still faced charges over the Yellow Rose of Texas affair. In a preliminary hearing in November, the matter was held over for trial to a date to be set in the New Year.

The media throng waiting outside the gates of the Canning Vale Remand Centre for Brian's release reflected the enormous public interest in the Mickelbergs. The local newspaper reported, 'Mickelberg took his first steps as a free man again arm-in-arm with his overjoyed wife Faye and their two teenage daughters. He was treated like a celebrity as relatives, friends and a host of news media representatives tagged along, all trying to speak to him at once. Behind him was the Canning Vale remand centre, where many prisoners could be heard cheering loudly.'[105] Brian spoke only briefly. He looked neat and trim, having lost fifteen kilos in prison and having shaved off his 'protest beard' when his wife told him his appeal was successful. Brian did not forget the inmates who had cheered his release so enthusiastically. As soon as he had the chance, he flew a light aircraft over the prison in a 'thank you' salute to those he had left inside.

The day after his release, Brian held a packed press conference in his Jandakot home and posed for photographs of him drying the dishes in the kitchen while his wife and daughters, Paula and Michelle, looked on. He said his time in prison opened his eyes to social and legal injustice. It had changed him from being selfish, concerned only for his family and himself, to wanting to work with civil liberties groups. Brian felt keenly the injustice of police 'verbals' and he was committed to achieving a total ban of this practice of fabricating confessions.

However, his top priority was to work with his fourth brother, serving army captain Graeme, to get Ray and Peter out of gaol. Graeme was in England when the Mint swindle took place but now, with the help of John Doohan, secretary of the Human Rights Watch Committee of Western Australia, he had formed a committee to secure a retrial for his brothers. Brian and his parents were convinced Ray and Peter stood a far better chance of securing release through a retrial than by relying on an appeal, in which they had little confidence of success.[106]

Even so, the incarcerated brothers continued to press for another appeal. Only two days after Christmas 1983, Peter lodged an application for leave to appeal against his conviction on all counts. Meanwhile, Peggy and Brian organised pub raffles to raise funds for the legal appeals and continued to collect names for a petition demanding the release of Ray and Peter.

CHAPTER 5
THE MICKELBERG STITCH

'We need to get this story out into the public, into the court of public opinion.'

As head of the newly formed 'Mickelberg Committee', John Doohan wanted to help the brothers take their story to a wider audience — and he knew just the man to help them. Avon Lovell was a journalist who was not afraid of treading on toes when pursuing a good story. In his role of secretary of the Human Rights Watch Committee, Doohan had worked with Lovell before and was confident he would be sympathetic to the Mickelbergs' cause. The brothers agreed Lovell was the man they needed to write a book revealing the real story behind the police investigation into the swindle.

Lovell was the publisher of a community newspaper, and when Doohan visited him at his Subiaco office in December 1983, he saw immediately that he was onto a big story. His excitement grew when Brian showed him the silicone finger cast that, Ray alleged, the police officers had taken from his home, and from which they had forged his fingerprint. This clinched it for Lovell. It may not have been enough to prove Ray innocent but it was enough to convince Lovell the police had framed Ray.

Within three months he had completed the first draft, which members of the Mickelberg family smuggled into prison for Ray and Peter to read. Overall, Ray and Peter were happy with the draft, although Ray initially had misgivings about some of the personal matters Lovell had included, such as Sheryl leaving him. The pressures of imprisonment had taken a toll on the marriage and there was now another man in Sheryl's life. Ray discussed his concerns with Lovell in letters smuggled out through his weekly visitors, but Lovell convinced him the personal matters were important in helping to shape the public perception of the brothers.

The book was progressing nicely, unlike their dealings with the criminal justice system. Ray was still despondent about the CCA's refusal to grant him an extension to appeal, as was Peter when, on 2 April 1984, Justices Wallace, Smith and Rowland dismissed his appeal against all of his convictions.[107] Peter had represented himself; the Crown was represented by Michael Murray QC and John McKechnie.

It never rains but it pours! In the depths of their despondency the Yellow Rose of Texas came back to torment the Mickelbergs.[108] This continuing thorn in their sides went to trial in June 1984 in the District Court of Western Australia, with Judge Francis Whelan presiding and the by now familiar faces of McKechnie and Yeats appearing for the Crown. Singleton represented Ray, Alan Fenbury appeared for Brian, and Garry Lawton acted for Peter. Jack Courtis, who was a vocal supporter of the Mickelbergs, defended the parents Peggy and Malcolm.

The ten-day trial was a very different matter to the Mint swindle trial of the year before. This time Ray, along with Brian Pozzi, pleaded guilty to charges of conspiracy to defraud. They each received maximum prison sentences of five years with a minimum of two and half years. Brian and Peter got eighteen months to three years maximum. For Peter and Ray, the sentences meant freedom was even more distant. But for Brian, the verdict abruptly brought his freedom to an end. The court found Malcolm not guilty but found sixty-one year old Peggy, who had no previous criminal convictions, guilty and sentenced her to eighteen months gaol but with the possibility of early release on parole.

The sentencing of the family matriarch incensed the brothers. 'You have sentenced an innocent woman,' Ray shouted at Judge Whelan as he was led away from the dock. Peter was even more agitated, shaking his fist in the air and spitting out, 'When will this state wake up?' More in hope than expectation, he added, 'Justice will be done.'

The Mickelbergs finally found some relief through the courts when, on 31 August 1984, the CCA in a two–one majority decision reduced the sentences of Ray, Peter and Pozzi.[109] Justices Peter have taken into consideration Pozzi's previous good character and reduced his sentence by nearly half. The cumulative sentences for the Mint swindle and Yellow Rose of Texas crimes of twenty-five years and seventeen years for Ray and Peter were too high in regard to their ages and should have been lighter on compassionate grounds. Dissenting Justice Alkin Wallace did not see any injustice with the sentences.

Peggy served just over six months and walked free from Bandyup Women's Prison on the banks of the Swan River in Upper Swan on 21 January 1985. Four days later, Brian walked out of Karnet Prison Farm in the Darling Ranges on the south-east outskirts of the city.

Lovell was now ready to release his book to the Perth public and beyond, but he lacked the financial resources to fund publication. Local independent book distributor Charles Thomas came to the rescue. With Thomas providing a letter of credit, Lovell was able to have the manuscript typeset in Melbourne and printed in Singapore. He had received legal advice that no printer in Australia could print the book without coming under serious threat of expensive defamation suits.

In early February 1985, Lovell flew to Singapore to supervise the printing of the book. While he was away, the state government announced the police would conduct an internal inquiry into the Mickelbergs' allegations that Ray's fingerprint on the WABS cheque was a forgery.

On 24 February 1985, while Lovell was still in Singapore, Channel Nine's iconic national Sunday night television current affairs program *60 Minutes* aired its report into the Mint swindle, focusing on the fingerprint forgery allegations. A *60 Minutes* reporter had interviewed Lovell, but two days before the program went to air Lovell withdrew his consent, concerned his appearance on the program might pre-empt the book launch he was planning.

Lovell arrived back in Perth on the Wednesday and the books arrived on the Friday evening, much to his relief. Saturday's *West Australian,* the state's only morning newspaper, was running a major news feature based on advance copies of the book. Lovell feared that if the story ran before the books arrived, the authorities would ban their entry into Australia.[110] With that fear now resolved, he was ecstatic when his mate, journalist Bob Howlett, came to his home to show him an advance copy of the news feature; it ran in early general news on page 3, spilling over to page 17. It doesn't get much better than that.

Within hours of the books arriving from Singapore, Thomas and his staff had distributed copies throughout Perth in what Lovell described as 'one of the slickest operations I'd ever heard of in the book industry.'[111] Bookstores and newsagencies around the city were soon doing a brisk trade in *The Mickelberg Stitch*.[112]

The public's appetite for the story was voracious and all main media were doing their best to feed this seemingly insatiable hunger. This was a story of intrigue, corruption and fabrication that read like fiction yet which, in the hands of a dedicated author, had a ring of truth to it. Lovell built an impressive case for the Mickelbergs, even though most of what he wrote had already been given in evidence in court. The difference was that now it was in book form, able to reach a wider audience.

While Lovell's introduction insisted the book did not take a position on the guilt or innocence of the brothers, he nailed his colours to the mast in declaring that the Mickelbergs were the victims of a terrible injustice.

Lovell did several radio interviews in the first week after the release of *The Mickelberg Stitch*, starting with a lengthy interview with Bob Maumill, the king of Perth commercial talkback radio. Maumill was well connected in Perth, particularly to the Labor side of politics and to many in the horseracing and football industries. He was on first name terms with the Premier of Western Australia, Brian Burke. Maumill gave Lovell the opportunity to tell his story without imposing his own views or interrupting the author's narrative.

Other media stories followed. In the first week of publication, television station Channel Seven ran a four-part series in their evening news. The media attention fuelled public interest in the book and the Mickelberg saga. But buying the book was about to become difficult.

On Wednesday 9 March 1985, the Mickelberg story moved up to the front page where the *West Australian* headline blazed, 'BOOK ON MICKELBERGS REMOVED FROM SALE'.[113] The story reported that the colourful John Quigley, resident lawyer for both the that the colourful John Quigley, resident lawyer for both the WA Police Union and the Prison Officers Union, had telephoned Thomas threatening to sue if he did not stop further sales of the book. Quigley viewed the allegations against the police as set out in the book as 'an outrageous and scandalous defamation' of his clients and he would sue any bookstore or newsagency which sold it, any newspapers which reviewed it, and any TV station which aired its contents.

Quigley's threat was enough to stop Thomas distributing the book. Some booksellers continued to sell it by ingenious methods — selling bookmarks for $8.95 with a free copy of the book attached, or selling a brown paper bag for the same amount, which just happened to have a copy of *The Mickelberg Stitch* inside it[114] — but there was no doubt that the threat of legal action had severely curtailed its sale. And it was only going to become more difficult.

Within days of the report in the *West Australian*, Quigley, acting on behalf of Sergeant Tony Lewandowski, sought and was granted an ex parte injunction (when the other party is not present in court) against Lovell, restraining him from distributing the book. Lewandowski had already instigated legal proceedings to sue Lovell. Later that day, acting on a tip off from the media, Quigley served the injunction on Lovell while he was selling the book at a hotel in Beaufort Street, just north of the Perth CBD.[115] This occurred in the full glare of TV cameras, print and radio journalists, and in the presence of eager buyers.

Lovell was in dangerous territory. He would be acting unlawfully if he sold another copy of the book. Lawyer John Hammond, a young associate of Quigley's, approached Lovell and asked to buy a copy, but another lawyer, Tony Black, alerted Lovell to the danger before the transaction could be completed.

A week later, on 27 March 1985, Justice Howard Olney refused an application to continue the injunction, the principle of freedom of speech influencing his decision. Quigley once again represented Lewandowski, and barrister Rene Le Miere, who was later to become a Justice of the Supreme Court of Western Australia, acted for Lovell.

Quigley made another application that afternoon. Justice Olney heard the new application on 29 March but again refused another application for Lewandowski at a later stage. Taking the opportunity, Quigley moved quickly and on 19 April, Le Miere and Lovell were back in court defending another injunction application. This time it was before Justice William Pidgeon in his chambers. Quigley was unable to attend and Laurie James, the principal partner of Quigley's law firm, represented Lewandowski. Three weeks later, to Le Miere's dismay, Justice Pidgeon found for Lewandowski, holding that the book contained serious defamatory allegations against the policeman and that banning the sale of the book would do little to harm Lovell.[116]

The police force despatched junior officers to bookstores and newsagencies to see that they were observing the injunction and to warn them that legal action would follow if they did not toe the line. One of their own had brought on the injunction and they were determined to enforce it.

Lovell had invested considerable time and money into researching and writing *The Mickelberg Stitch*, and the ban was hurting him. It was also bad news for Charles Thomas. Under a defamation threat from Quigley, he agreed to arrange the posting of notices on the walls of numerous shops, apologising to the police for any embarrassment or distress that the 'unsubstantiated allegations contained in the book' had caused them. The injunction remained in force until October 1985 when, after Lovell appealed to the court, Justices Olney and Kennedy, with Justice Wallace dissenting (as he had in the Yellow Rose of Texas sentencing appeals), lifted it.[117]

The fallout from *The Mickelberg Stitch* lasted a number of years and took many forms. Police officers filed defamation suits against Lovell, Thomas and some of the retailers.[118] The threat of law suits against other retailers was ever present, thus ensuring the distribution of the book was severely restricted. The Police Union bankrolled the legal action by imposing a special levy of $1 per pay from union members.[119]

In the months following the release of *The Mickelberg Stitch*, Lovell had to deal with more than just threats of defamation. The police announced they would conduct an inquiry not only into the allegations Lovell made in *The Mickelberg Stitch*, but also into those made by other people involved in producing and distributing the book.[120] Police Commissioner Brian Bull even publicly announced the police were contemplating bringing criminal charges against Lovell.[121]

Meanwhile, in July 1985 the *West Australian* reported that state government inquiries (led by the Crown Law Department) had found no substance in the allegation of forged fingerprints.[122] The investigators were not persuaded by the opinions collected by the Mickelberg committee to support their claim that the fingerprint was a forgery. This was a blow to the committee. They had canvassed fingerprint experts who were working, or had worked, for world-renowned policing forces and intelligence services, such as Scotland Yard, the FBI, US secret services, and the Royal Canadian Mounted Police.

The police inquiry took a darker turn when two CIB detectives visited the Wheatbelt town of Moorine Rock to interview a woman who had written a letter to the Minister for Police in which she expressed her concerns about the Mickelberg case. She wrote that she was disturbed after reading *The Mickelberg Stitch* and said a royal commission into the case was warranted. The woman, a member of the Western Australian Appeal for Justice group, later expressed her surprise and concern that the police should visit her because of a letter to their Minister. 'I wonder what this country is coming to when you send a letter to a politician and it gets passed on to the CIB.'[123]

The imprisoned Mickelbergs looked on dejectedly from the sidelines. They were happy with the book and the media attention it had attracted, but dismayed that the investigators had rejected the opinions of the fingerprint experts.

In early 1986, dejection gave way to grief. Brian was dead.[124] Forty minutes into a three-hour commercial flight from Jandakot Airport, the twin-engine Aero Commander 500 he was piloting crashed in thick bushland near Canning Dam in the Darling Ranges south-east of the Perth. One of the two passengers also died. The official explanation was that the plane ran out of fuel, a verdict the Mickelbergs and some of their brother's colleagues found difficult to believe. Brian was an experienced pilot; how could he run out of fuel so early into a designated three-hour flight? An inquiry into the crash failed to document any sinister revelations and found that in fact the aircraft had a faulty fuel gauge.

Peggy didn't buy the official version of events. She was convinced Brian's death was the result of foul play. In the week before the crash, Brian had told his mother someone was following him. At the height of her grief, just before Brian's funeral, Peggy took a phone call; there was no voice at the other end, just a recording of a plane crashing. A cruel practical joke? Or a message?

The family were in mourning for the loss of their son, brother, father and husband. For the incarcerated Ray and Peter, it was particularly difficult. Prison provided little privacy, little space for them to mourn. They were allowed to attend the funeral, with prison guards and police in attendance. The police and guards dispersed into the crowd of mourners as Ray and Peter joined other family members in paying their final respects.

After they had seen Brian laid to rest, Ray and Peter returned to prison. But *they* would not rest. For them, the fight went on.

CHAPTER 6
1987

There is a wry aphorism in show business that says that as one door closes another door slams in your face. That slamming door must have felt particularly vicious to Ray and Peter.

Desmond Dawson was dead.

Brian and Ray had met Dawson in 1981 when they sold him the aircraft Brian had flown twelve months earlier in the Yellow Rose of Texas fraud.

A wealthy property owner, Dawson had been a friend and racing associate of Detective Sergeant Don Hancock. He died when his utility mysteriously ran off a cliff on his farm at Hiawatha in country Victoria, just three weeks before Ray and Peter launched their new appeal in the Court of Criminal Appeal. His death meant the loss of another chance for the brothers to support their claim to innocence.

In 1985 Tim Boase, a pilot colleague of Brian's and a prominent member of the Mickelberg committee, learnt Dawson had offered to sell what he called 'Perth Mint swindle gold' for half its value to a Melbourne private detective, Frank Douglas.[125]

Boase asked the National Crime Authority to investigate Dawson's offer but they were not interested, saying that the matter did not relate to the criminal matters (organised crime) they were empowered to investigate and it was an issue for the WA authorities. However, after Brian's death, through a web of contacts between Mickelberg supporters, eastern states lawyers and the Victorian police, the WA police force took a renewed interest in Dawson and sent his old friend Hancock to Melbourne to investigate. To the surprise of no one in the Mickelberg camp, he reported there was no evidence to connect his friend to an attempt to offload the Mint gold bullion. The WA police were happy and the Victorian police were not interested. End of story! But not for Ray and Peter.

Over the previous eighteen months, Lovell and Boase had travelled to North America and the United Kingdom seeking expert evidence to support Ray's claim that there was fresh evidence to substantiate his assertion of forensic fabrication. Ray was also claiming that the sketch of Peter which police claimed they had prepared from eyewitness descriptions, was in fact prepared from a passport photograph.

Peter mounted his appeal on grounds similar to those Ray used. It stemmed from a petition he presented to the Governor of Western Australia, Sir Francis Burt, who as Chief Justice of the Supreme Court of Western Australia had presided over former appeals by Peter and Brian.

Under the then provisions of section 21 of the *Criminal Code 1913* (WA), the Attorney-General referred the matter to the CCA for consideration.[126] As well as challenging the authenticity of the fingerprint of the WABS cheque and the police sketch evidence, Peter repeated the assertions he made at trial that Hancock and Lewandowski subjected him to violence and combined to fabricate the statement they claimed he had made.[127]

Peter also raised questions about the Talbot note, allegedly written by the purchaser of the 1956 Ford Falcon sedan used in the swindle. At trial, the Crown had persuaded the court that Peter was the author. Peter now claimed that new expert handwriting analysis could prove he had not written it.

During the brothers' appeals, Justice Wallace said Peter's assertions raised 'the very serious allegation that the police fabricated the case against the appellants.'

In spite of the impressive list of forensic experts that Lovell and Boase were able to gather,[128] it was not plain sailing. First, the Crown alleged Lovell or Boase had prepared some of the affidavits which the pair said their forensic experts had prepared. These expert witness affidavits had been central to the request to Attorney-General Joe Berinson for an inquiry. The Crown's scepticism did not prove fatal though; while Lovell or Boase had in some cases written the affidavits, they were a true recording and reflection of the experts' opinions.[129] Of more concern for the Mickelberg committee and legal team were the perceived incidences of 'official nobbling'.

Lovell had engaged the services of UK Detective Francis Gardner of the Criminal Investigation Department (CID) at the Lancashire police headquarters in Hutton near Preston. Gardner had served almost twenty-six years with the CID, twenty-five years working with identikit, photokit and artist impressions. He had not worked for the defence before but there was no doubt he was a person well qualified to give expert evidence at the new appeal.

Gardner spent many hours testing the police sketch of Peter. He was amazed at how the sketch picked up the slight difference in one eye but not Peter's prominent buckteeth. This would be most unusual for a sketch drawn from eyewitness descriptions. In a signed sworn statement he sent to Lovell just six weeks before the new appeal, he concluded the sketch 'must have been traced from a photograph of the Mickelberg youth.' What's more, Gardner was willing to come to Perth to appear in person for the defence. Lovell thought he had hit the jackpot.

But with only weeks to go, Gardner telephoned Lovell to tell him he had some difficulties, although he did not say what they were. On 17 August 1987, Lovell telephoned Gardner, only to have his worst fears confirmed when the detective said, 'My job's on the line.' His superiors were asking questions about what he was doing, despite three previous written reports outlining his work for the Mickelberg defence. Now they were putting severe pressure on him. Why, is not clear, but it would be a fair guess that some high-level persuasion was coming from the antipodes. Gardner was due to retire in three years, his wife was sick and he needed his police pension. The Perth trip was off.[130]

For Ray and Peter, that revolving door had slammed on them once more. And before they could get up, it hit them again.

Robert Wagener, a supervising forensic specialist with the Sheriff-Coroner's Department in Orange County, California, had been involved in exposing fingerprint forgery in his home state in 1973. He filed his affidavit for the Mickelberg appeal, arguing that fingerprints can be forged or fabricated and that trial judge Heenan was wrong to say 'a fingerprint is, in effect, an unforgeable signature.' Wagener was scheduled to arrive in Perth on 21 August 1987 to give evidence in the trial. He did not turn up and would not take calls from the Mickelberg committee. More down under dirty work? Maybe.

Still, the Mickelbergs managed to assemble an imposing array of international experts. They also had an impressive legal team, with Ray receiving unlimited access to legal aid for the appeal while Peter received limited assistance. Counsel for Ray was Henry Wallwork QC, who had acted for Ray and Peter in their appeal on the sentence terms in the Yellow Rose of Texas matter. Solicitor Gary Lawton assisted him. Wallwork, the son of a chief magistrate, had done his articles at the Crown Law Department and was a leading silk at the Perth bar. In 1989, he would become a justice of the Supreme Court of Western Australia. Peter Searle from the Victorian bar represented Peter, with assistance from the Perth law firm of Lohrmann Tindal and Guthrie.

The Crown assembled an equally impressive list of expert witnesses and the formidable legal team of John McKechnie, a skilful cross-examiner who was to become Western Australia's first Director of Public Prosecutions in 1992 before being appointed to the Supreme Court bench in 1999. McKechnie had the able assistance of Mary Ann Yeats, who had spent considerable time on the Mickelberg case, travelling the world speaking to possible expert witnesses, including some of those on the Mickelberg side.[131]

The appeal went ahead on 24 August 1987 before Justices Wallace, Olney and Pidgeon, all of whom had previously been involved in the injunction hearings over *The Mickelberg Stitch*. That court had lifted the injunction, the only dissenter in the final hearing being Wallace.[132] If the brothers believed in omens, this was not a good one, particularly as Wallace was also one of the three justices who dismissed Peter's 1983 appeal.[133]

The new appeal ran over three weeks and was the most expensive appeal case in Western Australia's history up to that point. It also broke new ground by allowing witnesses to be heard in person to support the appellants' claims that they had fresh evidence.[134] Normally the bench decides appeals entirely on legal argument, without witnesses appearing in person.[135] Also somewhat unusually, Ray and Peter were given permission to leave their prison cells to sit at the back of the court and observe the proceedings.

On the opening day, Wallwork painted a picture of 'an aggregate of faults' at Ray's trial, many of which concerned evidence that it was Ray's fingerprint on the WABS cheque. Especially damaging, according to Wallwork, was the trial judge's direction to the jury that the fingerprint was an unforgeable signature. The directions did not acknowledge Ray's evidence that he had never seen or touched the cheque before police officers interviewed him. Moreover, Wallwork noted that earlier in 1987 the Crown conceded it was possible to forge fingerprints and that witnesses for the appellant would testify 'that the fingerprint in question cannot be scientifically proven to be a genuine fingerprint.'

Peter's counsel, Peter Searle, was even more provocative. In his opening address he proposed a new suspect. Showing exquisite timing, he did it early enough in the day to guarantee a front-page lead in that afternoon's *Daily News*. 'Mickelberg lawyer names new suspect. MINT SWINDLE: SECURITY FIRM ACCUSED' the headline screamed.[136]

In support of his proposition, Searle reminded the court that Arpad was one of the three security firms hired by the swindler to transport the bullion. Arpad employed a number of serving and past SAS soldiers. And, only one week before police arrested the Mickelbergs, the firm had appeared before the magistrate's court to answer charges of exceeding the terms of its security licence after gold worth $250,000 disappeared from a TAA flight in June 1982.

Ray's counsel at trial, Ron Cannon, had represented Arpad in that case.

We have here, said Searle, 'a clear conflict of duty and interest if one can establish the hypothesis that Arpad is in fact a very likely suspect, an alternative suspect, in relation to the Perth Mint swindle.' And that, he said, is a reasonable hypothesis. It puts 'Mr Cannon in a conflict of duty and interest of the most extraordinary degree.'[137] However, the matter was not fully developed during the appeal and the claim of Cannon having a conflict of duty and interest between Arpad's interests and the Mickelbergs' interest was not established.

Because Dawson was dead, Searle sought to amend some of the grounds of appeal. The CCA allowed the amendments but Justice Wallace expressed some disquiet that the court could now not test the Dawson allegations, and some others which the media had covered extensively. His Honour was at pains to allay any fears Crown prosecutor McKechnie might have had about the media coverage influencing the bench. 'If it is any solace to Mr McKechnie and those mentioned in the grounds now abandoned, we are all too conscious of the manner in which an endeavour has been made for this case to be tried by the media ... This court is not the media.'

The evidence of the international expert witnesses, which promised so much just a few weeks earlier, fell far short of the defence team's expectations. Too-long retired police officer James Proven lacked match practice and dropped the ball when McKechnie subjected him to aggressive cross-examination. He stood by his opinion that police artist Kenneth Pierce produced the sketch of Peter by tracing from a passport photograph rather than from the descriptions of witnesses, but gave the prosecution a free kick when he admitted that, in forming his opinion, he relied on information Lovell had supplied.[138]

Attempting to recover lost ground, the defence called on another retired police officer, detective Donald Cherry, the first full-time sketch artist employed by the Washington DC Metropolitan Police. Although more credible than Proven, he still came up short of expectations. In his affidavit, he said he believed the passport photograph directly influenced the police sketch of Peter. Now he told the court that a different photograph had influenced the police artist. He reached this conclusion because in both the police sketch and the photograph, the distance between the right eye and the hairline was shorter than between the left eye and the hairline. Moreover, he thought the artist drew the sketch freehand and had not traced it from the photograph.[139]

The police artist, Sergeant Kenneth Pierce, remained resolute under Searle's questioning. The Allens were mistaken when they testified at trial that Pierce made the sketch at their direction. He said their description of the young man who bought their car was imprecise; the only useful information was their description of his hair, which they thought was a wig, and the fact that the young man wore glasses. Pierce was only able to complete the sketch — using photofit strips — after Henry, who had seen the young man in the car park near Barker House, described his face.

By overlaying the hair and glasses onto the face described by Henry, Pierce produced the composite picture the prosecution had submitted as evidence.[140]

Now it was up to the fingerprint specialists flown in to testify that the fingerprint on the WABS cheque was a forgery. But they too vacillated. Under intense cross-examination and before three appellant justices in the state's highest court, what the four experts expressed in their affidavits as strong convictions that the fingerprint was a forgery now became equivocal. They were only prepared to claim that the fingerprint might have been from the silicone replica of Ray's hand.

These men knew the ropes. Former FBI senior fingerprint specialist George Bonebrake helped convict Martin Luther King Jr's assassin;[141] Robert Olsen was a fingerprint expert from the US state of Kansas;[142] Malcolm Thomson was a former senior fingerprint officer with Scotland's Edinburgh City Police;[143] Harold Tuthill lectured at the Ontario police academy in Canada;[144] and Reginald King was trained in science at New Scotland Yard and had more than thirty-six years experience.[145] They had earned their stripes and were not now going to compromise their professional integrity as experts in their field by swearing to something that might just be wrong. Olsen even went so far as to recant on his confident assertion, made on Channel Nine's *60 Minutes*, that the fingerprint was a forgery.

This was fatal news for Ray and Peter. In dismissing their appeal, Justice Wallace said, 'Not one of the appellants' experts had expressed the opinion that the crime mark was a forgery and that set against the opinions of the respondents' experts that indeed the crime mark was not a forgery is sufficient to dispose of these grounds in favour of the respondent.' Nor did the defence's expert evidence persuade the court that Ray's accusation of forgery was credible. Justice Wallace was especially scathing. The evidence, he said, could not 'be viewed in isolation when it is known that the rubber fingers supplied to Bardwell [a retired detective inspector formerly employed in the Queensland Police Scientific Bureau and engaged by the Mickelbergs] and by him to Queensland fingerprint expert O'Brien failed to provide a satisfactory ink impression when experimented with for that purpose.' His Honour was referring to a failed test before the

CHAPTER 6 • 1987

1983 trial in which Bardwell attempted to reproduce a convincing fingerprint using the bronze casting and a moulded synthetic rubber finger. Their respective failures put paid to Bardwell and O'Brien's claims to be credible expert witnesses. On the other hand, Crown witnesses were unequivocally convincing in arguing that the fingerprint was genuine.

Nor did the bench attach credibility to the evidence of former police officer Arthur Walsh, a man with criminal convictions who the force had dismissed for falsifying travel claims. Walsh claimed that, at a tavern on 16 July 1987, Lewandowski told him Hancock and he had 'fixed up' the Mickelbergs. He also claimed in evidence that, after making a complaint to the police, he received a middle-of-the-night telephone death threat. The court dismissed his evidence with disdain, preferring Lewandowski's vehement denial.[146]

The court also rejected the evidence about the Talbot note[147] from Peter's handwriting expert Geoffrey Roberts. According to Justice Olney, Roberts' evidence was 'unconvincing, lacked objectivity and was devoid of any probative value.' The Crown led evidence from another handwriting expert, John Gregory, who supported the Crown case and whose evidence was preferred. Gregory's opinion had in fact been sought by the brothers prior to the 1983 trial. His evidence at this appeal was consistent with what he had told the brothers before the 1983 trial, but their counsel had not adduced that evidence at trial. So as Justice Wallace noted, the evidence sought to be adduced by Peter's counsel in the appeal hearing was not 'fresh' evidence — evidence that has become available only after the trial — as an appeal court requires it to be. It was merely 'new' evidence, which is evidence that was available at the time of the trial, but which was not presented to the court. Such evidence cannot then be introduced at an appeal hearing.

Even Peter's tape-recording of a conversation with Hancock failed to dent the prosecution's case. (The recording had not been submitted at the trial because defence lawyer Ron Cannon was not convinced it was authentic.)

Peter claimed to have secretly recorded the conversation outside Ray's house on the day Hancock and his fellow officers roused the Mickelberg family in the early hours of the morning.

On the tape, Ray can be heard remonstrating with Hancock, who makes no apology but simply justifies his action as a way of putting pressure on Ray. Hancock says, 'I could have gone harder. We could have thrown them in and built a fence around them, too, and made it real hard.' Getting Ray to crack had become personal for Hancock. 'Pride comes into it,' he said on the tape. 'Don't ever challenge me to do something because I'll do it all right. You can rest assured about that.' And, 'I'm not a mean person but, I'll tell you what, I've done things in my life that you never did, and harder things, worse things, and if I've got to do them again, well, I'll do them again.'[148]

When the Crown called Ron Cannon to give evidence at the appeal, Cannon put the evidentiary value of the tape in doubt. Under questioning from McKechnie, he invoked legal professional privilege,[149] refusing to divulge the substance of any conversations with Ray — something he had never done in thirty-four years of practice as a criminal lawyer and something he wasn't about to start now. However, he admitted he hadn't submitted the recording at trial because he 'thought the tape was too good to be true.' He acknowledged that had the court admitted the tape as evidence, it would have corroborated Peter's allegations against the police. However, he said, 'I didn't believe it was a genuine tape or that the conversation had taken place.' He claimed he had only been prepared to submit the tape if the WA Institute of Technology (now Curtin University) could authenticate it. That didn't happen, he said. 'The tape was taken away and I never saw it again.'

In his original grounds of appeal, Peter had complained about the manner in which Cannon handled his case at trial, stating that Cannon had been neglectful in running the defence case at trial. However, the chance of succeeding with the negligent claim was always going to be difficult, so Peter withdrew that ground before the appeal began.

The court handed down its decision on 18 November 1987, unanimously upholding the 1983 guilty conviction. The so-called fresh evidence failed for want of credibility and there was no substance to the core arguments of the appeal — that police behaved corruptly and fabricated evidence. The overseas experts for the defence did not favourably impress their Honours, whereas the Crown's police and expert witnesses covered themselves with glory, it seems.

Justice Wallace, the Mickelbergs' judicial nemesis, delivered a caustic judgment on the case. The allegations made against Lazlo Bacskai and his firm Arpad Security troubled him greatly. The media had widely reported Searle's allegations, with the result that Bacskai and his firm 'may well have suffered in the eyes of the community.' He added, 'There has not been one iota of evidence to support counsel's allegation and yet the inference sought to be made remains and has not been withdrawn. In my opinion the attack made on Mr Bacskai is without foundation and scandalous.' Nor did he believe the serious charges made against the police were in any way substantiated. He concluded with the scathing observation that in the course of the appeal, the Mickelbergs cast their net wide and 'implicated innocent parties without justification.'

Peter did not take the verdict well. As he left the dock, he raised his arm and shouted in anger towards the bench, 'Justice one day! I can guarantee you.' Still boiling as guards led him to the Canning Vale prison van, Peter pointed to the assembled press on the other side of the cage separating them, demanding to know if they thought it right his brother should serve twenty-three years for crimes he had allegedly committed? 'I ask Judge Heenan tonight to turn and think to himself: "I sentenced Ray Mickelberg to twenty years. Can I sleep with that?"'

Before entering the prison van, Ray said to the media, 'I want to thank the thousands of West Australians who have supported us.' Then, in a reference to the police corruption that the Fitzgerald Royal Commission had exposed in Queensland, he said, 'I hope all West Australians will look at our judicial system and our police force carefully because in due course it will be exposed as it has been in Queensland.'[150]

The *West Australian* splashed Peter's angry cry for justice over its front page. Under the headline 'Faces of dashed hope', two photographs showed Peter in open neck shirt and casual jacket pointing to the media, his eyes blazing, and Ray in a three-piece suit, looking stunned and strained.[151]

On hearing the decision, Police Commissioner Brian Bull said, 'The decision of the three Supreme Court judges vindicates the findings of the inquiry within the police force and that of the Solicitor-General.' He also remarked that he was proud of the CIB and the forensic branch members involved in the Mickelberg case. They and their families should also feel proud.[152]

Five days after the decision, Premier Brian Burke announced that within two months a two-year trial of tape-recording and videotaping of police interrogations in Western Australia would commence. All police interviews of suspects would be tape-recorded in Perth and certain country centres and, where feasible, interviews involving indictable offences would be videotaped. The Law Society of Western Australia supported the announcement but WA Police Union secretary Ric Stingemore was critical. He said the taping would mean two standards of evidence and with cameras filming interviews, suspects might be more reticent to talk. He also said videotaping would not stop allegations against the police because suspects would allege the police engaged in improper conduct during breaks in the interview for meals or for changing tapes.

Police Minister Gordon Hill rejected union criticism. He thought the police would welcome measures that improved their ability to do their job and be seen to be doing it in a manner that was beyond reproach. He noted the many occasions when suspects had accused police of 'verballing' by writing false submissions into statements. 'We want to lay that allegation to rest once and for all.'

In the meantime, the Mickelbergs waited for another door to open.

CHAPTER 7
JUSTICE UNDER FIRE

The new measures for recording interviews so optimistically welcomed by Police Minister Gordon Hill on behalf of the police force might protect one flank. However, they would not provide cover against incoming fire from media, the public and the politicians. Nor would they shield police against friendly fire from within their own ranks.

The policeman's lot was to get a whole lot unhappier in 1988. A police officer charged with stealing government stores complained that the officers from the Internal Investigation Unit had verballed him, fabricating a confession to a crime.[153] In another instance, one of six detectives on trial for assault and conspiracy admitted inventing a statement he attributed to a man who police were questioning about stolen property.[154] And two officers — aka the 'Water Torture Cops' — were gaoled for punching and kneeing a suspect, and placing his head and left hand under boiling water from a coffee urn.[155]

Qualified support for the police came from an unlikely quarter. Ray Mickelberg wrote to the *Sunday Times* from his cell at Canning Vale Prison, agreeing with the WA Police Union secretary, Ric Stingemore, that the hours police wasted investigating public complaints against them reduced their effectiveness. However, he did not agree that many of the public complaints were stupid. 'I remind Mr Stingemore that police depend greatly upon the public coming forward with information. Many complaints may at first appear to be stupid and frivolous, however upon investigation they often lead to the solving of crime.' Ray believed establishing a 'three-man justice commission' to investigate complaints against the police would streamline internal investigations and help rebuild public confidence in the police force.[156]

But the public and the media had the justice system itself in their sights, especially judges. Crimes sensational enough to attract media attention were bound to draw public protests about judges' perceived big-heartedness to perpetrators when handing down sentences. The public reaction to the severity of the sentences handed down to the Mickelbergs was, therefore, something of an aberration.

A 1989 *Sunday Times* editorial claimed there were 'glaring inconsistencies' in sentencing.[157] 'Critics of the system point out that convicted rapists and killers can be released in a matter of a few years, or even months, while an "honest" thief, convicted of stealing gold but harming no one, can stay behind bars for more than 20 years.' Although the *Sunday Times* editorial did not name them, it left no one in doubt that it had the Mickelberg case in mind. Implicit in the editorial was the belief that the thief who did not physically hurt anyone was the less reprehensible offender. It was clearly not a view that police and Crown prosecutors shared.

The editorial followed shortly after Chief Justice David Malcolm's spirited defence of judges during question time at a Law Week lunch. Recently appointed to the chief justice position, Malcolm overcame a hundred years of judicial tradition by receiving his promotion directly from the bar, bypassing the Supreme Court bench.[158] In his role as an advocate, he probably had experienced moments of disappointment with judges' sentencing practices,[159] but he was now quick to counter suggestions from journalists at the lunch that sentencing was inconsistent. A journalist asked why perpetrators of violent crimes, including sexual assault, seemed to receive much lighter sentences than the twenty years and fourteen years handed down to Ray and Peter Mickelberg. The Chief Justice answered, 'It is a false comparison to take one of the most exceptional cases in our legal history and compare it with the general run of cases in another class.' In his assigning violence and sexual assault to the category 'general run of cases' one could infer that the Chief Justice was, if unwittingly, reinforcing the belief that the system did not value persons as highly as it valued property.

In a letter to the *Daily News* on 24 May 1989, Ray responded to executive director of the WA Law Society, Peter Fitzpatrick, who had criticised media sensationalism of some court cases and rebutted accusations of judicial bias against poor and non-white defendants.[160] Ray wrote that the media has a vital role in a free and open society of informing the public of court proceedings,[161] which generally they perform well. Furthermore, he wrote, 'truth cannot undermine a just system.' He also defended the public's right to comment on 'sentences that defy logic,' citing three cases of aggravated sexual assault where the sentences ranged from three years to eighteen months, even where in one case the victim was only five years old.

Ray also raised an October 1988 case in which a jury found that a forty-three year old intellectually disabled Aboriginal man with a mental age of seven was incapable of standing trial. But the judge ordered him to be held indefinitely at Canning Vale Prison. Despite letters protesting the decision, the Attorney-General and others in the justice system refused to deal with the matter. Ray wrote, 'This case is a very clear indictment of our judicial system and clearly demonstrates bias against the poor, the non-white and the handicapped.' He added that the courts are there to 'represent the people and are expected to reflect the values held by society' but 'they must be prepared to accept criticism.'

In his letter Ray called for more female judges. 'For too long the courts have been an exclusively male domain and they clearly place the value of a dollar before the value of human life and dignity. I am sure that the majority of West Australians join me when I say our society places human life above all else. Let this be reflected in our courts.'

A 'concerned' Perth resident questioned Ray's motivation in writing the letter and said the court got it right most of the time. Peter Fitzpatrick also responded forcefully. 'It is the half-truths and slanted views of the type presented in Mr Mickelberg's letter that pose a threat to the system and are likely to undermine public confidence in it,' he wrote in the *Daily News*.[162] He went on to say that most prisoners have an 'obsessive attitude ... towards those that commit sexual offences against minors.' Had he asked, he may well have found that most members of the public shared that obsession. Fitzpatrick also questioned Ray's capacity to make informed comment on the justice system. 'From the seclusion of his prison cell, Mr Mickelberg has sat as judge and jury on these selected cases, presumably on the basis of sketchy media reports. It is incomprehensible to me that without the benefit of hearing the evidence that was presented in court, or even the benefit of considering a transcript of these cases, he has arrived at the conclusion that the sentences were totally inadequate. From his remote position he takes for granted that he has a greater knowledge of sentencing parameters than the trial judges concerned, who collectively have about 100 years of legal training and experience.' Had his criticism been even-handed, he might also have levelled that same charge against the media and members of the public. He scoffed at Ray's call for more female justices.

In a rejoinder to Fitzpatrick's criticism, Ray said his stand against injustice was not motivated by his struggle to have his own conviction overturned but because of 'my unequivocal belief that all Australians have a fundamental right to justice.'[163] How, he wanted to know, could any reasonable person challenge his concern that a judge had imprisoned a forty-three year old man with a mental age of seven. He also claimed his earlier letter had prompted action to move the Aboriginal man from prison. He acknowledged he was not an expert on the criminal justice system but claimed he had spent many hours in prison following court cases and reading court transcripts. He ended, 'I concede to my critics that our judiciary has an exceptionally difficult task. But it must be remembered that members of the judiciary are public servants and the community expects them to reflect the values of society in their judgments.'

Two days after the *Daily News* published his latest letter, at the end of June 1989, the High Court of Australia handed down its decision on the Mickelbergs' 1988 appeal.

This was the Mickelbergs' first foray into the highest court in the land. Among their grounds of appeals was the claim that fresh and new evidence they had sought to rely upon in the 1987 Supreme Court appeals rendered the verdicts of the jury at trial unsafe and unsatisfactory.

The appeal had commenced on 25 October 1988.[164] The High Court had scheduled a half-day hearing in Perth as part of its annual national circuit trip. However, the court soon realised this would not be anywhere near enough time to hear the Mickelberg matter. Two full days had passed, with Crown Prosecutor McKechnie barely into his argument, when Chief Justice Anthony Mason called a halt to proceedings. McKechnie may have welcomed the respite, as he was under pressure to explain anomalies in police evidence about the photographing of the crucial fingerprint on the WABS cheque. Justice William Deane, later to become Governor-General of Australia, wanted to know why the police had waited for more than three weeks before photographing the crucial fingerprint on the fake WABS cheque after it had been treated with ninhydrin, a chemical used to highlight the impression. The absence of any record of photographing the fingerprint on 15 or 16 July 1982 also puzzled him, as did the uncertainty about what the police did with the fingerprint between 24 June and 16 July 1982. He thought it unbelievable that the police would send the fingerprint to Canberra for analysis without retaining a photographic record of it.

Just under a month later, the appeal concluded after a two-day hearing at the High Court in Canberra. The court dismissed Ray's appeal outright. Despite their efforts, the Mickelbergs' counsels, Wallwork and Malcolm McCusker QC,[165] lost the argument that the High Court should consider fresh evidence to right a wrong done to their clients. The majority of the High Court held that they did not have the power to receive fresh evidence when hearing an appeal from a state court exercising state jurisdiction if that evidence was not available at the time of the state court hearing, or was evidence that could not have been discovered with reasonable due diligence.[166]

Even Justice Deane, who was critical of the police evidence in relation to the fingerprint crime mark, did not find for Ray.[167] Justice Deane said there was no evidence that 'when the alleged fingerprint was sent to Canberra, there existed a mould or cast of Raymond Mickelberg's right index finger capable of producing a fingerprint.' He agreed with his colleagues that the CCA was justified in reaching the conclusion that new or additional evidence of 'the theoretically possible fabrication of the alleged fingerprint would not, if placed before the jury at the trial, have affected the outcome of the trial.'[168]

Peter fared better. The High Court allowed Peter's application for special leave to appeal,[169]and allowed the appeal itself, remitting the matter back to the CCA[170] to consider whether his conviction for conspiracy was inconsistent with the acquittal of Brian on the charges of conspiracy.[171] The court also held that the CCA had failed to determine the whole case referred to it and, as Justice Brennan noted, the evidence against Peter had 'not been subjected to the critical examination necessary to determine whether his convictions were supportable.' their Honours believed any appeal by Peter should also consider whether any of his convictions were unsafe or unsatisfactory. They also remitted these matters back to the CCA for consideration.[172]

Peter's joy was short lived. The CCA heard the appeal between the 11 and 14 September 1989,[173] handing down their decision on 2 November 1989.[174] Chief Justice Malcolm and Justices Wallace and Seaman were of the opinion that the jury's verdicts were well supported by the evidence presented to them and there was nothing in the trial judge's directions to the jury to warrant a conclusion that the verdicts against Peter were unsafe or unsatisfactory, or that his conspiracy conviction was inconsistent with Brian's acquittal of the same charge.

Another appeal door had slammed on the Mickelbergs' hopes. But, just like a good crime novel, the plot of this real-life drama was about to take another turn.

CHAPTER 8
GOLD

In the midst of their struggle for vindication, Ray and Peter were subjected to more speculation as a result of two bizarre incidents.

The first incident occurred in July 1989 when Channel Seven reporter Alison Fan received anonymously a gold bar worth $10,000. It had a serial number that matched the batch of gold from which the Mint swindle gold had been taken. However, nothing tied it to the actual gold stolen. Accompanying the bar was a note addressed to Fan, proclaiming the Mickelbergs' innocence. 'The Mickelbergs are rotting in gaol because of this gold. I have tried before to get those poor bastards of [sic] the hook. Doing things through the official system fails. You can do something on TV to help put things right. This gold is a small part of what has gone off. Most bullion that disappears is kept quiet. The fingerprint was forged all right and those guilty have already been named. Maybe this, the real thing, will do some good. I rely on you to make it public before the system covers it up. I can't do any more for them. A grass is nearly as bad as a bent pig.'

The second incident happened just days before the CCA rejected Peter's appeal in November 1989, while he was on a seven-day release from Canning Vale Prison. Alison Fan was again involved. This time, she received a note from an anonymous writer who told her she would find some of the gold from the Mint swindle in two plastic containers near the station's helicopter hangar within the grounds of Channel Seven's studios. When she investigated, Fan found a package of gold pellets just inside the gates.

Soon after, Fan received an anonymous call from a man who alleged that fifteen unnamed people, including a well-known Perth businessman, were connected with the Perth Mint swindle.

The caller claimed not to know whether the Mickelbergs were involved with the swindle and told Fan he was leaving the country and taking his share of the gold pellets.[175] Fan received a second call, from another mystery man who claimed the Perth Mint swindle was linked to two other unresolved gold hauls which occurred just prior to the 1982 Mint swindle. Gold bullion worth $350,000 from the North Kalgurli mine disappeared between Kalgoorlie and Perth and $250,000 worth of gold bullion disappeared from a TAA flight between Perth and Melbourne (the event which lead to Arpad having to defend itself in the magistrate's court, represented by Ron Cannon).

Where the gold pellets came from remains a mystery, but it seems they were not from the Mint gold bullion, although it took a long time to establish even that much. The police supplied seven pellets to mineralogist Dr Hugh Herbert at the Chemistry Centre in Perth for testing. However, lacking the equipment to conduct specialised tests (known as ICP-MS analysis or 'fingerprinting'),[176] he advised the police he would have to take the pellets to Queensland, where the necessary equipment was available. But Police Commissioner Brian Bull would not authorise the $2000 cost to finance the trip.

Herbert conducted what tests he could with his inferior equipment, but not for long. Somebody somewhere wanted him stopped. All Herbert could or would swear to in a statutory declaration was that Chemistry Centre director John Hosking ordered him to stop the tests and return the gold pellets to the police. The police denied they issued the order.

The statutory declaration formed part of Herbert's evidence in the 1991 Supreme Court hearing in which Avon Lovell was seeking to strike out a libel action against him by eight detectives he named in *The Mickelberg Stitch*.[177] During the hearing, Acting Master (who exercises some of the powers of a judge) John Adams warned Mines Department officials not to interfere with Herbert's ability to give evidence. The warning followed Herbert's testimony that, after giving evidence in court about the order to discontinue his 1989 tests, senior police officers visited his superiors who later 'carpeted' him.

In 1993 Herbert finally had the equipment he needed to conduct the ICP-MS analysis and, after Ray and Peter had asked new Attorney-General Cheryl Edwardes to review their case, she instructed Herbert to carry out the tests.[178] He did, but the result did not help the brothers. The pellets were not from the Mint bullion; the presence of deposits of osmium suggested the gold more than likely came from South Africa.

Whether the person who sent the gold bar also sent the gold pellets a few months later is uncertain, as the identity of the person or people responsible for depositing the gold with Fan, writing the note, and telephoning her, has never been established. Who would sacrifice such a large amount of gold in order to proclaim the Mickelberg brothers' innocence?

Hancock was willing to hazard a guess. Within hours of Fan reporting that she had received the gold bar, he told a packed press conference that he was not surprised and suggested it could be a publicity stunt to pressure the state government into holding a royal commission into the Mickelberg case.[179]

Ray and Peter denied they were involved in the gold bar incident, just as they later denied any part in planting the gold pellets at the Channel Seven studios. Ray later said the word around the traps was that the police believed he and Peter had organised the gold pellets ruse to stimulate interest in, and sympathy for, their cause ahead of their appeals. Ray scoffed at the suggestion because Peter and he were soon coming up for parole. If they were guilty, it would have made no sense to squander a large quantity of gold when they would soon have access to all the gold, now worth more than $1 million (at least as widely reported by the media), which they had allegedly stolen and hidden.

The brothers didn't put it past Hancock to be involved with sending the gold to Fan. Speculation that Hancock had framed the Mickelbergs because he himself was involved in the Mint swindle was widespread. But there has been no evidence to substantiate those rumours and, if they were true, what would Hancock have gained by muddying the waters of the appeals by throwing up the prospect of another perpetrator?

Hancock's superiors never took the speculation seriously but the Internal Investigation Unit did scrutinise his early handling of the Mint swindle investigation. A week before the CCA handed down its November 1989 appeal decision against Peter, Chief

Superintendent Bruce Scott, head of the internal unit, briefed the media. 'It could be said I am investigating Mr Hancock plus the crew that investigated the original Mint swindle because allegations have been made in the two notes that indicate the Mickelbergs were not responsible. And in view of that, if the Mickelbergs were not responsible and we have police officers giving evidence that they were, obviously there is room for an allegation to be determined in that,' he said.[180]

However, after Police Commissioner Bull claimed Peter's unsuccessful appeal vindicated the police, Chief Superintendent Scott was backtracking. He claimed the media had taken his words out of context (a familiar claim) and that there was no reason to investigate Hancock and his officers. Hancock, not surprisingly, denied he was under investigation and the matter went quiet.

It was not so easy for the police to escape criticism of their handling of other complaints against them. When Chief Superintendent Scott let the cat out of the bag about the investigation into Hancock and his officers, he was also reacting to the State Ombudsman's conclusion that internal investigation procedures were inadequate in controlling collusion and collaboration between police officers.[181]

The issue of police misconduct and police corruption was about to come under sharper focus due to the Argyle Diamonds investigation. In the 'greed is good' environment of the 80s and the spectacular excesses of Perth's 'four-on-the-floor entrepreneurs' — as Brian Burke once described them — the public's appetite for stories of scurrilous behaviour by the rich and famous was to be sated by another media feast and, for a change, the Mickelbergs were not on the menu.

CHAPTER 9
CORPORATE COWBOYS AND
ROUGH DIAMONDS

It was the end of the 1980s. Peter was out of gaol and for the first time in seven harsh years he could contemplate Christmas with his family. Ray, on the other hand, with two more years to serve in Canning Vale, had to content himself with writing Christmas cards — 120 in all — to friends and supporters who were still trying to get him out. As was Peter, who had pleaded in vain with authorities to release Ray in time for Christmas.[182]

The turbulent decade had ended, but the memories lingered on. Of entrepreneurs who played fast and loose with other people's money; of those who had gone to gaol, and those who had not — sometimes because they had friends in high places, including politicians and police officers. Some had stolen far more than the Mickelbergs were alleged to have stolen yet did only token time in prison — and sometimes none at all.

The Mickelbergs railed against what they saw as an unjust anomaly. Had they done the crime — which they continued to insist they had not — the scale of their punishment was inordinately disproportionate to the spoils. Unscrupulous entrepreneurs had got away with billions of dollars and, in the process, destroyed the lives of thousands of innocent investors.

Of all the Australian business tycoons the 80s spawned, a disproportionately large number came from the West. Alan Bond, John Roberts of Multiplex fame, Kerry Stokes, Len Buckeridge, Laurie Connell, the Holmes à Courts, and Lang Hancock, whose flamboyant and gregarious wife Rose kept his name in the spotlight. They made their fortunes through driving ambition and some through a cavalier entrepreneurial spirit. They climbed to dizzying corporate and social heights but some came crashing down, brought undone by tragic human frailties — greed among them — and an illusion of infallible omnipotence.

Many of the entrepreneurs seemed to regard corporate operating rules as mere recommendations, not mandatory sanctions — a useful starting point from which to develop their own modifications. It was Alan Bond who said, 'There was a sense in the business community that you could stretch the envelope.'[183] A royal commission and gaol terms for some politicians and tycoons alike subsequently showed that the envelope could only be stretched so far before it burst at the seams.

In corporate boardrooms across Australia and around the world, the corporate cowboys from the West were feted — and feared. Always looking for a deal, they might be boardroom guests today but hosts in that same boardroom tomorrow. Even that most astute businessman, Kerry Packer, took a haircut when he decided to get a piece of the Western Australian action.

In the mid 1980s, Packer sold Channel Nine network to Alan Bond for an inflated price of $1 billion. That was the good bit.

But Packer then became involved in another deal that would be a disaster. In 1988, with WA property entrepreneur Warren Anderson, he purchased a piece of prime real estate in Perth's CBD, known as Westralia Square. The state government, in partnership with Alan Bond and Laurie Connell, had bought the site for $33.5 million just two years before. They sold it to Packer and Anderson for $270 million. As part of the deal, the government wanted Packer to contribute $50 million to the rescue of Rothwells Bank. Packer had lost $10 million in an earlier salvage attempt and did not trust the bank's founder, Connell. When told of this condition by Anderson he spat, 'Tell them to fuck off.'[184]

The land deal went ahead anyway, and Packer tried unsuccessfully to develop the site for fifteen years before he gave up in 2003 and sold the land to Multiplex for just $19 million. After making a loss of over $200 million he declared that 'all West Australians are crooks' and that he would never do business in the West again.[185] That was the bad bit.

But true to the Packer heritage, he didn't get mad, he got even — and then some. When the Channel Nine network foundered and Bond Corp was on the brink of collapse, he bought the television stations back for $250 million. Later Packer famously said, 'You only get one Alan Bond in your lifetime and I've had mine.' And that was the very best bit.

Bond, the dupe of the Yellow Rose of Texas fraud, is the most prominent of the corporate cowboys. Through his Bond Group and private company Dallhold, Bond had a finger in corporate pies all over the world. He owned TV and radio stations, newspapers, global brewing empires, diamond mines, vast property developments and even an airship company. He was the quintessential entrepreneur, demonstrating what can be achieved with bold ambition and lots of other people's money; his rise and fall were equally spectacular.

One of Bond's ambitious plans was to develop a Yanchep sheep station into a satellite city for 250,000 people on Perth's northern fringes, which he promoted as Sun City. Realising the barren landscape of scrubby sand dunes would look unappealing in brochures, Bond had 20,000 acres of dunes painted with green bitumen paint to make them look like rolling hills. Bond never realised his Sun City dream, but he still made a profit by selling the project to Japanese investors and the WA government.

Following the 1987 stock market crash Bond teamed up with the WA government to rescue Laurie Connell's failing Rothwells Bank. The ongoing saga of this intervention would form the core of the legendary WA Inc scandal.[186]

In 1992, Bond was convicted over a secret $16 million payment Bond Corp received for its efforts in the Rothwells' rescue. The Crown case was that Bond and Connell privately agreed to this fee on 25 October 1987 and that Bond deliberately and dishonestly concealed this fact from the parties he persuaded to join in the rescue of Rothwells. Bond had persuaded other business people to join him, on apparently equal terms, in helping rescue Rothwells (as a matter of public interest), failing to tell them that, from a merchant bank that was haemorrhaging money, he alone would take a significant fee, at a time when every dollar was important to the bank's survival. The conviction relied on evidence given by Connell.

Bond's legal team, led by Ian Callinan QC, later a justice of the High Court, and Christopher Steytler QC, a South African trained lawyer (who later became a justice on the bench of the Supreme

Court of Western Australia and was to play a prominent role in the Mickelbergs' fight to clear their names), had the conviction overturned, convincing the court that new evidence would have led the jury to entertain a reasonable doubt as to Bond's guilt. The new evidence came from Max Healy, a long-time friend of Connell, who said that 'Connell had told him some few months before Bond's trial that Bond "didn't do anything".' Connell had in fact arranged the commission with Peter Beckwith, a senior executive of Bond Corporation. Beckwith died prematurely of a brain tumour before the matter went to trial. Connell intended 'to give false evidence in the Bond trial' because it would be in Connell's interests 'if other people were convicted of Rothwells' offences.'[187]

Bond's house of corporate cards collapsed in 1989.[188] Yet, even in failure, he could still set records. Bond Corp went into receivership, with the biggest debt Australia had ever seen. It was the country's biggest corporate loss (Bond Corp $1 billion); our biggest corporate collapse (Bond Corp $4 billion); and Australia's largest ever fraud (more than $1 billion). It left a $5 billion black hole in the Australian marketplace and many small-time investors, a lot of them 'mum and dad investors', in financial ruin.

It was a far cry from Bond's earlier record when, in 1983, he became a national hero after his *Australia II* challenge wrested the famous America's Cup from the New York Yacht Club, which had held it since winning against the Brits more than a hundred years before. Many had challenged; none had succeeded before Alan Bond. Even Prime Minister Bob Hawke got excited. At dawn in the Royal Perth Yacht Club, as the whole country watched *Australia II* cross the line to win the cup, the PM expansively declared, 'Any employer who sacks a worker for not coming in today is a bum.' Many Australians took the prime ministerial word to heart, especially in the West, where by lunchtime most of the bars in Fremantle were full. Such was Bond's charisma and influence. But it was this same personal charisma that had seduced so many mum and dad investors into entrusting him with their life savings. It was all part of the 80s delusion that the good times would never end. Whoever did the Mint job would not have that on their conscience.

As the Mickelbergs later noted with indignation, Bond's records did not extend to the amount of gaol time served. Although convicted on three different occasions in the 1980s for his dishonest business dealings, it was 1997 before they earned him a seven-year gaol sentence after he pleaded guilty to dishonestly siphoning off to Bond Corp $1.2 billion from Bell Resources, in which he held a controlling interest.[189] When Bond Corp subsequently crashed, it left Bell Resources in dire straits. Nevertheless, after less than four years inside, most of it spent on a prison farm, he was again free.

The High Court handed Bond his freedom on 9 March 2000, ruling he should only serve the original term of four years, not the seven he got after the Federal Director of Public Prosecutions appealed that sentence to the WA Appeals Court. The High Court held that because Bond had broken a state law, only the WA government could lodge an appeal – not the Commonwealth. The court said the Federal DPP could prosecute Bond by applying state laws because they mirrored federal laws. But those same laws did not allow the Commonwealth to appeal.[190]

On the ABC 7.30 Report on the day of Bond's release, reporter David Hardaker asked Emeritus Professor Tony Blackshield of Macquarie University whether he thought the decision was serving justice. Blackshield replied, 'The High Court – and especially perhaps, the current court – is taking the line in several cases now, it doesn't matter how unfair or unjust or inconvenient the result is. If that's what the Constitution says, that's what the court has to follow. This came to light in a High Court case last August, in an appeal from ... South Australia, where the same problem arose. The Commonwealth had appealed against sentence under the Corporations Law and the High Court said the Commonwealth law did not give power to do that. It's that same point that has now helped Alan Bond.'

WA Director of Public Prosecutions Robert Cock put on a brave face, saying he would try to have the High Court decision overturned. In his heart, he must have known the legal difficulties would be insurmountable. No appeal was ever mounted.

Bond served about forty-three months in gaol after having misappropriated the life savings of thousands of small investors. Just a day or so before he got out of gaol, a poor devil in the

Northern Territory was sentenced to one year for stealing cordial and biscuits worth $23. As the *Sydney Morning Herald* reported on 7 October 2000,[191] if the system had applied the same formula to Bond, he would have been in gaol for fifty million years.

But the system was kind to Bond. In 1995, the Bond family secured his release from bankruptcy (he had gone bankrupt in 1992 with a personal debt of more than $500 million) by paying creditors about 0.5 cents in the dollar — a total payout of $12 million. By 2008 Bondie (as he was affectionately known at the height of fame but now more often known to his former creditors by another B word) was again back in the BRW Rich 200 list, with an estimated worth of $265 million.

Laurie Connell is perhaps the Perth businessmen most befitting of the phrase 'corporate cowboy'. Although never as big as Bond, his actions, more than any other's, would ensure the downfall of the 1980s state Labor government and many of Perth's most successful corporate entities. Connell didn't play by the rules and was happy to bribe, cheat and coerce those around him to achieve his goals.

He had many connections, including well-known Northbridge identity John Kizon. He had a close relationship with the state government and was a major donor to the Labor Party in the 1980s. He also employed former Liberal premier Ray O'Connor as a consultant, a move that helped blunt Parliamentary Opposition attacks over his questionable business dealings with the Labor government of the time.

One of Connell's most entrepreneurial corporate acts was the creation of Rothwells merchant bank in the 1980s. Tired of borrowing money from banks, he created his own. When all else failed, businesses knew they could usually rely on Rothwells to help them out, albeit at equally entrepreneurial interest rates, leading some to dub him 'last resort Laurie'. Following the 1987 stock market crash, Rothwells was on the verge of collapse and the state government secretly decided it would mount a rescue operation. The government initially injected $300 million, but within months it realised more bail-out money was needed. Over the next few months, the government pumped vast amounts of money into Rothwells and often made it a condition of unrelated business deals that other parties would invest in the bank.

Not all responded with Kerry Packer–style bluntness. Robert Holmes à Court, although probably sharing Packer's sentiments, nevertheless did contribute the $50 million the government wanted in return for it buying BHP from Holmes à Court. It was not enough. Rothwells collapsed in November 1988, losing the state of Western Australia over $1 billion.

While Rothwells was teetering, Connell remained heavily involved in the Perth horseracing scene, where he was known for placing huge bets. Rumour had it he was not above giving those huge bets a bit of a helping hand at times.

Disbelief and claims of foul play echoed through the crowd at Ascot racecourse after Connell-owned Rocket Racer blitzed the field to win the 1987 Perth Cup. Although run on a searing New Years Day, the horse continued running after completing the two-mile race, and only stopped when on the verge of collapse; six attendants had to carry the horse from the track. It has become folklore that the horse was drugged with Etorphine, or 'elephant juice', to ensure victory.[192] Connell reportedly won half a million dollars on the race and ordered champagne all round while his horse lay dying in the stables outside.

Although Connell was never charged over the Rocket Racer saga, his involvement in another horseracing scam was beyond question and eventually led to his imprisonment. The 'Bunbury hop-off' involved Connell paying his jockey, Danny Hobby, $5000 to 'fall' from his mount to ensure his horse didn't win the 1983 AHA Cup in Bunbury. When it became apparent the fall would be investigated, Connell paid Hobby over $1 million to leave the country for a number of years. Hobby eventually returned to Australia, admitted his involvement, and was gaoled for three years.

Connell was charged with perverting the course of justice and orchestrating the fraud. He was convicted for his involvement in keeping Hobby out of the country, but not for his part in the initial race fraud. He was sentenced to five years in prison and served some of that time before his death in 1996.

Robert Holmes à Court was a more urbane character than Bond and Connell but was nonetheless a very shrewd businessman, feared as one of the world's most ruthless corporate raiders. He moved to Perth from South Africa to study law at the University of Western Australia in 1961. He began his own practice in 1967, of which Nicholas Hasluck would later become a partner.

Holmes à Court's empire began to take shape in 1973, when he acquired Bell Brothers, a well-known West Australian transport and contracting group, for $9.6 million. Bell Brothers later became Bell Resources, his flagship company. He was involved in countless hostile takeovers of companies; some successful, others not. His most audacious and almost successful bid was for BHP. Even when unsuccessful, his raids generated significant profits as companies paid Holmes à Court to cease the takeover bids. By the mid-1980s, the Zimbabwean born-lawyer was feared in Australian and overseas boardrooms and renowned for his ability to walk away from unsuccessful bids with substantial 'compensation' for his efforts.

Holmes à Court's raids were funded by debt and he suffered heavily following the 1987 crash as lenders disappeared overnight. Merrill Lynch alone withdrew a $1 billion credit line from the Bell Group. As the Bell Group began to buckle under the strain, the unholy alliance of Alan Bond and the Western Australian government appeared on his doorstep, offering him the opportunity to complete what was his last big, and perhaps most successful, deal. Selling his own company allowed Holmes à Court to survive the 80s relatively unscathed, with almost half a billion dollars of Bond and government money in his pocket. He died of a heart attack in 1990 at the age of fifty-three — intestate![193]

Buying Bell was to guarantee the government its place in the infamous corporate history of Western Australia.

The story of WA Inc embraces Western Australia's corporate history from 1983 up to 1990. It snared three successive Labor premiers — Brian Burke (1983–88), Peter Dowding (1988–90) and Carmen Lawrence (1990–93). And to the last of these embattled premiers, Carmen Lawrence (Western Australia's first female premier), fell the task of cleaning up the mess.

Lawrence was under relentless pressure. With voter support at an all-time low, she finally succumbed and on 19 November 1990, announced a royal commission into WA Inc. The Royal Commission into Commercial Activities of Government and Other Matters was to investigate a number of matters relating to Rothwells and a scheduled list of other government business activities and matters relating to the Stirling City Council. Most of the matters dealt with activities during the Burke and Dowding administrations, but some involved the previous Liberal National Coalition governments of Sir Charles Court and Ray O'Connor.

The three commissioners were Supreme Court Justice the Hon. Justice Geoffrey Kennedy; retired Supreme Court Justice the Hon. Peter Brinsden QC; and former High Court Justice and President of the Human Rights and Equal Opportunity Commission Sir Ronald Wilson. The commissioners commenced hearings in March 1991.

The formal hearings did not end until 30 June 1992. They sat for over 278 days, heard from 681 witnesses and took 44,000 pages of evidence. Most of the key players in the WA Inc years were called to give evidence, including Bond and Brian Burke.

The six-volume report was tabled in Parliament on 20 October 1992. It made findings of impropriety, conflicts of interest, inappropriate use of money and abuse of office and public confidence. It found that Brian Burke 'acted improperly, his conduct being discreditable and amounting to a substantial breach of the standard of rectitude to be expected of a person holding the office of Premier.' Of former deputy premier David Parker, it said, 'By any normal measure of the conduct of a minister of the Crown, his behaviour was grossly incompetent, if not absurd.' The royal commissioners found that Premier Dowding was evasive and unconvincing. Subsequent to the royal commission, Burke and Parker faced criminal charges. Burke resigned his Ireland ambassadorship and was gaoled for two years in June 1994 for 'false pretence' for illegally claiming $17,179 in travel expenses from taxpayers between 1986 and 1988. He served seven months before release on parole. In March 1997, he was gaoled for three years on multiple counts of stealing a total of $122,585 in campaign donations. In his defence, Burke, a keen philatelist, said he used money donated to the party leader's account to buy stamps as an investment for the ALP but had not notified anyone of this. He served six months before the convictions were quashed on appeal, on the grounds that the money was Burke's to use as state leader 'as he saw fit.'[194]

In 1994 David Parker was charged with stealing $38,000 from his election campaign funds between 1986 and 1989, although this offence did not specifically relate to WA Inc business. He was sentenced to one year's imprisonment, which he served out, but the High Court later acquitted him.[195] In 1996 Parker was charged and convicted of committing perjury before the WA Inc Royal Commission. He was sentenced to eighteen months imprisonment, of which he served four months before being released on parole from the minimum security Wooroloo Prison Farm.

Ray O'Connor, who succeeded Sir Charles Court as premier of Western Australia in 1982, did not escape the clutches of the WA Inc Royal Commission, which implicated him in the theft of a cheque for $25,000 that Bond Corp executives had given him to pay Stirling City Councillors to expedite approval to build the Observation City hotel. However, he kept the cheque for himself and was tried in 1995 and gaoled on charges of stealing and criminal defamation.[196]

The Royal Commission findings did not surprise Ray and Peter. They were only sorry that a similar investigation into the police force seemed unlikely. Richard Court's Liberal government, which had taken power after defeating the Lawrence government in the 1993 election, balked at the idea, with some politicians nervous about holding a royal commission into a police force they liked to consider was without blemish.

In fact, for some time the police force had been conducting an internal investigation into alleged illegal activities involving Argyle Diamonds.

In the late 1980s, a well-organised criminal syndicate stole diamonds on a regular basis from the Argyle Diamond Mine in the Kimberley, in Western Australia's far north. The Argyle Diamond Mine is the world's largest supplier of rare and valuable pink diamonds, and annual sales were carefully regulated. An alternative source of pink diamonds was therefore attractive for both buyer and seller. Although the level of security at the mine was seemingly high, members of its own security department were siphoning off rough diamonds onto the black market.

A Perth organised crime figure had recruited a highly placed security employee to implement the systematic theft of rough diamonds from the mine site. The Perth criminal acted as an intermediary in shipping the diamonds offshore. Once overseas they were cut, processed and reportedly moved through a highly reputable dealer in Switzerland before being sold through legitimate outlets in the Hong Kong and European markets. Embarrassed over the breach of their security measures, Argyle Diamonds was reluctant to reveal the number and value of stolen diamonds and the figures were never established at trial, although the loss clearly ran into the millions.

The Argyle chief of security had already conducted initial investigations before informing police in late 1989. In total, the police undertook three investigations into the thefts. The first two produced no results, while the third led to the conviction of three people for conspiracy to steal diamonds.

Allegations that high-ranking police officers had deliberately frustrated the first two investigations rocked the police force. Security employee Lindsay Roddan had associations with a number of police officers who, according to the allegations, acted corruptly to protect him. Although the Crown laid charges against some police officers, they dropped them on the eve of the trial, leaving a cloud of suspicion hanging over the force. The affair only received a new airing in 2001 when Geoff Gallop's Labor government established a royal commission into police corruption. A thorough review was conducted and more than 100 of the 600 pages of the 2004 Royal Commission final report were devoted to the affair.[197]

The Royal Commission found no evidence that senior police officers deliberately frustrated the Argyle Diamond investigations. Instead, it found that significant management failures and faulty internal communication hampered investigations. It was these failures that led to the persistent allegations of corruption, and the negative public perception of the police force.

The Mickelbergs' hopes that revelations of corporate, political and police corruption would help their case were dashed. The police, the judiciary and the government were unmoved. Ray was soon to be released, but that was not the end of the matter as far as he was concerned. The brothers would continue to use the courts and court the media to get their version of the story heard.

CHAPTER 10
TANGLED WEBS AND THE DECEIVERS WHO WEAVE THEM

Free at last to join Peter on the outside, Ray Mickelberg was a man on a mission. He had scores to settle with those who, he claimed, had snared the brothers in a web of deceit. WA Inc may have been the primary target on the media radar in April 1991, but just below the horizon, the Mickelbergs were coming in hot.

True to his SAS heritage, Ray was determined to dare — and to win. The reverberating clang of the closing prison gates had hardly faded away before he launched his first attack. Calling a media conference, he likened the imprisonment of the Mickelberg brothers to the wrongful conviction of the Birmingham Six. After serving sixteen years in prison for an IRA bombing attack on a Birmingham pub, the six gained their freedom when sophisticated testing, using Electro Static Deposition Analysis (ESDA),[198] showed conclusively that the police had fabricated their alleged confession and that they were innocent victims of a gross miscarriage of justice.

Simultaneously, Ray launched a legal action to have the police release their so-called confession documents for ESDA testing in the UK. Meeting Johnny Walker, one of the Birmingham Six, in Perth in November 1991 strengthened his resolve to pursue the ESDA testing. He and Peter were going to storm the courts, the politicians and the media. In the court of public opinion, some had nailed their colours to the mast declaring emphatic belief in the brothers' innocence. Others, just as emphatically, thought the Mickelbergs were guilty as sin. Many just didn't give a damn. But in the only court that truly mattered, new battles were about to be joined.

Malcolm McCusker QC had previously worked with Henry

Wallwork QC, who had since joined the Supreme Court bench. Now McCusker was acting solo for Ray and Peter, assisted by instructing solicitor Gary Lawton. In the Supreme Court on 10 December 1991, McCusker applied to Chief Justice Malcolm to have certain exhibits from the Mickelbergs' 1983 Perth Mint swindle trial released for testing in the UK, the US and Germany. The exhibits comprised Lewandowski's notes, which contained the unsigned statement in which Peter allegedly admitted his involvement; forensic scientist Dr Kobus's negatives in relation to the fingerprint of the WABS cheque and his affidavit that he had treated and photographed the print; and the police file on Ray, which related to his conviction for an offence in 1976.

McCusker asked that, in the 'interest of justice' for the Mickelbergs and in the wider interests of the community, 'the court consider the possibility, however repugnant, that the administration of the justice system could err,' and order the state to examine 'the possibility that by scientific evaluation a wrong may be uncovered.'

Mary Ann Yeats, who by now knew the Mickelberg case inside out, appeared for the Crown. She argued the Mickelbergs had 'been given extraordinary opportunities to explore all possible scientific and factual defects in the evidence against them, with public assistance,' and that it had never been the law that a convicted person could continue to test the evidence against them in the hope that at some stage a fault may be found. She forcefully submitted to the Chief Justice that 'the interests of justice compel the rejection of post-trial and post-appeal fishing expeditions, which is really what it is.'

However, McCusker's argument prevailed and on 1 April 1992 the Chief Justice made detailed orders allowing for the release of the documents.[199] He said granting the application did not suggest there was any support to the allegations of a miscarriage of justice; it did 'no more than grant access to the documents for the purpose of testing or examination.' The Chief Justice held that, given the repeated allegations of police misconduct, it was in the interest of justice to allow further testing on the exhibits 'whether the results are favourable to the Crown or the applicants, or whether they are inconclusive.'

He rejected the submission that the court needed the Crown's consent before the exhibits could be tested because, even if the exhibits were the property of the Crown, they were now in the custody and control of the court. Therefore, he had 'jurisdiction as a single judge of the court to order that the documents be made available for examination and testing, so long as there are appropriate safeguards which will ensure that the documents remain in the custody of the court and that the integrity of the documents will be preserved.' His orders required an officer of the court to travel overseas with the documents while they were tested.

Yeats made an eleventh-hour bid to have the exhibits tested by Sergeant Hofstee of the Document Examination Section in the Forensic Branch of the police department. An angry McCusker wanted to know why the Crown was making this last-ditch effort to prevent overseas testing when the police, who had possessed the equipment to do the same test for the past ten years, had not done so. In an interview with *The Bulletin*, Ray declared that the Crown was 'frightened of the results.' He told the magazine, 'The point to be made here is that police did have the technology available ten years ago to prove or disprove that confessions had been fabricated. Were they not morally obligated to advise government they could effect such tests to prove or disprove [our claims] and solve the situation once and for all?'[200]

McCusker also challenged Hofstee's independence, given that he took part in the raid on the Mickelberg house in July 1982 and had been a Crown witness at the trial. Chief Justice Malcolm agreed.

Yeats would not let go. What about letting Peter Munson, a forensic document examiner with the Perth office of the Department of Immigration, Local Government and Ethnic Affairs, have a go at the exhibits before the Crown handed them over to the Mickelberg experts? 'I don't think so,' said the Chief Justice, perhaps privately wondering if Yeats thought he had come down in the last shower.

Although they knew there was a long way to go, the Mickelbergs and their supporters were euphoric. Feeding their euphoria were the findings of two British handwriting forensic experts, Peter Radley and David Baxendale, a former Home Office officer whose findings of police fabrications led to the release of the Birmingham Six.[201] After testing Peter's alleged confession, Radley's report said in part, 'There is clear evidence to demonstrate that the original interview notes written have been modified by the current pages 2 and 3 having been written after page 14 and then substituted for the original pages 2 and 3. Page 1 may also have been substituted.' Baxendale reached a similar conclusion. 'The present pages 2 and 3 are not the original second and third pages but are substitutes which were written on sheets of paper which had been resting underneath page 14. The two pages cannot therefore be contemporaneous.'

Peter presented these findings in an affidavit to the Supreme Court on 13 May 1992 in support of the Mickelbergs' application for court permission to submit further evidence for forensic testing. Ray and Peter held a media conference on the same day. Ray said fabricated evidence had convicted him and his brothers. He added, 'We have always maintained that there has been a major conspiracy to pervert the course of justice in this case. We have struggled for ten years to prove it and we now call upon the Attorney-General, and indeed the Premier, to take action quickly.' Peter said, 'These reports, by world leaders in their fields, conclusively demonstrate that the case against us was fabricated. The point is that, if the police lied about these matters, the veracity of the whole Crown case has to be thrown out.'[202]

The report from the handwriting experts was not the only reason for Ray and Peter's rekindled optimism. A report from world-renowned US document examiner Richard Brunelle provided tentative support for Ray's claim that his fingerprint mark on the WABS cheque was a forgery. Brunelle argued that someone in the police department could have forged the fingerprint from a fingerprint they had on file from Ray's minor 1976 offence, even though the police had claimed they destroyed the print in the same year.

A one-line entry on the top of Ray's police file dated 11 June 1976 said, 'Fingerprints destroyed by request.' However, preliminary testing from Brunelle indicated the ink used for the notation was not manufactured until 1986. After further testing he concluded, 'In (my) professional opinion the entry ... could not have been written in 1976 as the ink used was not manufactured until at least 1978.'[203]

Brunelle's findings did not provide the smoking gun Ray was looking for, but they did raise the possibility that the entry on the official police file was false.

Peter's affidavit, with the reports from Radley, Baxendale and Brunelle attached, sparked renewed interest in the Mickelbergs. State parliamentary upper house members, Independent Reg Davies and Liberal Peter Foss, were asking questions of Attorney-General Joe Berinson and Police Minister Graham Edwards. Enlisting the support of Independent (formerly Labor) lower house member Dr Ian Alexander and Opposition spokeswoman on law matters Cheryl Edwardes, they pressed the state government to take measures to secure all evidence in the matter held by the office of the Director of Public Prosecutions and the police department and for an inquiry to take place. Davies didn't mince words. He said the recent expert evidence obtained by the Mickelbergs demonstrated that the police had fabricated evidence. Berinson cautioned Davies against making such allegations and did not agree to an inquiry.

Don Hancock, the man with most to lose, came out fighting. He conceded that the latest evidence created the distinct possibility of another inquiry into the Mickelberg case. Taking the initiative, he agreed to a *60 Minutes* interview with hard-nosed interviewer Richard Carleton, and later to an extensive interview with the *Sunday Times*.[204]

Carleton went straight for the jugular. 'Would you accept that if page two of these notes ... had in fact been rewritten after the event, then you perjured yourself?' Hancock parried, 'If they were rewritten after the event, yes I would probably say that. But they weren't. I am not prepared to elaborate on that, but there is a logical explanation for what is being once again bandied around by the Mickelbergs and, at the appropriate time and in the appropriate place, the right forum, that explanation will be given.' He sought to avoid further questions on the subject, saying he could not discuss it in the media because of the likelihood of a future court case. In fact, no case was pending at that time, although the Mickelbergs were champing at the bit to lodge another appeal.

Two weeks later, in his interview with Jim Pollard of the *Sunday Times*, Hancock's concern about future litigation didn't hold him back. This time it was not the Mickelbergs in his sights, but Chief Justice Malcolm. He was blunt: Malcolm got it wrong.

In granting the Mickelbergs' application to conduct further testing, the Chief Justice wrote: 'the notes purport to be a complete and contemporaneous record of a conversation between Detective Hancock and Peter. Detective Hancock and the then Detective Lewandowski stated on oath at the trial, and at the appeal, that these notes represented an accurate record of the entire interview of Peter at Belmont' and Lewandowski had taken them down word for word as the conversation took place. Detective Lewandowski also stated on oath 'there was nothing in the notes which was written in later.' The Chief Justice noted that defence counsel had put it to Lewandowski he had not made the notes in the way he had sworn, but had fabricated them after the interview. Lewandowski denied the claim. In the event, the notes constituted an unsigned record of interview, which the prosecution relied on heavily in making their case to the court. The Chief Justice could not have been more emphatic.

Malcolm counterattacked Hancock's claim vigorously. 'I don't believe that is right because the handwritten notes of interviews contained very little information in the way of outright confessions.' Yet during the trial, Crown Prosecutor Ron Davies referred to the interview of Peter on 26 July 1982 as 'the breakthrough' and trial judge Heenan left the jury in no doubt about the importance of the police interviews.

With the sorrowful air of a misunderstood nice guy, Hancock bemoaned the absence of videotaping of police interviews when Lewandowski and he were interviewing the brothers. 'It would have saved us a lot of trauma.' Had he forgotten how strenuously the WA Police Union had opposed Premier Burke and Police Minister Hill in 1987 when they announced a trial of this procedure?

Hancock said it was a lie that the police had targeted the Mickelbergs only after the Yellow Rose of Texas fraud charge. He claimed he only became aware of the fraud two months after charging the Mickelbergs with the Mint swindle.

He dismissed the Mickelbergs' unremitting allegations against the police, and their cultivation of the media, as politics. Ray, he said, had an enormous ego which he needed to feed constantly.

'He just never stops. He's got the biggest ego I've ever seen. He just can't take a beating. He probably got it from the SAS, the mental training they drum into them. He's a most unusual man.' Ray may not have agreed that his SAS training had given him an inflated ego, but he knew it had made him mentally tough and persistent. He also knew how to seize the moment, as he did when Premier Carmen Lawrence was a guest on 6PR's *Sattler File* on 21 July 1992.

As early as 1990, in his weekly *Sunday Times* column, Howard Sattler had pressed for Ray's release from prison. Although not asserting the brothers were innocent, he did think Ray especially had been hard done by. He wrote, 'Officially Raymond Mickelberg is a criminal. But his story now shows that he was the biggest loser from his alleged escapade. The part of his twenty-three years that Ray has already served has cost him, his family, his home and his business. Unlike scores of others with whom the courts have been more generous, Raymond Mickelberg presents no physical threat to the community. It is time the government agreed he has paid his dues.'[205]

Ray grabbed the opportunity to phone the Premier live on air to tell her he had received over 240 telephone calls of support after the airing of the *60 Minutes* segment. He then challenged the Premier to accept a personal briefing from him and Malcolm McCusker. The Premier rejected the suggestion, saying it was important politicians did not become intricately involved in the judicial process.

The Mickelbergs were determined to have another day in court. The overseas testing of the police confessional notes and Ray's police fingerprint records only made them more resolute. For the second time, Peter petitioned Governor Sir Francis Burt for the right to lodge a special appeal under section 21 of the *Criminal Code 1913* (WA).[206]

Under the state's constitutional monarchical system, while the consent of the Governor of Western Australia was required, the State Attorney-General determined whether the matter should proceed to court.[207] Attorney-General Berinson agreed, and announced that the Director of Public Prosecutions, John McKechnie, would investigate the allegations contained in the petition, which included the evidence of Messrs Baxendale,

Radley and Brunelle.

To the cynical observer, McKechnie's appointment may have seemed disingenuous because of his central role in prosecuting the Mickelbergs in the first instance. Although sceptical, the brothers could do no more than hope McKechnie would not allow any lingering prejudices to compromise his impartiality. McKechnie clearly recognised the dilemma, and refused to make any final recommendations at the end of his 65-page report because of his role in prosecuting the Mickelbergs.

The media had a field day. During August 1992, the *West Australian* and the *Sunday Times* each ran major articles. The month started off favourably for the brothers with a *Sunday Times* story on 2 August headlining the disclosure that Don Hancock regarded rules in police work as nothing more than guidelines.[208] That revelation had come from Peter's tape-recording of the conversation between the brothers and Hancock in December 1983 — the recording Ron Cannon had decided was 'too good to be true.'

However, by mid-month the brothers were on the defensive. On 14 August, the *West Australian* headlined a 'Mickelberg bombshell'.[209] Its revelation came out of the blue from a surprising source and threatened to derail the Mickelberg appeal train just as it was developing a full head of steam.

The source was Peter Holz, a defence witness at the original trial who claimed to have been a friend of Brian Mickelberg. Now he was telling the *West* he had lied to protect the brothers. Holz, a boat builder, first met the Mickelbergs in 1982 when he agreed to build a blue water yacht for Brian. Sometime later Ray and Peter also visited Holz's workshop in the south-east metropolitan suburb of Maddington. Holz didn't take to Ray; he was cold and never smiled. Peter, on the other hand, talked a lot and seemed very impressionable. Ray showed great interest in how Holz did the bronze castings for portholes and chain plates and asked if Holz would let him try his hand at casting moulded lead ballast for the hull of the yacht Holz was building.

Not long after the Perth Mint swindle, Brian, his wife Faye and their two children visited Holz, telling him the police had treated Brian badly. Holz said that Peter had also visited him, and told him he had bought a car at Armadale while wearing a wig and he thought the police would not be able to prove anything. Later, Peter also purportedly discussed the possibility of the brothers doing gaol time, apparently telling Holz, 'We are prepared for it. In any case, half a million will only bring one or two years. With good conduct we will be out in one year.'

The *West* reported that after the initial visit, the three brothers again called in on Holz at his factory to ask for a favour. Ray wanted Holz to attest in an affidavit that on 22 June 1982, he was sailing with Brian between 2 p.m. and 6 p.m. Holz assumed the date was accurate and agreed. He claims he did not check his diary at the time because he relied on Brian accurately recollecting the date. It was not until two weeks before the 1983 trial that he checked his diary and realised Brian and he had gone sailing on 23 June 1982, not 22 June. But because he had already signed the affidavit he felt trapped, he said. During the trial, he tried to skate over the issue by telling the court he recalled sailing with Brian on a Tuesday but could not remember the month.

Not so easily explained was why he also agreed to Ray's request that he tell the police he saw Peter and Brian working on a fence at the Mickelberg family house on the day of the Mint swindle, even though he had not. At trial, he refused to give evidence on the matter.

Also not easily explained was why Holz told the *West Australian* he had decided to speak out now only because he had recently received a phone call about the case from an unidentified caller. What did the unidentified caller say that prompted Holz to recant on the evidence he had given at the trial? According to the *West*, Holz said he was not out to help the police 'with any controversies they might be involved in,' but that 'I just want to set the record straight' and 'I feel sorry for the Mickelberg supporters, for all the time and effort they put in, without knowing the truth.'

On 16 August 1992 the *Sunday Times* reported that Holz had been offered protection from the police and that the CIB told him to go to the media because, 'If I come forward, some of the heat would go off the police.'[210] The police refused to confirm or deny Holz's statement.

Ray was incensed. Noting the allegations were only now being aired after the release of the findings of the Mickelbergs' overseas experts, he demanded an open inquiry into every aspect of the case, including purportedly new or fresh evidence. 'In the interests of justice and to clear the name of the police force, if it could be cleared, then the only avenue is a full and open inquiry.'[211] Peter joined in. Explain, he challenged, how the alterations to police interview notes occurred. The challenge was not taken up.

With a change of state government in February 1993, the Mickelbergs gained a sympathetic ear in the new Attorney-General, Cheryl Edwardes.[212] After receiving the McKechnie opinion, she appointed Adelaide based QC Brian Martin, who had acted as counsel assisting the WA Inc Royal Commission in the early 1990s, to conduct an independent inquiry into the Mickelberg case and to study the 65-page opinion dealing with the factual merits of the section 21 petitions by Ray and Peter. The Attorney-General said that at the conclusion of Martin's investigation she would be left with three choices — reject the section 21 petitions, allow the petitions to take their course through the courts, or quash the convictions.

A number of people, including Avon Lovell and the Western Australian Legislative Council Select Committee on the Western Australian Police Service (set up in 1993), wanted to see McKechnie's opinion and Martin's report. McKechnie sought to block the release of his opinion, but was unsuccessful. However, he had more luck with preventing the release of the Martin report, claiming legal professional privilege and public interest immunity.[213]

Avon Lovell was anxious to get his hands on the McKechnie DPP opinion, hoping it would help his damages case against Lewandowski, in which he was asking $400,000 for lost sales of his book, *The Mickelberg Stitch*.[214] He hoped the opinion would also help his defence in the defamation action the eight high-profile police officers (including Hancock, Assistant Commissioner Edward Billing, Superintendent Ken Henning, and Lewandowski) were bringing against him. Lovell was particularly anxious to get his hands on Lewandowski's attempt to explain how the Mickelbergs' British experts were able to show someone had altered two pages of notes from the police interview with Peter on 26 July 1982.

McKechnie's opinion included Lewandowski's explanation that he had to rewrite the two pages because they were illegible.

He didn't change them, he said, just 're-copied' them. While the opinion acknowledged the international reputation and credibility of Radley and Baxendale, it viewed Lewandowski's explanation, which Hancock corroborated, as innocent and not sinister.

Radley and Baxendale were not convinced. Baxendale said the explanation was possibly legitimate but not convincing and Radley said he found no evidence to support the view that the words written on the original pages 2 and 3 of the notes of the interview with Peter were poorly written or illegible. Furthermore, the explanation bore little resemblance to the evidence Hancock and Lewandowski gave under oath in the 1983 trial.

One of the terms of reference of the Western Australian Legislative Council Select Committee on the Western Australian Police Service required it to inquire into and report upon 'whether the self regulatory role of the Internal Affairs Unit (IAU) within the Police Service is effective or desirable in the public interest and if not, what method of detecting, punishing and preventing corruption within the Police Service should be implemented.' The terms of reference also gave the Select Committee authority to hear evidence from Ray and Peter. At least two members of the Committee were acknowledged sympathisers with the Mickelberg cause – the Chair, Hon. Derrick Tomlinson, and the Deputy Chair, Hon. Reg Davies. The other members were Hon. Nick Griffiths, Hon. Philip Lockyer and Hon. Murray Montgomery.

Over the course of three days in late 1995, Ray and Peter took the Select Committee through their allegations of police misconduct and described how the legal and political system had thwarted their efforts to seek justice. Unlike their defence counsel at trial, who had let the police off the moral hook by labelling their attempts to nail the brothers as 'noble corruption', Ray and Peter didn't pull any punches. They asserted that far from doing just a little bit extra to nail those they were sure were guilty, the police knew the brothers could not have done the crime. In fact, they claimed, it was a distinct possibility the police were looking for scapegoats to protect a guilty person or persons within the police force itself.

They scathingly rejected McKechnie's resort to legal professional privilege in denying the brothers, Lovell, and the Select Committee access to the Martin report, and they questioned McKechnie's personal integrity by alleging that he lied in his 65-page opinion.

In its interim report on the third term of reference, the Select Committee expressed disquiet and disappointment in not being able to access the Martin report. The committee wrote, 'A request to the Hon Cheryl Edwardes MLA for access to Mr Martin's report was denied on the ground it was the subject of legal professional privilege. That is unfortunate. Whatever opinion it contains and whatever justification of that opinion it offers, the Martin report would have been of interest to the Committee. It might have helped resolve, or alternatively have confirmed, some of the doubts held about the integrity of the case against the Mickelbergs.'

The committee was receptive to the Mickelberg cause. They made that clear when they wrote, 'The Committee has considerable disquiet about the information presented to it in lengthy hearings. On the face of it, there is strong evidence to suggest the police case against the Mickelbergs was contrived. Whether the Mickelbergs committed the crime, they were convicted and imprisoned. At law they are guilty, but they may have been convicted on evidence about which there are grave questions.'

However, the committee was not prepared to go further and seek answers to these 'grave questions'. They said they didn't have the resources to do so. There may have been more to it than lack of resources. The committee comprised some very experienced politicians who would have been acutely aware of the potential political sensitivities and fallout from delving too deeply into the police and judicial system and processes of the state. Fortunately for the committee, they had a legitimate out. Although an independent judicial inquiry was 'necessary to prove whether the police handling of the Mickelberg case was beyond reproach,' they said the matter of the convictions in law was for the courts.[215]

Now the brothers were before the Court of Criminal Appeal again. Attorney-General Edwardes had referred their section 21 petitions to the highest appellate court in the state for another appeal; in all this was Ray's seventh appeal and Peter's ninth. The government had granted Peter an ex gratia payment to finance the appeal,[216] but not Ray. Once again, he would have to rely on the generosity of his supporters and legal team. And once again, the wheels of justice would turn slowly. It was now late 1995. The appeals were not heard until 1998.[217]

In the meantime, the police faced further claims of police corruption and sinister dealings with the underworld.

CHAPTER 11
RED EMPEROR — THE ONE THAT GOT AWAY

'ALARMING REPORT' the headline blared.

So began the public saga of the search for the truth about police corruption in Western Australia. The day this headline ran in the *West Australian* (19 June 1996), the newspaper's editorial writers were already composing copy for the following day which would accuse the state government of playing politics with police corruption. The all-party Select Committee report, the editorial said, 'confirmed the worst fears of many people in Western Australia in its finding of significant police corruption and a police culture that allowed it to flourish with impunity.'[218]

The Select Committee report not only criticised the Mickelberg investigation, it also recommended judicial inquiries into the Argyle Diamond affair and the death in custody of Perth teenager Stephen Wardle, neither of which eventuated. As well, it proposed an independent Police Anti-Corruption Commission with royal commission powers of investigation into allegations of police graft and corruption.[219] It slammed the police department's Internal Investigation Unit and the Internal Investigations Branch as equally ineffective in combating police corruption and in dealing with complaints against the police. It also found evidence of selective leaking of confidential information to the media; advance warnings of police investigations to persons involved in gambling or drug operations; interference in criminal investigations; tampering with evidence; colluding to conceal evidence; selling drugs confiscated in police raids; accepting bribes from organised-crime figures; and receiving corrupt payments to protect prostitutes and drug traffickers. That pretty much covered all police operations except writing out speeding tickets.

Corruption, the committee said, was endemic, especially in the drug squad, and remained uncovered only because of an institutionalised code of silence intended to protect the reputation of the force at all costs.[220] The committee was especially worried that some officers at the highest levels in the force were active in weaving the web of corruption.

Although the code of silence may have insulated the police from widespread public scrutiny, there had always been plenty of gossip around town. In pubs and at dinner parties, there would be somebody who had heard from 'someone who knows' stories about criminals, the rich and powerful, and politicians who had mutually useful contacts with copper mates. Perth had long been a city with strange and tangled webs of connections, some clearly visible, others hidden. Most of the nightlife centres on Northbridge, Fremantle and one or two of the western suburbs in between. Only those who are fringe dwellers of the vibrant subcultures that make up the city of Perth could describe Western Australia as an isolated 'dullsville'.

Its proximity to Asia and its long, poorly monitored coastline also make Western Australia an 'ideal backdoor for drug importation,'[221] while the vastness of its outback provides opportunities to grow large marijuana crops which are hard to detect. This has brought drug growers and organised crime groups over from the east and for years there have been significant underworld links between Western Australia and the rest of the country. A 2005 report by the Corruption and Crime Commission of Western Australia traces the thread of organised crime back to the early 1970s. It names the chief sources as criminal networks, ethnic-based crime groups, motorcycle gangs and paedophile networks.[222]

The leading figure in Western Australian organised crime during the 1980s and early 90s was Bruno 'The Fox' Romeo.[223] He was the leader of the Italian crime group N'Dranghita and had close family connections to the Calabrian drug barons of the Griffith region in NSW. These groups played integral roles in the events that finally led to the Royal Commission into the NSW Police Force in the 1990s. There was also suspicion that Romeo and his associates were connected to the 1994 parcel bombing at National Crime Authority (NCA) headquarters in Adelaide in which one officer, Geoffrey Bowen from Perth, was killed and another officer blinded. At the time of the bombing, the NCA was conducting major investigations into Western Australian criminal syndicates. Suspicions came to light at the inquest into Bowen's murder, but never hardened into evidence.[224]

Police arrested Romeo in 1994 for cultivating an $8 million cannabis crop on a pastoral lease in the state's north. He was gaoled for ten years. Romeo's departure left a gap at the top for some ambitious entrepreneur prepared to walk on the dark side of the law. A brash young man named John Kizon,[225] who grew up in Perth's northern suburbs and began his early adult life as a star boxer, decided he was the man.

Perth people have an insatiable fascination with Kizon, not unlike that which draws them to the Mickelbergs. Each has featured prominently in newspapers and TV news services for many years, always proclaiming their innocence. However, one would be hard pressed to find members of the public — or of the police force — who would link the brothers to organised crime. Kizon is a different proposition. Usually described in the media as a 'well-known Northbridge identity', the sobriquet has little impact on the public perception of him as a denizen of the underworld, and not only in Perth. In 1998, he was a pallbearer at the funeral of murdered Melbourne crime figure Alphonse Gangitano. His propensity to somehow drift into the spotlight when dramatic events occur, including nightclub shootings, the death of a star witness and the sudden dismantling of a high level police operation into the Kizon syndicate, continue to stimulate the public's fascination with a man who seems larger than life, both in physical stature and the public imagination.

Kizon's criminal record is brief, and has been gathering dust since 1990 when the court found him guilty of opening false bank accounts. He had two prior convictions, one for heroin trafficking in 1982 for which he served time, and one for assault in 1985. Since then, the Western Australian Police Force, the Federal Police and the National Crime Authority have conducted many intensive investigations into the Kizon syndicate, mostly without success. Try as they might, the police have been unable to pin anything on him. He has survived unscathed many attempts to prosecute him.

Perhaps taking its name from the superb white-flesh fish in the seas off Western Australia, Operation Red Emperor began on 10 March 1997. Police Commissioner Bob Falconer was determined to reel in the big fish that had got away in previous undercover operations conducted by the NCA and Federal Police. The plan was to infiltrate organised crime activities presumed to be connected to John Kizon. The officer in charge was Senior Sergeant Peter Coombs, a highly decorated policeman known both for his innovation and determination to get the job done.

Red Emperor was supposed to run until March 1998, but ended in shambles in November 1997, having fragmented into isolated and conflicting sub-operations brought in from other areas under the Red Emperor umbrella. As these sub-operations became increasingly independent and uncontrolled, there were fears of potential corruption and a growing apprehension that the operation had been compromised.[226]

Nevertheless, in the seven months before it disintegrated, Red Emperor revealed a wealth of information on organised crime in Western Australia and the occasional walks on the dark side by some police officers as they got too far down into 'the mud and the blood and the beer' where the crims were. Particularly shocking was the revelation from recorded phone conversations of extensive police corruption in the Andrew Petrelis affair.[227]

Andrew Petrelis died from a heroin overdose in a Queensland apartment on 11 September 1995. Police found him naked, crouched, with one arm resting on a chair and the other behind his back. A hypodermic syringe lay close by. The door to the apartment was locked from the inside. Investigating officers recorded that, although Petrelis was right-handed, the injection was in his right arm and there was no tourniquet or spoon. The death had far greater implications than the loss of yet another young junkie's life. At the time of his death, Petrelis was living as Andrew Parker under the Western Australian police witness protection program after agreeing to give evidence against Kizon and his associate Michael Rippingale in relation to a drug bust.

Petrelis did various jobs around Northbridge for Kizon, including serving as driver for Kizon's girlfriend. He did one job too many and it cost him his life. Acting on instructions, he collected several garbage bags containing $150,000 worth of cannabis, buried in Kings Park, and took them to a self-storage unit in Perth's northern suburbs. The storage centre owners became suspicious when they saw that the door to the unit, which had not previously been locked, was now padlocked. They notified police, who had no trouble sheeting the crime home to Petrelis because he had leased the unit in his own name. Petrelis agreed to testify against Rippingale and Kizon, for whom he said he was working, in exchange for immunity against all charges.

On 22 November 1994, Rippingale went to the storage depot to collect the bags. To his dismay, he found them filled with lawn clippings, and immediately phoned Kizon to break the bad news. Rippingale and Kizon leapt to the wrong conclusion: that Petrelis had done a number on them.

What they did not know was that police already had phone taps in place as part of another investigation, and it was they who had substituted the lawn clippings. The police had cracked the trifecta — the boss and his conspirator, and their errand boy ready to grass on them both. They charged Kizon and Rippingale with conspiracy to supply cannabis. Happy days!

But not for long. Petrelis, who had moved to Brisbane where he was living under the assumed name Andrew Parker, died a month before he was due to testify. His death delayed the trial. In November 1999, a jury acquitted Rippingale and Kizon of all charges. The DPP believed the loss of Petrelis's evidence significantly undermined the prosecution case.

Bad luck? Or a bad apple or two in the barrel? As a protected witness, Andrew Parker's details were restricted and any violation of access should have been automatically flagged at Internal Affairs Unit (IAU), which would immediately investigate. Nevertheless, two police officers, Murray Shadgett and Kevin Davy, unlawfully accessed his covert details four months prior to Petrelis's death.

The dubious manner in which Petrelis died fuelled speculation that someone had murdered him, presumably to prevent him testifying at the forthcoming trial of Kizon and Rippingale. Speculation intensified when it emerged the police failed to give Petrelis a new identity once they knew someone had blown his cover.

A raft of ultimately futile investigations followed. The IAU tried; the Queensland coroner had a go and found that Petrelis had died from a self-administered heroin overdose; the Anti-Corruption Commission thought it might uncover what the others had failed to do; the 2003 Police Royal Commission chimed in. A final review in 2007 by the Corruption and Crime Commission (CCC) reluctantly conceded that, although it was clear that unauthorised persons had been told Petrelis's new identify, no conclusive evidence linked that disclosure to his death.[228] This meant the Queensland coroner's finding that Petrelis died of a self-administered heroin overdose stood.

The 2004 Police Royal Commission report did, however, strongly criticise police handling of the case and their failure to discipline the officers who illegally accessed the file, describing the conduct of Sergeant Shadgett and Constable Davy, and the system they operated in, as unacceptable in a modern police force.

Sergeant Shadgett had accumulated more disciplinary charges than any other member of the Western Australian police force at that time. He was friends with several known criminals and regularly provided them with confidential police information. The police had been aware of this behaviour since the mid-80s and had disciplined him for his association with criminals — many of whom were close associates of Kizon — who were at times under surveillance as part of major NCA and Federal Police drug operations. These agencies made sure the WA police knew about his activities and by 1992 Shadgett was on his last warning. He was advised that 'any transgressions whatsoever' would result in his immediate dismissal, yet Shadgett continued to provide information to criminals. By 11 September 1995, when Petrelis died, the force had still taken no action against him.

Sergeant Shadgett accessed Andrew Petrelis's covert details four times in May 1995 and on each occasion his unauthorised entry into the computer records was transmitted to the Internal Affairs Unit. He claimed he was helping a friend who suspected that the man to whom he was supplying drugs was actually an undercover officer. The man was in fact Petrelis and none of the inquiries has concluded otherwise. Despite everything, Sergeant Shadgett remained free to continue divulging information until he retired in 2000. The police feared that if they dismissed him it would alert his criminal associates that they were under surveillance, and thereby damage existing operations. Also, the NCA supplied information to the IAU on the understanding that it could not be used for internal disciplinary action because to do so might compromise NCA active operations.

By 30 June 2000, the police had had enough. Having drawn together enough evidence for a criminal prosecution, they prepared a notice of discharge on disciplinary grounds. Shadgett beat them to the punch, announcing his retirement for medical reasons on 6 July 2000. There was one final bizarre irony — the Police Commissioner's standard letter of appreciation to Shadgett in which he wrote, 'The Commissioner of Police acknowledges your faithful service to the community of Western Australia over the past 29 years and expresses regret that your medical condition has necessitated your early retirement.' Shadgett has never been charged.

The view may be clearer in hindsight, but Davy's reasons for accessing the restricted file would surely have caused his supervisor to raise an eyebrow. When questioned, Davy initially said he checked the Parker file because he was an Elvis fan and he was thinking about Colonel Tom Parker, the star's legendary manager.

The slightly more rational explanation that Davy also offered was that he accessed the Petrelis file because an associate asked him to check the credentials of two business investors, Thomas Clay and Andrew Parker, who had offered to invest in his taxi business.

Davy had only been a police officer for a short time and had already faced a misconduct charge for an earlier unrelated disclosure of confidential information. He resigned because of this other charge and was never charged over the Petrelis affair.

Davy accessed the Parker file on 31 May 1995, two weeks after Shadgett first accessed it on 18 May 1995. The man who asked Shadgett to access the information was also involved in the request to Davy to check the credibility of Clay and Parker; he was also a close associate of both Kizon and Rippingale. It is possible Shadgett's associate had been given these names and used Davy's associate to further check them out. It is highly improbable that there actually existed two business investors named Parker and Clay. Thomas Clay was in fact an officer assigned to the Petrelis case.

Officers involved in Red Emperor had little doubt the Kizon group was trying to track down Andrew Petrelis. Kizon himself had an alibi the weekend of Petrelis's death, having checked into hospital complaining of heart problems (although this of course would not have prevented Kizon from 'ordering' someone else to murder Petrelis). All investigations failed to uncover direct evidence of a link between the separate file breaches, Petrelis's death and Kizon. Yet there remain many apparent connections. The alternative is a series of extraordinary coincidences that ultimately led to the death of a man in witness protection and to the acquittal of those against whom he was to testify.

The Royal Commission was very critical of the way police handled the Petrelis affair and in particular its approach to Sergeant Shadgett. The ease with which the security of the witness protection program could be breached was worrying, as was the failure of the police to provide Petrelis with a new identity once they knew his cover was blown. Although the Royal Commission agreed internal investigations might need to yield to operational considerations, nevertheless procedures must exist to protect the security of sensitive information. That police could be aware that an officer was providing confidential information to known and significant criminals for over a decade without taking action is certainly remarkable and disquieting.

While regularly handing over potential corruption cases to Internal Affairs, Red Emperor itself became the target of Anti-Corruption Commission (ACC) investigators, who forced officers working in the operation to hand over all documents to the ACC who began an operation of their own.

On 8 September 1997, police management commenced an internal review of the operation. The review found, among other things, that Coombs had been allowed too much latitude, leading to protocol breaches and inadequate operational focus. It recommended removing Coombs immediately and winding up Red Emperor. Deputy Police Commissioner Bruce Brennan did not wait for the ACC to complete its investigation. On 5 November 1997, he ordered the immediate closure of Red Emperor.

Management gave no explanation to Coombs or other officers for the decision to shut down Red Emperor, leading to speculation that the review had uncovered widespread corruption. The official report handed to the 2003 Police Royal Commission claimed that the primary reason was that the operation was consuming substantial resources with little evidence to lead to a successful prosecution of the primary targets. Police Commissioner Barry Mathews stated that although covert operations officers felt they were getting very close, it appeared they would never get close enough to achieve actual results, especially as there were indications that the target group was becoming suspicious. The ACC felt the operation was hopelessly compromised. Although some questioned the wisdom of shutting down the operation when it may have been close to a major breakthrough, it had consumed significant resources over many years without success. In any event, it appears due process was followed.

Sergeant Coombs and another officer, Chris Cull, were suspended following the completion of ACC investigations and Cull resigned soon after, citing disillusionment with police leadership.

Expensive bait and no fish, that's the Red Emperor wash-up.

Meanwhile John Kizon continues to be a person of interest to the police whenever anything dodgy is going down in Northbridge. He proclaims his innocence and repeats his cry of police vendetta, while the media feed off any titbit that falls from the celebrity tables at which he appears to dine regularly.

For the Mickelbergs, all this talk of police corruption and links with underworld crime was just a subplot to their story. They grabbed onto it eagerly because it made more plausible their allegations that equally corrupt police officers had stitched them up so long ago. Though they had served their time they were still determined to settle the score with their nemesis — Hancock, the Silver Fox. It was time to head back to the courts.

CHAPTER 12
1998: COURT GIVES RAY THE FINGER

Ray and Peter were still pinning their hopes on concocted confessions and fabricated fingerprints in their 1998 appeal before the Court of Criminal Appeal. They believed they had fresh evidence that would point the finger of suspicion directly at Hancock and Lewandowski. The court would review the whole case,[229] but this was to be the crux of their appeals.

Money was a problem. The state government had granted Peter $132,000 to fund his appeal. But once again, Ray was struggling. The government at first rejected his pleas outright, eventually relenting to the extent of $60,000[230] — not nearly enough for the cost of his appeal. Even though their legal team worked for significantly reduced legal fees, even pro bono in some cases, an appeal in the highest appellate court in the state was still an expensive business.[231] The DPP even refused to assist in producing Ray's 1500-odd page appeal book, without which the appeal court would not hear his case. Ray set out to raise the money and ended up back in gaol.

From time to time, members of the public offered the brothers financial assistance. So when Lindsay Treby, a stranger to Ray, offered $1000 for the legal fund, Ray arranged to meet him at the Raffles Hotel on the banks of the Swan River in Applecross. However, in return for the donation, Treby, a convicted drug dealer, wanted Ray to stash some cannabis at his home until a friend called to collect it. Ray agreed. He needed the money.

Ray was unaware that the police were keeping a watch on his Trigg home, which he shared with his teenage son Ross: he and Ross were seen handling cannabis in nearby bush. On 14 May 1997, Ross's nineteenth birthday, the police pounced, discovering 2.82 kilograms of cannabis, worth around $155,000. They charged father and son with conspiring to possess cannabis with intent to sell or supply.

At their District Court trial in April 2000, Ray admitted to storing the cannabis, but both he and Ross pleaded not guilty to conspiring to sell or supply the drug. He admitted that he had acted stupidly in agreeing to store the drug and explained that he had decided to move the stash to nearby bush because the quantity of cannabis — seven garbage bags — had surprised him.

At the end of the two-week trial, the jury cleared Ray and Ross of the charge of conspiring to possess cannabis with intent to sell or supply, which carried a twenty-year gaol penalty. But they found Ray guilty of two charges of possessing cannabis with intent to sell or supply and convicted Ross of the lesser offence of possessing cannabis. Judge Groves imposed a $900 fine on Ross and said he was a good young man who had grown up bearing the stigma of the Mickelberg name. He added, 'I wish you well as you go back to your normal life. Good luck.' Ray, neither young nor, it seems, lucky, got two years with parole.

Ray appealed, and four months later the Court of Criminal Appeal, in a two–one decision, overturned his conviction, holding there had been a miscarriage of justice because Justice Groves had erred in his directions to the jury.[232] He failed to leave it to the jury to decide whether Ray stored the cannabis with intent to sell or supply, or whether he was holding the drugs for safekeeping as he had always maintained. The appellate court upheld the charge of possession but decided that the four months he had already served was enough. Free again!

Of course in 1998, the drug conviction was still to play out in court. For the moment, it was just another of the many things exercising Ray's mind as he and Peter prepared once more to challenge their convictions for the Mint swindle.

Once again, Ray drew the short straw. Although they would have preferred to have the appeals heard together, Ray had to sweat out a seven month wait while the court heard Peter's appeal. Again, the Mickelbergs were represented by the forensic advocacy skills of Malcolm McCusker QC, a man at the height of his professional standing. Considered to have one of the sharpest legal minds in the West, he had been involved in many high profile civil and criminal cases, and was in demand on both sides of politics on any number of inquiries. Gary Lawton again acted as instructing solicitor.[233] The Crown relied on two of their more senior lawyers, Stephen Pallaras and Joe Randazzo. The bench for both appeals comprised Chief Justice David Malcolm, now well versed in the Mickelberg case; South African–born and trained Justice David Ipp;[234] and the first female justice of the Supreme Court, Justice Christine Wheeler, who had worked as a Crown solicitor and whose partner was a police officer.

Their Honours were to consider whether the fresh evidence would have left a jury with a reasonable doubt as to the guilt of the Mickelbergs.[235] In law, fresh evidence and new evidence are not the same. Fresh evidence is evidence that did not exist or which could not, with reasonable diligence, have been discovered or known at the time of a trial. New evidence is evidence that did exist and which could have been known at trial with reasonable diligence.[236] In the Mickelbergs' 1989 appeal to the High Court, Justices Toohey and Gaudron had stated the legal position that only fresh evidence is admissible in an appeal to decide whether there had been a miscarriage of justice or whether a jury would have reached a different verdict had they been able to consider the evidence.[237] The difference between fresh and new evidence is not always clear. However, in *Ratten v The Queen* Chief Justice Garfield Barwick said, 'It will probably be only in an exceptional case that evidence which was not actually available to [an accused] will be denied the quality of fresh evidence.'[238] There was no doubt the Mickelbergs had fresh evidence for their 1998 appeal.

The essence of the challenge McCusker laid before the court in his submissions, examination in chief and cross-examination of witnesses during the two-week appeal in early May was whether the fresh evidence provided by Radley and Baxendale would have raised reasonable doubt in the jury about the police case against Peter. McCusker argued further that not only was the evidence of Hancock and Lewandowski — in particular, the police notes of the confession — fabricated, but also the jury would have been entitled to infer that all the police evidence against Peter was false.

Adding urgency to McCusker's advocacy was the fact that, although the court was to consider their appeals separately, there was no doubt that the outcome of Ray's forthcoming appeal was inextricably linked to the success or failure of Peter's. Should Peter succeed, then so should Ray, because it would raise the likelihood that a jury would also have doubted the veracity of the alleged admission that Ray made to Hancock and Round on 15 July 1982.

Unlike many of the expert witnesses used by the Mickelbergs in their unsuccessful 1987 appeal, Radley and Baxendale, the documentary forensic experts from the UK who had conducted the ESDA testing on Lewandowski's notes, were no less a class act than McCusker. Like McCusker, they were well versed in their craft, and they were experienced technicians totally prepared for any vigorous cross-examination. So well prepared, in fact, that the Crown did not dispute their evidence. Baxendale was confident that they had served it up to the police so convincingly, there was no way any jury would have convicted Peter. Game, set and match — they thought.

Radley and Baxendale told the court that the pressure impressions they found on page 4 of the notes did not match up with the writing on pages 1 to 3. This suggested that someone had rewritten the first three pages. The experts presented further evidence that they both had found an ESDA impression of page 14 of the interview notes on the rewritten page 2 of the notes, with the impressions only being on the top portion of page 14. The two experts inferred that when the lower portion of page 14 was written, it was resting on something different to that on which it was resting when the top half was written.

The Crown called Hancock and Lewandowski to refute the inference invited by Radley and Baxendale's evidence. The former detectives gave pretty much matching explanations, though as McCusker pointed out, these differed from the accounts they had given at the 1983 trial, in their 1992 statement to the McKechnie inquiry and in their affidavits for the 1998 appeal. Faced with the evidence of Radley and Baxendale, they had again changed their version of what happened.

In oral evidence, each admitted that they did get together to discuss their recollection of events before making their 1992 statements, before swearing their affidavits for this current appeal and before appearing to give oral evidence. But still they denied emphatically they had concocted the notes of the 26 July interview with Peter.

The former detectives each claimed to have hazy memories of some parts of that 1982 interview because so much time had elapsed. But when they got together a couple of days before the appeal to review their notes, go over transcripts from the trial and examine the evidence of Radley and Baxendale, the haze lifted to reveal a near perfect recollection of what happened on that night.

Lewandowski says he rewrote the first three pages because others would find them illegible. He re-established legibility after page 3 because by that time his writing rhythm was swinging along nicely to the pace of the interview. During a break in the interview, at page 14, when Hancock was on the phone, he read the notes to Peter and rewrote the illegible first three pages before continuing the interview. His meeting with Hancock two days before the appeal had so refreshed his memory he could even recall that when he resumed note taking, at page 14, he was writing on a different surface. He had discarded the original pages as he didn't believe they would be of any further use.

McCusker asked why private investigator Terry McLernon had given evidence of a conversation in which Lewandowski had told him he was worried about being charged with perjury for evidence he had previously given and had considered seeking a certificate of immunity from prosecution. Lewandowski scoffed at the idea as the chances of the prosecution giving him a certificate were remote. 'From the allegations against me, probably I would be the last person — if I had done anything wrong — to have been given a certificate.'

McLernon also gave evidence that in November 1993 Lewandowski, with his wife, son and two friends present, admitted he had changed the notes of the interview. 'He said he had signed up that he had done it without Hancock's knowledge and that it seemed inevitable he would go to gaol.' The Crown called on Lewandowski's wife to refute McLernon's story.[239] However, in cross-examination by Pallaras, McLernon revealed that he had deep hostility towards Lewandowski, which of course affected his credibility.

Other witnesses the defence called proved equally unreliable.

Paul Allardyce, Gloria Bounsell and Arthur Walsh all testified that Lewandowski had said he had perjured himself at trial and had verballed the Mickelbergs with fabricated evidence. But the Crown had done their homework; it revealed ill feeling between Lewandowski and Allardyce, an insurance claims assessor who worked for a company in which a Mr Buckley and Lewandowski were the principals. The Crown also revealed that, after a falling out in their business, Buckley and Lewandowski had an acrimonious parting of ways. Gloria Bounsell was married to Buckley, and did not like Lewandowski. As for Walsh, the nature of his evidence had already been tested at the 1987 appeal; the bench did not like him any more now than they did then.

The smooth sailing the defence had enjoyed during the Radley and Baxendale evidence was turning choppy. Although the Crown had decided not to use Peter Holz, the boat builder, because the court had scuttled his credibility on his last appearance, they did have his former first mate — Brigitte Holz. Although her marriage to Peter Holz ended in 1985, she was nevertheless prepared to corroborate much of his story about what happened at his workshop when she was still his wife. Pallaras led her through her evidence to reveal that she was at the boat building workshop in Maddington when, on several occasions, one or more of the Mickelberg brothers came to speak to her husband. She said she overheard Peter boasting that the police would never be able to prove they had stolen the gold and of how 'he had bought the car through the *Sunday Times* from a couple and that when he did so he had used a wig and given a false name' and thought that was 'pretty funny'. He had also boasted that, being a diver, he knew some good hiding places. He even suggested that the gold would fit nicely into the ballast compartment of the boat that Peter Holz was building for Brian.

Brigitte also testified that a solicitor (apparently representing the Mickelbergs) had come to see Peter Holz to ask for a statement confirming Brian Mickelberg and he were sailing together on the afternoon of the Perth Mint swindle. She knew that was not true and added that 'Peter Mickelberg and Raymond Mickelberg also talked about creating other alibis that my ex-husband could help them with. These alibis included going sailing together and working on a fence. Other suggestions were also discussed but I cannot now remember the details of them except to say that they involved my ex-husband falsely agreeing that he was doing something with the Mickelbergs at the relevant time. The Mickelbergs kept coming up with different suggestions to try to make it easier for my husband to remember the details.'

Pallaras was enjoying his time at the helm. There was no question that Brigitte Holz's account of events was fresh evidence; she did not go the police until 1996, after her former husband suggested she might be of some help to them.

McCusker was unable to dent her credibility in cross-examination and he had no doubt a reasonable jury would believe her.[240] It was time to reveal some skeletons in her closet. Brigitte Holz had a number of shoplifting convictions over the period 1981 to 1994 and had undergone psychiatric treatment to cure her compulsion. But she had stopped seeing a psychiatrist in 1995 and had stopped taking her prescribed medication 'for nerves' by the time the police saw her in 1996. She said that she was under a lot of stress around that time as her son was ill with AIDS. He died in August 1996.

McCusker argued the court should not admit Holz's evidence as it did not directly rebut any fresh evidence submitted by the appellants. However, the court allowed it, saying that 'a reasonable jury' might find that evidence of Peter having admitted certain things to other people 'bears directly on the cogency of all of the appellant's fresh and new evidence (and the inferences to be drawn there from), and the credibility of their witnesses, other than the experts.'

Brigitte Holz's evidence hit the defence hard. For McCusker it was a double blow. If it damaged Peter's appeal, then Ray's chances of persuading the same bench later in the year would be slim. If he was to get the appeal back on course, it was time to change tack.

McCusker began his summing up to the court with a blistering attack on Hancock and Lewandowski.[241] He submitted that they had deliberately attempted to deceive the jury at the 1983 Perth Mint swindle trial. There had been a conspiracy to fabricate evidence to frame the Mickelberg brothers and that conspiracy started at the top with the head of the investigation — Hancock. He said the trial judge and the Crown prosecutor had put to the jury that it was a contest between the police evidence and that of the Mickelbergs. But, McCusker submitted, 'the fresh evidence in this case shows that what the officers said at the trial is not what they are now saying' and 'all of these things taken together add up to a significant possibility that the jury would be left in a reasonable doubt.' Hancock and Lewandowski's explanation as to why they had changed their evidence in relation to the making of the police notes 'smacks of recent invention and something which is less than credible.' What's more, if the conspiracy started at the top with Hancock, it was open to any reasonable jury to question seriously the veracity of all the police evidence.

McCusker moved on to condemn Lewandowski and Hancock for physically assaulting Peter at Belmont, but the court stopped him in his tracks, reminding him that the physical assault allegations lacked independent verification or support. The Chief Justice, clearly unimpressed, also told McCusker that it was not the responsibility of the bench to point out the deficiencies in the case. McCusker tried to recover by denying the case was deficient, but he had lost the momentum. The court had already heard evidence from Assistant Commissioner Bob Kucera that on the night of 26 July 1982 he was the police officer in charge of Belmont police station. He had spoken to Peter outside the interview room and Peter had not mentioned having been assaulted; nor did he show any signs of damage or injury to his body.

McCusker had objected to Kucera's evidence on the ground that it was not fresh. Their Honours acknowledged that the Crown did know of the evidence at the time of the 1983 trial but had not considered it necessary to call Kucera because they had enough evidence from other officers to refute Peter's allegations. Furthermore, the defence had not asked the trial court to consider the issue of evidence fabrication. Now, however, the appeal court held that it should consider Kucera's testimony to be fresh evidence and admissible because it 'tends to contradict or weaken the evidence given by Peter and on his behalf.' McCusker had lost the initiative and now desperately tried to regain it by seeking the indulgence of the court to call Dr Ian Guy, who had examined Peter two days after his police interview.

Not unlike a mercy dash to a hospital emergency, Guy rushed

to the court. He told the court he examined Peter on 13 July 1982 and provided him with a medical certificate, which Peter had told him he needed for his future employment as a driver. Peter consulted him again on 28 July, at which time he went into detail about his arrest and the assault at the police interview. On examining Peter, he found a graze to the front of his chest and a bruise to the right of the chest area.

Guy also told their Honours he had been reluctant to give evidence at the trial because he was busy. But Chief Justice Malcolm said that not calling Guy was a 'missed forensic opportunity' and as his evidence was known at the time of the trial, it came under new and not fresh evidence. The distinction between Kucera's fresh evidence and Guy's new evidence seemed contrived — as if the Court of Criminal Appeal was working to a preferred outcome — however, the court did not completely throw out Guy's evidence when considering their deliberations.

The Chief Justice ended the proceeding by reserving the appeal court's decision, explaining that its task was now to consider what a jury would have decided had all the evidence been available.[242] There was little likelihood of a decision before the court reconvened later in the year for Ray's appeal.

In November the legal team began preparing for Ray's appeal, in which the fingerprint on the WABS cheque would be the centre of attention. The Crown had relied heavily on this so-called 'crime mark' to convict Ray and his brothers.

The Court of Appeal was to hear detailed and complex argument, a lot of which differed significantly from that presented at the original trial where Ray said he had touched the cheque when Hancock showed it to him at the police interview on 15 July 1982. He did, however, repeat what he had argued in the 1987 appeal: that he had not made the print with his natural finger but that someone had fraudulently applied it by artificial means. Also, the court was to hear about two other prints, evidence of which only came to light after the original trial and which now formed part of the fresh evidence at the appeal.

At the trial, the Crown had presented a chronology starting from 24 June 1982, the day on which Sergeant Henning of the fingerprint section of the police force received the three Mint fraud cheques, which he examined for fingerprints by immersing them in ninhydrin.[243] He found fingerprints on two of the three cheques. Henning visited the Mint the next day and eliminated the fingerprints of Mint staff who would normally have handled the cheque. That evening, 25 June, he went on a week's leave after arranging for another member of the fingerprint section of the police force, Sergeant Neville, to do further tests. Neville's tests eliminated the employees of the various security services who had handled the cheques. At the end of the elimination exercise, only one unidentified print remained — the crime mark.

Henning returned from leave in early July and on 5 July recorded for the first time the ninhydrin treatment that he had applied to the three cheques prior to going on leave. He did not record the existence of an unidentified print.

By 7 July, the Mickelbergs were firming as suspects and around that time, the police discovered the record of Ray's 1976 Commonwealth offence of forging a document. The Commonwealth Police took his fingerprints at that time but, after the court discharged Ray as a first offender, they sent the prints to the Western Australian police and Henning himself had destroyed them in accordance with police policy.

Yet in 1982 the Commonwealth Police and the Central Fingerprint Bureau still had possession of Ray's 1976 fingerprints. Henning did not ask for help from either of them and police made no effort to take Ray's fingerprints until 15 July 1982 — two days after Sergeant Billing, the police handwriting expert, told Hancock and others in the team he had identified Ray's handwriting on the application for the Gulley account with the PBS. Around noon on 15 July 1982, a Constable Gaspar took a set of fingerprints from Ray on a P62 form and handed the prints to Henning, who had taken part in a search of Ray's home earlier that day.

Later that day, after Ray's interview with Hancock at the East Perth lockup, Constable Van Den Elzen also fingerprinted Ray and recorded the prints on a P62. Between 7 p.m. and 8 p.m., Constable Muhleisen received the form at the fingerprint section. Muhleisen was not yet a fingerprint expert but had completed five years in the examination and classification of fingerprints and was engaged in a course of study under the tutelage of Henning. He asked Sergeant Billing if he could compare the prints on the

P62 with the crime mark. Billing agreed and Muhleisen found five or six points of identification on the crime mark.

When Billing did his own assessment, he found six or seven points of identification, which was below the police standard requirement of at least twelve points before they could use a fingerprint as evidence in court for identification purposes.[244] Not long after Billing concluded his assessment, around 9 p.m., he telephoned Henning with his findings. On returning to the office the next morning, Henning for the first time compared the crime mark with Ray's fingerprints. On that morning, 16 July, Billing photographed the crime mark and a police officer in the photographic section, a Sergeant Thomas, made photographic prints of it.

Billing, Henning, Sergeant McCaffrey and the head of the fingerprint section, Sergeant Devaney, met to discuss the quality of the prints and whether it could be identified as belonging to Ray. Although they agreed the fingerprint was Ray's, it lacked sufficient points of identification to be used in court.

Hancock and his investigating team agreed they should send the cheque to Dr Kobus, a forensic scientist based in Canberra, for further examination. Kobus had recently developed a procedure involving the application of zinc chloride to ninhydrin-treated fingerprints. The investigating team hoped the new procedure might make more points of identification visible.

Kobus started work on 20 July and within a few days had completed his treatment and returned the cheque and a series of negatives to Henning on 26 July. The crime mark was now clearer and Henning found sixteen points of identification; he marked twelve to be used as evidence in court. That day, police arrested Ray and searched his home again, seizing 'metal castings' of hands.[245]

That was the Crown fingerprint evidence at trial. In his grounds of appeal, Ray had advanced many arguments but he chose only to pursue some of them at the 1998 appeal hearing. McCusker fired his first salvo, arguing a conspiracy of deceit and corruption on the part of a number of police officers and others unknown to Ray. He submitted that the perpetrators of the Perth Mint swindle found Ray's PBS passbook, which Ray claims he lost on 27 May 1982, and used it to obtain the cheque the courier handed over for the gold.

McCusker argued that when the police first suspected Ray, they compared the prints on the cheques with the 1976 prints they had on record and found they did not match. This would explain why the police did not seek Ray's prints from the Commonwealth Police or the Central Fingerprint Bureau.

He claimed the police seized the silicone hands on 15 July, not 26 July as they claimed, and that later that day, a police officer bleached the cheque to clean it and used the silicone finger to place the crime mark on the cheque. McCusker claimed they used the same technique to plant two other prints, which now formed part of the fresh evidence. To cover all bases, McCusker advanced an alternative hypothesis: that the unidentified forger used adhesive tape, or something similar, to lift Ray's fingerprint from some surface he had touched at the police station and applied those prints to cheque. McCusker offered a third possibility, although not as strongly: that the forger might have used a combination of the silicone finger and the lifting procedure to produce the three prints. Someone then applied ninhydrin to the cheque to make the artificially applied latent prints visible. He thought it possible the forger again used bleach to eliminate any defective prints from the cheque. He asked, rhetorically, how likely was it a criminal would deliberately press his right index finger not once but three times, at the same angle, on the back of the same cheque? How likely was it the criminal would do that three times without leaving a thumbprint on the front of the cheque?

This was a careful and meticulous forgery, which McCusker argued took place on 15 July between lunchtime and around 7 p.m. The 'window of opportunity' closed at around 7 p.m. because shortly after, Muhleisen (who McCusker did not think was part of the conspiracy) would have received Ray's prints and compared them to the crime mark.

There was more. It takes time for ninhydrin-developed prints to reach their optimum. Therefore, McCusker argued, the police forgers did not photograph the crime mark on July 15 but waited until the cheque came back from Canberra so that the prints had developed well enough to guarantee sufficient points of identification to use in court. They destroyed the photographs of the cheque taken on 24 or 25 June, as well as the records that had been made of the receipt of the crime mark and the 1976 record of fingerprints. To cover their tracks, Henning fraudulently noted on Ray's 1976 police docket that the fingerprints were destroyed in 1976.

McCusker had cast the conspiracy net wide, beyond Hancock, the head of the investigation team, to take in many other police officers. Previous appeal court hearings had not bought the conspiracy theory, but Ray was optimistic that this court would see that it was plausible enough to raise reasonable doubt in the collective mind of a jury. His counsel had fresh evidence to submit in support of his claims, much of it centred on the opinion of Terry Nesbitt, a private consultant from New South Wales.

Nesbitt was confident, prepared to back his own judgement, and not easily intimidated. He testified that he had serious concerns about the genuineness of the fingerprint crime mark. It was clear someone had cleaned the cheque chemically, giving rise to his opinion somebody had introduced the fingerprint(s) after the cleaning. He was unequivocal, unlike Ray's expensive expert witnesses of 1987, and aggressive enough to challenge the Crown to let him test the procedures and findings of their experts in court.

Pallaras wanted no part of Nesbitt's theatrics. The Crown's experts would not expose themselves to his challenge; tests belonged in the laboratory, under controlled conditions. Judges had allowed in-court tests before, but Chief Justice Malcolm told McCusker he should have applied earlier so that the court could have put appropriate arrangements in place to guarantee the scientific integrity of the tests. It seemed this court wanted no last-minute diversion.

The Crown's fingerprint experts were sceptical of Nesbitt's opinions. Kenneth Luff, a former head of the fingerprint section of Scotland Yard, said even though it was almost impossible to distinguish genuine prints from well-made forgeries, he was convinced Ray's fingerprint on the WABS cheque was genuine. In cross-examination, McCusker asked why, if it were almost impossible to tell, he would not at least consider the option that the print was 'a well-made fabrication'. Luff replied, 'That is an option which I turned down.' He would not move from this position, which was hardly an answer to the question.

Kenneth Henning, now retired from the police force, was only slightly less inflexible, even admitting he had given partly incorrect evidence at the 1983 trial when he testified that about midday on 15 July, Constable Gaspar had given him a set of Ray's fingerprints. Now he said he was at Ray's home at the time and did not return to police headquarters until about 3 p.m., by which time Gaspar had left work for the day. He now claimed he first saw the prints at 7 a.m. the next day, 16 July, when he returned to the office. McCusker put it to him that he changed his 'story to suit the circumstances.' Henning responded, 'No I have not.'

Henning also conceded that he erred at trial when he testified that police photographed the WABS cheque before sending it to Canberra. Now he acknowledged that in fact police photographed the cheque after it was returned by Dr Kobus. This was an innocent mistake, he claimed; he had not deliberately sought to deceive the jury.

It was nearly the end of the third week of Ray's appeal hearing. McCusker was into his closing address to the bench, continuing to hammer away at the credibility of the police. It was not credible the police would have delayed matching Ray's fingerprints with the print on the WABS cheque. He was their prime suspect, the alleged mastermind but, according to the police, they waited some seven and a half hours before checking whether they had their man. Such a delay 'defies belief' and gives credibility to the argument that in fact the print on the WABS cheque did not exist — well, not until some police officer forged it.

McCusker did not know who that police officer was. He said several officers had put themselves 'in the frame,' including Hancock, Henning and Billing. Finally, he exhorted the court not to dismiss the appeal because they thought it inconceivable police officers would stoop so low. 'One does not know what motivates police to frame people but we know it happens.' Perhaps, he offered, one of the reasons was that the police 'thought the men guilty and set out to frame them.' A reprise of the theme of 'noble cause corruption'.

In his summing up, Pallaras said there was no miscarriage of justice. None of the so-called fresh evidence Ray had submitted amounted to a miscarriage of justice, because it would not create doubt in the minds of a reasonable jury. Nothing before the court would have raised the possibility of a different jury verdict to that handed down in 1983. The Crown expert witnesses, from Western Australia and overseas, spoke with one voice in asserting the fingerprint on the WABS cheque was genuine. Nothing that Terry Nesbitt had put forward cast even the slightest shadow over the scientific findings of the Crown's experts. Nesbitt, the witness Ray played as his trump card, had failed to shift them.

Pallaras said Ray's appeal raised allegations against many police officers, 'almost the entire' WA Police Service got a guernsey. He said, 'It seems everybody in this case who has given evidence contrary to Ray Mickelberg's case is either wrong or lying.' Pallaras did not deny there were corrupt police officers but Ray's 'enormous allegations' were so sweeping as to unfairly tarnish the reputations of many officers of good character — officers who would have refused to be involved in the behaviour Ray alleged in his police conspiracy theory. This was wrong and unfair, the allegations were untrue and the court should dismiss the appeal.

It was over. Now Ray and Peter could do nothing but sweat out the seemingly interminable wait until the three justices delivered their reserved decision.

Christmas and New Year came and went. Listlessly, the brothers endured the long hot summer until, on 12 February, the court handed down its joint judgment. Ray and Peter were in court to hear the decision.

Appeals dismissed.

The brothers sat drained and dispirited as Chief Justice Malcolm delivered the court's unanimous decision.[246] Considering all the evidence presented by the appellants and the Crown, they were not convinced a jury would have reached a different decision. Their Honours thought that a jury would find Hancock's and Lewandowski's explanations about the police notes credible and that the contents of the notes were not 'inherently suspicious' but reflected what might be described as a considerable amount of 'fencing' between the interviewer and Peter, and revealed an obvious reluctance on Peter's part to divulge information. Questions based on direct allegations elicited nothing by way of detail. Peter refused to make express admissions. Indeed, the admissions made by him, as recorded in the notes, were almost made despite himself and were essentially implicit. They were capable of being explained by Peter being disconcerted (on the police version) by having been recognised by Henry, having been told (as recorded on page 2 of the notes) the couple who sold him the Falcon recognised him from the photo of himself with a wig and spectacles superimposed, and that the police handwriting expert identified his handwriting on the Talbot note. His confidence may also have been affected by the police knowledge of the identity of Otto Kleiger. In their Honours' view, 'the content of the notes, generally, demonstrates no obvious signs of concoction.'

In the end, the most powerful individual factor influencing the court's decision was the testimony of Holz and Kucera, and the break in page 14 of the police notes. They acknowledged the admissibility of Holz's and Kucera's evidence was contentious. Thus, the court expressed their conclusion in two parts: one excluding Holz and Kucera's evidence; the other including them.

Their Honours said the break on page 14 was a strong corroborating feature of the testimony of the police officers. The explanation given by Hancock and Lewandowski for the break seemed most reasonable and as such, their Honours said, 'This appears to be fundamentally inconsistent with a complete fabrication of the notes. It is to be borne constantly in mind that the case of the appellants is not that the police tampered with the notes of interview, but that the notes are a complete fabrication. Having regard to the break in page 14 alone, the probabilities are very much against the notes being completely fabricated.'

The court acknowledged that if one excluded the evidence of Holz and Kucera but considered all other evidence, including the break in page 14, that matter is 'finely balanced'. However, 'the combination of the factors constituting the remainder of the Crown case is so compelling in its totality that there is no significant possibility that a jury acting reasonably would bring in verdicts of not guilty.'

Their Honours then went on to say that Kucera's evidence, which they considered credible and cogent, added 'another dimension to the case of the Crown.' But Brigitte Holz's evidence was the sealer. Their Honours wrote, 'The testimony of Mrs Holz, in our opinion, would be regarded as final and conclusive proof of guilt. Her evidence is so cogent, powerful and damning, and the impression she would — in our view — make on a jury so strong, that we consider that once her evidence is taken into account, there is no possibility that a reasonable jury, on hearing her evidence, and all the other evidence in the case (even excluding Kucera), would come to a verdict other than guilty.'

On the fingerprint argument, the cornerstone of Ray's appeal, their Honours again came down on the side of the police and Crown version. The court was most impressed by the credentials of the Crown's experts. In contrast, Nesbitt was less experienced and lacked the eminence of the Crown's experts. The court had no doubt a jury would attach considerably more importance to the Crown's experts and added that Nesbitt 'gave the impression of being closely and enthusiastically identified with Raymond's case.' Ray was mystified why the court would single out Nesbitt for one-sidedness. The Crown's witnesses were not exactly detached in the way in which they demonstrated their expertise.

Pointing to Ray's performance under cross-examination, their Honours also thought a jury might doubt his credibility. His explanation as to 'how he came to lose the Gulley passbook' was unconvincing. They also doubted a jury would accept his account of why he drew the various bank and building society cheques in small amounts (in particular, the cheque in favour of C. Wilson on the Gulley PBS account). And his 'various withdrawals that were capable of bearing a relationship with the rental payments for the Barker House premises in Subiaco' also undermined his credibility.

Then there was the court's scepticism about the truth of what Ray said to and about the police. The story his counsel had told at trial about the police tricking him into handling the incriminating WABS cheque had been abandoned. In his 1987 appeal, Ray implied the police seized the silicone hand from his house on 15 July but he failed to persuade the 1987 court that this was the case and no evidence presented in this appeal changed that. The court said also 'the hypothesis advanced by Raymond (and supported by Nesbitt)' was in many respects 'based on a series of speculative assumptions ... that are highly improbable.' Added to the evidence of Brigitte Holz, their Honours had no doubt a jury would draw adverse inferences from these incidents.

The court referred to the 1989 High Court appeal where

Justices Toohey and Gaudron said there was a 'high level of improbability of the print having been forged in the manner hypothesised.' Chief Justice Malcolm and Justices Ipp and Wheeler said, 'When regard is had to the whole of the evidence, the Crown has established a powerful and compelling case that the crime mark was made by Raymond's natural finger. There is cogent and compelling evidence to this effect. The Crown case is not refuted by the hypothesis advanced. In our opinion, there is no possibility whatever of a jury finding that the crime mark was not made by Raymond's natural finger. Accordingly, we would reject Raymond's arguments advanced during this stage of the appeal.'

Outside court, Pallaras praised the efforts of the police. He said, 'In solving this notorious crime, Don Hancock and his team did a tough job well and the community owes those men a debt of gratitude.' He then took a swipe at what he perceived as biased reporting by the media. 'This case is a timely reminder of the disservice done to our community in having a media that is all too willing to zealously take up the cause of disaffected and disgruntled citizens without proper and mature regard of the evidence,' he said.

Ray and Peter were devastated and angry. Ray called the decision 'gutless ... two police officers know I am speaking the truth — I challenge them to be man enough to come forward and tell the truth.' Peter said, 'I'm angry and frustrated but determined to keep going.' How angry was to be revealed to the packed media scrum outside the court and on the evening news and in the *West Australian* the following morning.

Don Hancock also was in court to hear the verdict. As he left the Supreme Court building via a side exit, media representatives pursued him, falling over themselves on the steep stairs as they tried to snap pictures and shoot video footage. They got more than they could have hoped for, because there was Peter, also in hot pursuit.

As journalists with microphones and notebooks in hand yelled for a comment, Hancock, who had not been happy with the media's coverage over the years, told them, 'Go and talk to your scumbag mates.' This was too much for Peter, who repeated Hancock's outburst to any of the journalists who might have missed it. Hancock goaded him further by adding 'and a criminal.' This was like a red rag to a bull. Peter picked up his pace to draw level with Hancock and for the next couple of hundred metres, they went at each other hammer and tongs. It was an unedifying spectacle, and the media loved it.

Peter and his brother were torn. They wanted to continue the fight but they also wanted out. They sought unsuccessfully for leave to appeal to the High Court[247] before deciding to migrate to New Zealand to buy a small farm and establish a timber business. But the land of the long white cloud rejected Ray's immigration application, allowing him to stay only a few days before sending him packing. Peter had no trouble, but Ray's rejection put paid to their plans to start a new life.

New Zealand law prevented Australians from settling in that country if they had been given prison sentences longer than five years.[248] Letters of support from politicians Cheryl Edwardes, Derrick Tomlinson and Julian Grill did not persuade the New Zealanders to change their mind. The Western Australian public only learned about the letters of support after Ray's 2000 conviction for drug possession. It was an embarrassing moment for the parliamentarians, particularly the high profile Edwardes who admitted meeting Ray when he sought her help to gain residency in New Zealand. As the matter did not go to court until 2000, and the politicians wrote their letters in 1999, there was no suggestion that they set out to mislead New Zealand authorities. The letters didn't mention Ray's drug charges but the politicians' defence was they didn't know about it when they wrote the letters in 1999.

After serving his four months in 2000 for the drug possession incident, Ray contemplated what to do next. He and Peter still wanted to clear their name, but they were beginning to doubt they would ever find a court to side with them against the police and two of their former officers — Hancock and Lewandowski had both now retired. Peter was still hoping that one day Hancock's luck would run out. And run out it did.

CHAPTER 13
THE EVIL THAT MEN DO ...

Late one chilly October evening, six members of the Gypsy Jokers bikie gang sat around an outback campfire. Suddenly, a shot rang out from nearby bushes and one of their number fell dead.[249]

Had the person who fired that fatal shot foreseen the fury his action would unleash, perhaps he would have stayed his trigger finger.

It was Sunday 1 October 2000. Most Australians were glued to their televisions watching the spectacular closing ceremony of the hugely successful Sydney Olympic Games. That's what they were doing in the tiny settlement of Ora Banda, fifty kilometres north-west of Kalgoorlie-Boulder, itself 500 kilometres east from Perth. The streets were empty. The historic Ora Banda pub had closed its doors for the night.

Billy Grierson and two of his mates had been kicked out of the pub and had joined three other Gypsy Jokers down at the old racecourse, about 200 metres away. Their beloved Harley-Davidsons, along with a Ford 100 ute, were parked on the oval. The ute carried supplies for the gang and was powering a fluorescent light which hung from a tree. Enough light to illuminate them as they sat in companionable array on a long bench, enjoying a beer, but not enough to spoil the pitch-blackness of the outback sky in which the Southern Cross hung brilliantly.

In the Ora Banda pub Billy, distinguishable by his long beard, had been drinking with Fats and Charlie. They drank too much and too loudly, becoming increasingly unruly and obnoxious. When Charlie swore at the barmaid, the owner of the pub decided that was enough. He ordered them out and closed the front bar. They objected heatedly, but there was no violence. The publican was Don Hancock. He had long dreamed of returning to the Goldfields, the place of his birth, and now owned and ran the Ora Banda pub with his wife Elizabeth, his daughter Alison, who tended the bar, and one of his two sons, Stephen.

The shot that killed Billy Grierson was not the first fired that evening. Only five minutes earlier, a bullet had struck the campfire but only Charlie realised someone was firing at them. By the time it dawned on the others that they were in danger, it was too late. Billy, the father of an eight-week-old baby boy and two daughters from a previous marriage, died in the front seat of the ute as his mates rushed him to the nearby Cawse mine site nursing post.

When the police arrived to investigate, no one at Ora Banda was willing or able to help them in their inquiries. Those who made statements had nothing useful to contribute. Hancock, among others, had nothing at all to say. But within an hour of the shooting, he had hired himself a silk — the colourful and high profile QC, Brian Singleton,[250] Peter's counsel at trial. On the phone, Singleton advised Hancock and Elizabeth to keep silent. No problem for Hancock; he had plenty of practice at that.

As it turned out, however, talking to the police was the least of his worries. Less than two weeks after Billy's murder, two explosions rocked the pub just before midnight. Stephen Hancock had just left the premises. Although severely damaged, the pub was still standing, and somewhere out of sight, a bomber was probably ruing the fact that he had not packed the explosives properly. Still, it was enough to scare Hancock and many other residents of Ora Banda away from the tiny settlement.

A month later, on 5 November 2000, more explosions shattered the peace of the six or so residents who had decided to stay after the first attack. One bomb exploded in the general store attached to the pub, the other at a gold battery some 300 metres away. The explosion destroyed Hancock's house and his Goldfields dream. The irony of the date would not have been lost on Hancock. It's a fair bet that when he was a kid, he celebrated Guy Fawkes night the way all kids did in those days: building a bonfire and setting off fireworks.

Still no one was talking. The police suspected all three bombings were a revenge attack by the Gypsy Jokers for the murder of their mate Billy. The Gypsy Jokers had made no secret of the fact they believed Hancock was the sniper.

As police inquiries progressed, Hancock became the prime suspect for the murder, although there was insufficient evidence to take the matter further. If he didn't actually pull the trigger, he would have known who did, the police thought. Nevertheless, he was one of theirs, so the police offered him protection and a new life interstate. He refused, choosing instead to slip quietly back into Perth where he hoped the Gypsy Jokers would forget about him.

In the meantime, police were waiting for the coronial inquest,[251] which they hoped would compel Hancock and other persons of interest to answer the questions they had been putting fruitlessly over the past several months. Unfortunately, yet another bizarre and violent act was to dash their hopes.

On Saturday 1 September 2001, Hancock and his longstanding friend, racing identity Lou Lewis, were spending the afternoon at the Belmont races, as they usually did. After the last race, Lewis drove Hancock back to the former detective's Lathlain home, less than a ten-minute drive from the track. It was 6.30 p.m. As Lewis pulled into the driveway, an explosion that was heard kilometres away ripped his Holden station wagon apart, hurling debris 200 metres away. Hancock died instantly. Neighbours administered basic first aid to Lewis but he died at the scene.

Although police were never able to confirm it, they speculated that the explosive had been planted while the station wagon was parked at the Belmont racecourse and was triggered by remote control. Witnesses claimed to have seen several bikies in the race crowd that day.

The *West Australian* newspaper left no one in any doubt who it thought responsible for the double murder. The front page of Monday's paper carried a large colour photograph of the bombed vehicle under the banner headline 'BIKIE REVENGE'. One of Billy Grierson's sisters was reported as saying, 'They [the Hancock and Lewis families] are just another group of people whose lives have been destroyed by this group of parasites [the Gypsy Jokers]. When are they going to stop; can't they just lock them all up?'[252]

The police also thought it was a revenge killing. Assistant Commissioner Tim Atherton refused to point the finger at the Gypsy Jokers when he fronted a media conference the day after the murders,[253] but he did say the police found the Gypsy Jokers difficult to deal with. 'We cannot reason with them and they show that they do not respect law and order.' He announced police would ramp up their efforts to control the motorcycle gangs, adding, 'I would not like to be a member of an outlaw motorcycle gang over the next few months.'[254]

Within twenty-four hours of the Lathlain murders, police swarmed onto the Goldfields' headquarters of the Gypsy Jokers, searched the homes of some members, and raided the gang's fortified Maddington clubhouse in Perth's outer suburbs. They also announced the establishment of a 200-strong task force dubbed 'Operation Zircon' to investigate the murders and offered police protection to anyone coming forward with information. Those who did know anything might have found the offer less than reassuring, given the police had so miserably failed to protect Andrew Petrelis when he was on a police witness protection program six years earlier.

The state government also got in on the action, hoping to break the bikie code of silence with a $500,000 reward for information leading to the murderers of Hancock and Lewis.[255] Police Minister Michelle Roberts said 'the reward is very large but we are dealing with organised crime' and 'this is an attack on the administration of justice in Western Australia and we are treating this matter very seriously.'[256]

Operation Zircon eventually resulted in two Gypsy Jokers being charged with the Hancock and Lewis murders. One of these, Sidney Reid, pleaded guilty and was sentenced to fifteen years imprisonment. The other, Graeme Slater, was acquitted on 27 October 2003 after a trial in the Supreme Court.[257]

More than 2000 mourners attended sixty-four year old Hancock's funeral at Fremantle Cemetery. They included family members, police officers, racing personalities and politicians. In a glowing tribute, the October 2001 *Police News* wrote that the huge number who came to pay their respects was 'an indication of community support for the former detective chief,' a man the police force had honoured by awarding him the Australian Police Medal for distinguished service before he retired in 1994.[258] Commander Daryl Balchin, Superintendent Murray Lampard, retired Superintendent Jim King and Police Union secretary

Michael Dean read the eulogies.

Balchin said Hancock was a compassionate, down-to-earth man with great energy, enthusiasm and loyalty, a mentor to many in and out of the police force and 'a wonderful example of what a man should be — one of nature's gentlemen.' Dean said it was a humbling and difficult task to present a fitting eulogy for such a unique and special individual. Hancock was 'one of the Police Force's finest investigators — very professional and always well respected by the people he dealt with.' He was 'a detective of the old school who was hard but also fair.' King also spoke in glowing terms of his former colleague.

Lampard recited the CIB poem 'The Calm Before the Storm', which featured Hancock. The opening stanza went, 'And the word went around the corridors — Ora Banda was the spot, And just as quick, the question came: "Ora bloody what?" "Never heard of it," said one bloke. "Is this some kinda dream?" but Hancock's mob just closed their ranks and formed a cricket team.' Hancock was the captain of the team, marshalling the troops. The poem ended: 'We've got fasties, we got slowies, we got spinners, we got swing, we'll belt the ball all round the ground, this team's got everything. Our fasties smash the wickets, so we brought a spare or two, we got a new six-stitcher which no doubt will cause a blue. The keeper's never missed a ball and never dropped a catch and we're known to have a drink or two throughout a hard-fought match. The media and townsfolk will welcome us with fuss. Now remember, act with dignity and don't fall off the bus. Ninety-two at Ora Banda will go down in the books as front-page news says CIB "has whipped the local sooks" ... but if our team gets nobbled (which can happen to a club) we'll pool all our resources and buy the bloody pub.'

Had they known what was to come to light later, they might have opted instead for Mark Anthony's speech at the funeral of Julius Caesar: 'The evil that men do lives after them. The good is oft interred with their bones.'

Two weeks after the murder, with the world dealing with the aftershock of 9/11, the Hancock killing was still front-page news. Under the by-line 'Tony Barrass and Trevor Robb', the *West Australian* ran an article titled 'Dark Horse' which posed a number of questions. 'Was he a corrupt detective or a defender of the good and just? Did he shoot bikie Billy Grierson or was his refusal to help investigating police just a well-publicised diversion from a cold blooded killer?'[259]

The article provided no answers to whether he was the murderer of Billy Grierson but it quoted former police colleagues who strongly refuted the suggestion. Hancock's many friends stayed loyal to him and his reputation remained intact, 'despite constant references during the controversial Mickelberg saga, which now drags well into the second decade.'

But, as Michael Dean had eulogised at the funeral, Hancock came from the old school of policing 'when rules,' Barrass and Robb wrote, 'were bent to get results.' He was the hard man of the CIB and 'crooks used to break into a cold sweat when he and his workmates came calling in their black Ford Galaxies.' Like his mates from the old school, Hancock believed passionately that the CIB was 'the last line, the defenders of society.' His policing philosophy was simple: 'You know they did it, they know they did it, just make sure the jury knows they did it.'[260]

Ray and Peter Mickelberg knew first hand how Hancock operated and they disliked him, even hated him, but they did not rejoice in his murder. They felt for his wife and three children. They also felt that, with the death of the Silver Fox, any chance of clearing their name had evaporated for good.

But, unlike Shakespeare's Mark Anthony, the world was not ready to 'let it be' with Hancock.

CHAPTER 14
LEWANDOWSKI COMES TO THE PARTY

'Now that Don Hancock is dead I cannot harm him and I am now telling the truth.' With these words, Tony Lewandowski prepared to bare his soul to the court of appeal.

The years of pressure had taken their toll. The former detective, now wracked by alcoholism and depression, wanted to clear his conscience, even though it meant ratting on his 'best friend'. He had not been able to bring himself to do it while his former colleague and mentor was alive. Now he could speak, Lewandowski hoped the truth would set him free from the intolerable burden of guilt he had carried for all these years.

On 5 June 2002, just shy of the twentieth anniversary of the Perth Mint swindle, Malcolm McCusker hand-delivered an affidavit, sworn by Lewandowski, to Director of Public Prosecutions Robert Cock. A few minutes later, Lewandowski, accompanied by his lawyer, walked into the DPP office to negotiate an agreement with Cock for limited immunity. The DPP agreed it would not use the contents of the affidavit against Lewandowski.[261]

The contents were dynamite.

Lewandowski swore: 'When the Perth Mint swindle first came to light a squad was formed to deal with it and I became a member of that squad, which was under the leadership of Detective-Sergeant Don Hancock. At the time of the inquiry I came to the view that the three Mickelberg brothers had perpetrated the Mint swindle. I believed to get the three people to fit the pattern of events would be impossible. However, at the time they were charged with the offences on July 26, 1982, I said to Don Hancock that I didn't believe we had enough evidence and he said to me, "Don't worry, it will get better."

'Early on the same day, 26 July 1982, I was with Don Hancock and we were returning from Midland. He requested other officers to pick up Ray, Brian and Peter Mickelberg. He gave instructions that Peter Mickelberg was to be brought to Belmont CIB offices. When Peter Mickelberg arrived and other officers had left, Don Hancock came into the room and told me to make Peter strip naked.

'I ordered Peter to get undressed and he did. At this time I am not certain if I put handcuffs on him but he was definitely stripped naked. I went through his clothes and found a letter written by his solicitor, Ron Cannon, which we just chucked aside because Don called it "Cannon's Joke". Don then went up to Peter and gave him two or three quick punches in the solar plexus. At different times, I would grab him and push him back in the chair and into the wall. Throughout the time he was there, about four hours, he never really said anything other than he wanted to talk to his brother Ray and then he would talk to us. We never did the record of interview until much later, about two months later after we found a series of photographs of how Ray Mickelberg and Brian Pozzi made the gold nugget they called the Yellow Rose of Texas.

'The statements which were purportedly taken from Peter Mickelberg at Belmont CIB on 26 July 1982, were in fact not taken in Peter's presence that day but were a fabrication made by Don Hancock and myself shortly after 2 September 1982. I believed at the time and I believe now that the Mickelbergs did the Mint job. When we saw the Yellow Rose photographs both Don and I knew that they were the right people.

'The statements, when made, were based on later information. For example, about the burnt and dumped car. Peter said nothing about that because we did not know that until later. So we put that in the fabricated statement.

'Basically the evidence given by Mr Radley and Dr Baxendale in the 1998 Court of Criminal Appeal was correct. Don and I just sat around adding in what we reckoned we needed. When we did Ray's statement I can't recall using his diary but terms were used which Ray used during our various conversations. There were certain terms used and we put them in the statement. We did Brian's statement at the same time after we got the Yellow

Rose photographs.

'At the Mint swindle trial we thought we would get Ray and Peter but we thought we would lose Brian because we didn't give Brian enough. We didn't tell enough lies. The notes that were compiled for the trial were basically completed in one day. There were bits that were rewritten or portions that were rewritten but basically they were compiled over one day.

'I gave evidence at the Mint swindle trial and at numerous appeals over the years as well as providing information at a number of internal inquiries. All that evidence in relation to the so-called confessions of Peter Mickelberg, Raymond Mickelberg and Brian Mickelberg having been true statements of those three brothers was false. The statements were fabricated by Don Hancock and myself some time early in September 1982.

'A lot of the evidence that Hancock and I gave in various courts, I was amazed at what we got away with. In respect to the fingerprint, I never saw the original cheque and even though I was basically second in command to Don in the Mint inquiry, he never said anything about a fingerprint and the first I knew was when the cheque was sent to Canberra for scientific work.'

Lewandowski went on to detail his friendship with Hancock, the guilt he had carried around for so long, and the toll it had taken on him and his family.

'I considered Don Hancock to be my best friend. He was a hard man but I considered him a fair man. I could characterise myself as being a great follower but a terrible leader. Don was definitely the leader and over the period of years when Don was alive there was no chance of me going against his wishes. A couple of times I wanted to come clean but there was no way I could go against Don. We talked many, many times about the confessions to keep the story going.

'I said to Don one particular day, "Don, you are going to die, you know, a long time before me and then I am going to be copped with all this shit." He said, "No you'll be all right mate, but whatever happens, just do your best."

'I have never copped a penny out of this, I have lost 20 years of hell. I have basically had enough. I lost my business. I have lost my wife, I have lost my son. I have gained nothing out of this. I am now telling the truth. I have told lies and I am not proud of it.

'I make this statement fully knowing that I have committed offences, but I am doing it without coercion of any kind and of my own free will. I have had enough. Now that Don Hancock is dead I cannot harm him and I am now telling the truth.'

This was the moment of truth for which the Mickelberg brothers and their supporters had waited so long. For some others, it didn't change a thing: the cops might have lied but the brothers were still guilty. However, for most, this latest twist in the Mickelberg drama merely reinforced the truism that truth is stranger than fiction. Even the way in which the affidavit came about could have been the work of an inventive crime novelist.

Bitterly disappointed after their unsuccessful 1998 appeal, the Mickelbergs had engaged private investigator Terry McLernon to try to persuade Lewandowski to admit the fabrication of the police confessions. McLernon had been a constable at Fremantle police station in 1978 when Lewandowski was stationed there as a detective. Despite the fact that McLernon had given evidence against Lewandowski at the 1998 appeal, the brothers hoped there could still be some empathy between two old colleagues. So too, no doubt, did McLernon. He was working on commission — he would get his fee only if he persuaded Lewandowski to talk publicly about the fabricated evidence and if the Mickelberg brothers successfully extracted a compensation payout from the state government.

McLernon buttered up Lewandowski with money, alcohol and a prostitute for a weekend at a Yallingup holiday unit. Ray and Peter didn't approve of this approach, but that wasn't a concern for long, because when, just before Christmas 2001, Lewandowski discovered McLernon was working for the Mickelbergs, that was the end of McLernon's influence over Lewandowski.[262]

In a lovely piece of irony, Lovell, the pugnacious investigative journalist and long-time supporter of the Mickelbergs, was to have more luck. Lewandowski had been the first of eight police officers to sue Lovell for defamation over the contents of *The Mickelberg Stitch* back in 1985.[263] Lovell had counter-sued the lot of them and in 1996 new Police Union secretary Mike Dean thought it best to settle the matter, with the union reaching an out of court settlement, agreeing to pay Lovell over $250,000.[264]

Mick Buckley, private investigator and friend of the former

detective, brought Lewandowski and Lovell together. The old foes formed a mutual respect for each other, which, considering the history between the pair, was no mean feat.

Lewandowski came to trust Lovell. When he confessed to him, a great sense of relief engulfed him. The twenty-year burden of lies and deceit had taken a toll on his health, contributed to the end of his marriage and strained relationships with family and friends. He felt the guilt strongly. His mother recalls how on many mornings of his various court appearances he would lie down on the floor in her living room, look up at the ceiling and shake with fear.

Not long after Lewandowski visited the DPP's office, Lovell whisked him away to a secret location outside the country under the protection of Buckley and Lovell's son Rohan. Many assumed it was to Bali, a place Lewandowski knew well and where he had business interests. In fact, the hideaway was in Phuket, Thailand.

The Mickelbergs knew nothing about the Lewandowski confession bombshell until Lovell turned up at Ray's house to tell them. Stunned but delighted, the brothers could finally see an end to their battle to convince the judiciary of the truth of what they had claimed for so long. But of course, nothing happens to the Mickelbergs without controversy.

A few days later Attorney-General Jim McGinty made the affidavit public, justifying its release on the grounds of public interest. It created a storm on many fronts. Police Commissioner Barry Mathews, for one, was livid. He had received a copy of the affidavit on 6 June before heading to his native country of New Zealand on holidays; he expected the contents to remain a secret. He told radio station 6PR, 'I was stunned. I got a ring in New Zealand ... to say that the Attorney-General had released the thrust of the contents of the affidavit to the media. I am concerned about why it was done. I think it should have been left to the royal commission.'

McGinty didn't take this swipe by the state's top cop lying down. He let fly with a haymaker of his own, claiming he had done nothing wrong, as Lewandowski's affidavit went to the heart of public confidence in the police and the administration of justice in Western Australia. 'I hope Mr Matthews is not suggesting the government should have swept it under the carpet and tried to keep it secret. It was not something that either could have or should have been kept secret. If police can't get their internal communications together that's a matter for Mr Matthews to sort out.' The *West Australian* reported the dispute under the headline 'LAW MEN CLASH'.[265]

However, in what must have seemed to him like a tag-team wrestling match, McGinty was also taking a pounding in Parliament. Before he released the affidavit to the public, McGinty had referred it to the Royal Commission into Police Corruption. But he had later also revealed its contents to Bob Kucera — before Cabinet had discussed the matter. Kucera was by then Health Minister in the Geoff Gallop Labor government. Coincidently, Kucera's son was married to one of McGinty's daughters.

The government was under pressure. As *Sunday Times* columnist Gary Adshead wrote, 'It seems the pillars of power and influence have been severely shaken by the Lewandowski confession. Mr Lewandowski says his dishonest evidence put three brothers in gaol twenty years ago and his lies since made sure the guilty tag stuck. Now his supposed honesty threatens to put ex-colleagues in gaol and is undermining the career of a minister whom the Premier says it is an honour to know.'[266]

The Liberal Opposition smelled blood and went on the attack.[267] Why, they asked, had McGinty discussed the matter with Kucera when there was a standing position that Kucera excuse himself from all deliberations in Cabinet on matters dealing with the royal commission? Now the heat was on Kucera. The Opposition demanded he be stood down from Cabinet until the commission investigated his role in the Mickelberg affair. However, Premier Gallop stood by his Health Minister; he said Kucera's role was to fetch hamburgers and coffees for the interviewing officers while they interviewed Peter at Belmont police station, hence his nickname 'Hamburger Bob'.

Kucera maintained he did no wrong and received support from an unlikely source — Avon Lovell. Lovell said on ABC radio that Kucera's role, if any, was peripheral and he was a decent man. Privately, Lovell was also concerned that the continual heat being applied to Kucera might put McGinty offside on the matter of another appeal and the issue of ex gratia compensation.

McGinty, a Cabinet heavyweight with immense political skills, played a game of brinkmanship with Lovell. He queried whether the affidavit might be tainted by inducements, a suggestion Lovell vehemently rejected. McGinty also said that if Lewandowski did not return to Perth to face questioning by the police royal commission on the contents of the affidavit, he might not be able to recommend to the Governor that the Mickelberg matter once again be referred to the Court of Criminal Appeal. Lovell countered that Lewandowski feared for his safety if he returned to Perth: Buckley's wife had received phone calls threatening his well-being.

Meanwhile, Lewandowski's public confession had inspired a raft of similar complaints about police treatment, as well as fresh claims that others were responsible for the Perth Mint swindle. Former Detective-Sergeant Frank Scott resurfaced, reiterating a number of allegations about police corruption he had made in 1995. He also admitted he was involved in the bashing, verballing and isolating of suspects during his period in the CIB.[268]

Scott told the media, 'I was taught that way and so I didn't think there was anything wrong with it ... everybody did it. I didn't see it as being corrupt because there was no financial benefit; you were simply doing your job, which was to catch crooks.'

He also said, 'Half the time, because of the restrictions on admissibility of evidence, a jury didn't know what police knew. But if the jury was able to get the same information as police had then they would have come to the same conclusion.' Scott saw the corrupt method as an investigative tool to be used against hardened criminals, not against the innocent or against white-collar criminals. It was not a method he thought the fraud squad should use.

According to Scott, the methods the CIB used on the Mickelbergs were commonplace. When the CIB was based at police headquarters in Adelaide Terrace, opposite cricket's iconic WACA Ground, 'it was not uncommon to take someone to a suburban CIB to do the interview where you could give them a hiding without everyone around the place hearing the interview.' He insisted that verballed confessions of suspects by certain CIB officers were admitted as evidence in trials before the introduction of videotaped police interviews in the 1980s, when unsigned or uncorroborated statements became generally inadmissible.

Reflecting on the culture of the CIB during the 1980s and before, Scott said many of the officers were lazy and not prepared to do the hard work to obtain the evidence needed to convict someone they believed was guilty. In fact, 'some of those blokes could solve any crime in Perth almost without leaving the saloon bar.'

Peter Duvnjak, the courier who delivered the stolen Mint gold to Jandakot Airport, also spoke to the media.[269] He told the *West Australian* that as he waited behind Barker House in Subiaco for instructions to collect the 'mineral samples', he was watched by two men in a car. Police interviewed him a few days after the swindle, and took his diary, where he had written down the registration number of the vehicle with the two men. When they checked the number they found it was a police car, and became hostile to him. '[A detective] said "it's not that number" and tore the page out of my book and wouldn't give it back. Then the police went right through my car. There was a camera in the back and they took the film.' He wondered where all this fitted into the scheme of things. He also wondered why the detective tore the page out of his diary and why the police did not follow up the information about the police car. 'Why weren't these guys called in and questioned?'

Andrew Foster, the brother of Peter's girlfriend at the time of the swindle, also came forward to reveal how the police physically assaulted him during an interview on 12 October 1982.[270] Foster maintains police physically abused him, with Lewandowski and others repeatedly pushing him against the wall, and a police officer held a sharp storeman's knife against his neck. He was a young man at the time and very fearful for his life. About thirty minutes later Hancock appeared and sought to induce him to confess to being involved in the swindle along with the Mickelberg brothers. When Foster's father complained to Hancock about what happened, Hancock rejected his charge but also said, 'That was the way they did things.'

Maverick politician John Fischer, a member of the One Nation Party, tabled an affidavit in the Legislative Council of the Western Australian Parliament prepared by private investigator Michael

Murphy, in which Murphy linked two Perth businessmen, property developer Barry Waller and entrepreneur Roger Byers, to the Mint swindle. Waller and Byers vehemently denied the allegations.[271] (For a long time, Murphy had sought an investigation into his claims that $30 million worth of gold was stolen from his goldmine in the early 1990s. He believed there was a government conspiracy to cover up the crime. The allegations went nowhere.) Nor was Fischer given much credence by his parliamentary colleagues, and not only because he came from the One Nation Party; he frequently used his nightly ten-minute speech in Parliament to allege that the state political and legal system was mismanaged and corrupt.

On top of this rash of complaints and conspiracy theories, the Lewandowski confession also put in motion a media hunt for the now disgraced CIB detective. This was turning into the story of the century. Media outlets were desperate to secure exclusive interviews with Lewandowski and the Mickelbergs, and Lovell secured exclusive media deals to the tune of $130,000 with Channel Seven and the *Sunday Times*.[272]

A Channel Seven news crew was soon flying out of Perth to Lewandowski's Thailand hideaway to film an interview for the station's flagship tabloid current affairs show, *Today Tonight*.[273] The interview by Alison Fan was an unedifying spectacle. Bloated and guilt-ridden, Lewandowski had been drinking heavily and could not wait to spill the beans on TV. Lovell, the relentless investigative journalist now turned minder, did his best to control what Lewandowski would say on camera. Perth journalist Victoria Laurie captured it vividly: 'As the cameras rolled, the scenes became farcical. The crusading campaigner for truth was captured on tape standing over his charge, a bullying figure telling him not to answer certain questions. A bewildered Lewandowski protested feebly, "I've got nothing to hide." Lovell insists he was protecting Lewandowski, who had limited immunity from the public prosecutor over the content of his affidavit: "What he said could be actioned by police and others."'[274]

Lovell was right. When the *Today Tonight* broadcast of some of Lewandowski's admissions, including those of fabricating evidence, was played before the Royal Commission into Police Corruption, DPP Robert Cock expressed surprise. He said he could not understand why Lewandowski had admitted to criminal conduct on TV as he did not have immunity from prosecution in such circumstances. 'The Channel Seven tape amounts to self-incriminating evidence against him. This evidence goes beyond the undertaking that I gave him.'[275] Cock said Lovell was not serving Lewandowski well and had a conflict between his own personal interests, Lewandowski's interests and the interests of the Mickelbergs.

Long-time Mickelberg supporter and Channel Seven employee Tim Boase was also critical of Lovell. He was concerned with Lovell's handling of Lewandowski and the spending of money various media had paid for interviews — Lewandowski never saw any of the money. Boase reminded Lovell he was not the story; that the real mission was proving the innocence of the Mickelbergs.[276] But this was all water off a duck's back for Lovell, who didn't care what people said about him.

Even Ray and Peter, who admired Lovell for the way he had tenaciously fought their case over the years, were annoyed. Although not prepared to criticise him in public, they were exasperated when Lovell initially refused to appear before the royal commission. What is more, they wanted Lovell to bring Lewandowski back to Perth to appear before the commission. They were worried about his safety and mental state in Thailand, and were concerned McGinty would continue to delay referring their matter back to the Court of Criminal Appeal while Lewandowski remained out of the country.

Ray and Peter turned up to the royal commission but Lovell failed to materialise, even though he had been subpoenaed.[277] He was to be the commission's first witness. As far as Lovell was concerned, the royal commission was not the forum to test the veracity of Lewandowski's affidavit: he wanted the matters referred to the Court of Criminal Appeal. However, he did reconsider and agreed to appear, as a matter of courtesy, two days later.

Lovell's appearance on 17 July 2002 turned into a farce. He entered the commission late, sought to table submissions, refused to move to the witness box as directed by Royal Commissioner Geoffrey Kennedy QC and senior counsel assisting Peter Hastings QC, and then proceeded to tell the commission it was acting outside its powers and outside its terms of reference in seeking to deal with the Lewandowski affidavit. At one stage, Kennedy told Lovell he was talking nonsense and reminded him the commission had powers similar to those of a court and could charge him with contempt. Undeterred, the man who had fought so hard alongside the Mickelbergs to prove their innocence stormed out of the commission a mere fifteen minutes after arriving. On his way out he told the media scrum to 'get stuffed' and 'get fucked.'[278] But he had pushed his luck a little too far. He was arrested and charged with contempt of court.

Once again, Ray and Peter could only watch in amazement and disbelief. Still they were unwilling to criticise publicly the champion of their cause, the man who got Lewandowski to confess. Peter told the media Ray and he were 'the meat in the sandwich' and that the media should not allow Lovell's actions, over which the brothers had no control, to prejudice their reporting. But he also expressed disappointment that McGinty had referred the Lewandowski affidavit to the royal commission rather than directly to the Court of Criminal Appeal.[279]

A week after Lovell's dramatics in the commission, McGinty reversed his position and, after seeking advice from the Solicitor-General in consultation with the royal commission, decided the Mickelberg matter should go to the Court of Criminal Appeal without waiting for the Lewandowski affidavit to be fully tested by the royal commission. McGinty said it would be unfair for the Mickelbergs to face further delay because of the antics of others not under their control.[280]

Lovell escaped a prison term but the Supreme Court found him guilty of the contempt charge and slapped him with a $30,000 fine.[281] He avoided a spell inside after writing a letter of apology to the commission and promising to cooperate with it in future. His promise was never put to the test as he was never called again.

Lewandowski arrived back in Perth on the weekend of 10–11 August 2002. The Mickelbergs paid for his return after their call for the state to cover the costs fell on deaf ears. Although by now used to the Crown snubbing him, Ray thought this was most unfair. 'You have to ask yourself whether he would be allowed to stay in Thailand if he had evidence to give in the bomb plot against the former CIB chief Don Hancock. You would expect the Crown would give a witness of that importance a new home, money, new identity and even a facelift if required.'[282] But the DPP was not about to ignore what amounted to twenty years of Crown precedent. They would not help the Mickelbergs, even if, in this matter, the issue of police corruption was at stake.

It is hard to understand why the DPP adopted such a dog-in-the-manger stance. The royal commission also wanted Lewandowski back in Perth. They had sent two investigating officers to Thailand to interview him and served him with papers to return to Perth to appear before the commission. He did give evidence to the royal commission when back in Perth but with the Court of Criminal Appeal now to test the affidavit, the commission was no longer investigating the Mickelberg matter.[283]

As soon as Lewandowski arrived back, the Mickelberg legal team applied to the Supreme Court to take the evidence of Lewandowski as a matter of urgency. They were concerned with his health and mental state. They were also concerned with his safety — the police reviled him because he had gone over the infamous police 'blue wall of silence, the code, brotherhood, secrecy, loyalty, solidarity and protecting your mates ... the constructs upon which traditional assumptions about police culture have been built.'[284]

Lewandowski looked fragile and haggard as he made his way into the Court of Criminal Appeal on the morning of 27 September 2002. Clearly, the tranquillity of the Supreme Court Gardens through which he walked on his way to court did nothing to alleviate his stress. The man had endured the mental agony of guilt for too long. It had contributed to his drinking more; the break-up of his marriage; and two spells in the psychiatric ward at Fremantle Hospital. He had hoped swearing his affidavit would assuage his anguish. It didn't.

Life had been no easier in his hideaway in a foreign land, where his diet was dominated by alcohol, cigarettes and valium. Nor would it be any easier when he returned home to rumoured death threats, a hearing before the police royal commission and ostracism by his former work colleagues. He had ratted on his own including his mentor, the Silver Fox. He was concerned about spending time in prison where police officers could make life hell for him.

The issue of immunity from prosecution played heavily on Lewandowski's mind as he took the stand in the Court of Criminal Appeal. He had requested and was granted permission to be in a different room from the Mickelberg brothers, the justices and the lawyers. The thought of being in the same room was too much for him; he was to give his evidence on closed circuit TV from another part of the Supreme Court.[285]

McCusker asked Lewandowski to confirm that the contents of his affidavit were true. The response dumbfounded the QC. Lewandowski said, 'I decline to answer that question on the ground that it could incriminate me.' Peter and Ray were stricken with anxiety. Not again! Surely, their nightmare was not going to continue. Surely, the man who could end that nightmare, the man who finally had agreed to come to the party, was not going to leave without delivering his gift.

Chief Justice Malcolm, sitting in between Justices Steytler and Murray, reminded Lewandowski that pursuant to Section 11 of the *Evidence Act* 1906 (WA), immunity from prosecution could only be granted after evidence has been given. He said to Lewandowski, 'You may be entitled to a certificate of indemnity if the court forms the opinion that your evidence which you give in response to the questions which are put to you today has been given in a truthful and open and appropriate manner.'[286]

The Mickelberg brothers let out their collective bated breath as Lewandowski then confirmed that the content of his affidavit sworn on 5 June 2007 was correct. This is all they wanted to hear. McCusker had no further questions.

Now it was the turn of Simon Stone from the DPP to cross-examine Lewandowski, once a star witness for the Crown. Stone had a difficult task ahead of him and took the predictable approach: that Lewandowski was a self-confessed liar and therefore had no credibility as a witness of truth. How then could the court now rely on the truthfulness of an affidavit sworn by a man who admits to lying to the court in the past? Lewandowski did not try to hide his past lies but insisted he had only ever lied about the Mickelbergs. He admitted to becoming a skilled liar over the Mickelberg matters, deceiving judges, prosecutors, police officers, his own family and the community at large. He was amazed that he and Hancock got away with it. He said when he and Hancock 'were going through appeals I was reading my evidence time and time and time again. It got to the stage where I nearly believed it myself that it was true.' But now he was sure what was fact and fiction as he gave evidence in this latest appeal.

Stone asked, 'And your evidence, do you say, Mr Lewandowski, was designed to mislead the judges, the District Court, the Supreme Court, the Court of Criminal Appeal and the High Court of Australia?'

Lewandowski replied, 'Yes, that's correct.' But he did not accept that his lies had put innocent men behind bars. When Stone asked, 'Were your lies designed, Mr Lewandowski, to send innocent young men to gaol?' Lewandowski was adamant: 'I did not believe, and I still do not believe, that the Mickelbergs are innocent.'

Ray and Peter were obviously not happy with such a comment. However, they could not help but feel a bit sorry for a man who had leapt the 'blue wall' and was now enduring the agony of ostracism from an organ of the state that had for so long been an essential part of his life and of his own sense of personal identity. Lewandowski craved companionship and he desperately wanted forgiveness from the Mickelbergs. After his court appearance he would intermittently ring Ray (but not Peter, the person he had assaulted), just to have a talk and repeatedly say how sorry he was. Ray listened and talked, though he found it difficult to forgive the man who had been instrumental in putting his brothers and him in gaol.

In cross-examination, Lewandowski denied Mickelberg allegations that he had made threats against Ray's wife and children; that he told Peter a certain prisoner would rape him in Canning Vale Prison; and that he threw telephone books at Brian while interviewing him. But he confirmed he slapped Peter in the face, slammed his head against a windowsill and kicked him. He also confirmed he witnessed Hancock punching and kicking Peter.

Stone asked Lewandowski whether he received payments from Channel Seven and the *Sunday Times* for interviews stemming from his 5 June 2002 affidavit. Lewandowski said he was unaware of any media agreements. 'I was never under the impression that we [he and Lovell] were getting any money, anybody was benefiting financially out of it.'

He said since returning from Thailand he had had very little contact with Lovell. Stone ended his cross-examination by asking, 'If Mr Lovell should abandon you along the way, Mr Lewandowski, are you going to tell another story about what happened at Belmont?'

Lewandowski replied, 'No. I haven't come all the way of my own volition from Thailand to sit here and tell a pack of lies and I'm here today on my own volition.'

In re-examining Lewandowski, McCusker went straight to the issue of money. He asked Lewandowski if he had received any money from Channel Seven. Lewandowski said he had not. He confirmed he had very little money; he was worth only about sixteen cents.

McCusker: 'When you decided earlier this year that you wished to make a confession as to the fabrication, did you do so for the purpose of receiving any money?'

Lewandowski: 'Definitely not, sir. I had a complete breakdown over the whole issue and Don was dead and I thought, "I'm the only person that can be hurt now."'

McCusker: 'You said very early in your evidence in cross-examination this morning that you were aware that you had deceived, over the years, the courts, various courts, the DPP and counsel and the community at large. Remember that was put to you this morning and you said, "That's one of the reasons I'm here today." Would you like to explain what you mean by that?'

Lewandowski: 'That I was very, very sorry for what I'd done, the cost to the people of Western Australia. It's just been playing on my mind for twenty years.'

After a few more questions, Lewandowski's day in court was over. It was nearly 4.30 p.m. The day's hearing had commenced at about 10.30 a.m. It had been a long and demanding ordeal for the former CIB detective. But at the end of the day, the court granted him his certificate of immunity.

For Ray and Peter, the end of the day simply meant a return to something at which they had become quite expert — waiting. Chief Justice Malcolm adjourned the court to a date to be fixed.

If there is any truth in the old saying 'time flies when you're having fun', then time was going slowly for Ray and Peter as they waited for the Court of Criminal Appeal to reconvene.

Lewandowski wasn't having much fun either. He scarcely had time to catch his breath before being arrested less than a week after giving evidence. When three Anti-Corruption Commission officers arrived at his mother's home in Kardinya with an arrest warrant, she told them he was not there. Two hours after the officers left, Lewandowski emerged. With his head covered by a blanket, he was driven to St John of God Hospital in the nearby suburb of Murdoch, where he was admitted under a false name before being transferred to the psychiatric ward of Fremantle Hospital. Shamed by his role in framing the Mickelbergs, shattered by his betrayal of his old colleague, this shell of a man was suicidal. He had no prospect of peace in Perth and now, it seemed, any chance of returning to his safe haven in Thailand was gone.

It was only a temporary reprieve. The next day the ACC officers arrested him at the hospital. At a bedside hearing before a magistrate, Lewandowski was charged with twenty-one offences, including fifteen for perjury,[287] covering the period from the 1983 trial to the 1989 appeal. The other charges related to attempting to pervert the course of justice, fabricating evidence and providing a false statement. The magistrate refused bail and remanded him in custody for seven days for psychiatric assessment at Graylands Psychiatric Hospital.

Many of the players were angered and many others confused by the decision of the Acting Director of Public Prosecutions, Simon Stone, to arrest Lewandowski. The charges brought against him seemed to be an abrogation of the limited immunity granted by Robert Cock, the Director of Public Prosecutions, and of the certificate of immunity issued by the Court of Criminal Appeal.

High profile criminal defence lawyer Laurie Levy, who represented Lewandowski, complained angrily that Stone had breached the immunity agreement his client had reached with Robert Cock.

In very general terms, an immunity is an exemption from liability for prosecution for a criminal offence given by the Attorney-General or the Director of Public Prosecutions, normally on condition the person being granted the immunity gives evidence on behalf of the Crown.[288] It is an agreement not to prosecute rather than a pardon. An immunity can relate to the involvement of a person in a crime or crimes, or to the use of evidence given by the person in specified proceedings to prove the commission by the person of a criminal offence.

In what seemed like a cute piece of lawyerly tap dancing, Stone argued that the agreement did not say Lewandowski would never be arrested, just that he would not be arrested on his return to Perth from Thailand. And because he had waited two months before arresting him, hadn't he honoured the agreement?

Stone also argued that the immunity was limited to Lewandowski's June 2002 affidavit and his evidence before the police royal commission and before the Court of Criminal Appeal in relation to the affidavit. He claimed the charges the DPP brought related to statements Lewandowski made to the media, particularly his admissions of criminal conduct in the now notorious Channel Seven interview with Alison Fan. Anti-Corruption Commission chairman Terry O'Connor said the undertaking by Cock did not mean evidence gathered outside the agreed areas could not be used to instigate criminal proceedings against Lewandowski.[289]

Stone's arguments did not bedazzle policy science academic Allan Peachment from Curtin University. He thought Stone should be sacked. He said the arrest would deter whistleblowers, as they would be suspicious of any agreement offering immunity from prosecution. Member of the Legislative Council and Mickelberg sympathiser Derrick Tomlinson agreed,[290] as did McCusker, who said, 'What this does is present a great discouragement to people who might otherwise come forward and be prepared to give evidence — whistleblowers in other words — when they find they have to look very carefully at the technicalities to see whether the indemnity's words are sufficient to cover them.'[291]

On the night of the attempt to arrest Lewandowski at his mother's home, Ray had made the same point, telling the media other police officers would now be scared off from telling the truth. 'Tony Lewandowski was the first to come forward and will be the last,' he said.[292]

Indemnity from prosecution is a most important issue for whistleblowers. Derrick Tomlinson argued that 'indemnity is the most powerful weapon to encourage people to turn State's evidence.' The Andrew Petrelis case had already shown how easy it was to compromise police protection or witness program protection. If immunity from prosecution were not to mean what it said, who would be mug enough to blow the whistle on crooks — inside or outside the police force? Lewandowski was also a protected witness in the sense that supposedly he was protected from prosecution. But the system that was 'meant to protect Mr Lewandowski aided in his demise.'[293]

The *West Australian*, which had been extensively reporting the events of the Mickelberg saga since 1982, wrote a highly critical editorial on 4 October 2002 titled 'Immunity-deal spirit breached'. The paper said Lewandowski deserved 'every bit of the contempt West Australians feel' for the self-confessed perjurer and corrupt cop and it was difficult to feel sympathy for him. But, 'it is difficult to endorse the actions of the authorities that have arrested and charged him.' The paper added that, casting legal niceties aside, Lewandowski made the affidavit and had given evidence in the recent appeal based on immunity from prosecution 'over matters associated with the Mickelberg case.' The editorial argued that Lewandowski's confession might have the effect of overturning an unsafe conviction — correcting an injustice.[294] It continued, 'The issue is not whether the Mickelberg brothers were guilty of the 1982 Perth Mint swindle of which they were convicted. It is whether their trial and appeals were fair.

'If it is accepted that some police evidence given at these hearings was fabricated, then clearly they were unfair. Regardless of Mr Lewandowski's motive, his confession could serve the public interest. If it leads to flawed verdicts based on concocted evidence being set aside, then it will help to increase public confidence in the justice system and its capacity to arrive at fair judgments.

'However, the arrest and charging of Mr Lewandowski have raised new questions about the fairness or otherwise of elements of the justice system. These acts have breached the spirit — if not the letter — of the undertakings given to him.'

The editorial went on to say Lewandowski's arrest would have a negative effect on whistleblowers coming forward because they would not be able to trust the authorities. In the long term, the paper argued, this would not be in the interest of the community.

The editorial concluded, 'Certainly, Mr Lewandowski deserves to be put behind bars for what he did as a police officer — but not like this.'

Three days after the editorial appeared, Lewandowski was behind bars. Fremantle magistrate Michael Wheeler refused bail; knowing of Lewandowski's intention to return to Thailand, he considered him a flight risk. However, after only eleven days, the court relented and granted bail.[295] Finally, on 20 May 2003, Chief Justice Kevin Hammond of the District Court set Lewandowski free from the fear of a lengthy term in the slammer when he ruled that prosecuting him on perjury and related charges would be an abuse of process.[296] Hammond criticised the actions of Simon Stone and gave him a judicial scolding for not honouring the agreement struck between the DPP and Lewandowski.

Outside court, Lewandowski said to the waiting media, 'It has made me sick. I just want this to be the end of it. Thank God it's over.'

But it wasn't quite over. The former detective had not long before been diagnosed with tumours on his bladder. He was a tormented soul, condemned by society and by his former work colleagues, and by the body he had abused with alcohol. He was free from gaol but not from his demons. Over the next year he continued to ring Ray, sounding lonely and depressed. He finally freed himself from his demons when he hanged himself at the rear of his home in Parmelia on 20 May 2004.[297]

His funeral took place six days later. Ray and Peter were there, as were a few police officers, though not in uniform. No guard of honour for this former copper who had exposed to the harsh glare of public scrutiny the repugnant undercurrent of police operations in Western Australia at that time. In the process of exposing one flaw in the justice system of Western Australia, he had prised open a can of worms that would be still seething into the twenty-first century.

CHAPTER 15
THE JUSTICE SYSTEM: FLAWED AND FLOUNDERING

As several judicial reviews in the early part of the new century would show, the Mickelberg case was neither the first nor the last conviction gained by corrupt, careless or incompetent justice system operations. Two of the more celebrated were the Beamish and Button cases.

In April 1961, Darryl Beamish, a deaf mute, was remanded in custody in relation to a number of sexual assault charges on four young girls, each of whom was four or five years of age. While in custody on these charges, Beamish was questioned by Detective Sergeant Owen Leitch in relation to the 1959 Cottesloe Brookwood Flats murder of twenty-two year old Jillian Brewer, heir to the MacRobertson chocolate fortune. Initially he denied any knowledge of the Brewer murder but later confessed. He repeated his confession in written responses to questions put to him in writing by Leitch.

Beamish's trial for wilful murder commenced in the WA Supreme Court on 7 August 1961 before a jury and Chief Justice Sir Albert Wolff. Beamish's 'confessions' or 'statements' to the police were crucial to the prosecution's case: there was no other evidence linking him to the crime scene, although in February 1961 Beamish had gone to the Brookwood Flats to see a Susanne Delaney even though she no longer lived there. Beamish gave evidence at the trial through a sign language interpreter. When examined by defence counsel, Beamish denied the confessions. He said that during one of the police interviews, Leitch shook him and had his fist in his face. Also, he gave evidence that Mrs Florence Myatt, a public relations officer and interpreter for the WA Adult Deaf and Dumb Society, who interpreted for Beamish at some of the interviews, suggested the answers he should give in relation to Leitch's written questions. At trial, Myatt denied this was the case, although she said that because of Beamish's limited English vocabulary, she modified or amended the questions Leitch had asked her to convey to Beamish. She also denied Leitch had thrust his clenched fist towards Beamish's face.

The jury found Beamish guilty, leaving Chief Justice Wolff no option but to sentence him to death, despite the jury making a strong recommendation for mercy. However, because of the state government's policy towards people with disabilities, the governor commuted Beamish's death sentence to life imprisonment with hard labour.

Shortly after the trial, Beamish appealed and the appeal commenced before the Court of Criminal Appeal on 19 September 1961. At issue was whether the chief justice should have used his discretion to exclude Beamish's statements to the police made on 7 and 8 April 1961 because they were not shown to be voluntary. The court dismissed the appeal and Beamish was incarcerated in Fremantle Prison.[298]

Jillian Brewer's murder was the forerunner of a short reign of terror which shattered the illusion of Perth residents that their streets, or even their homes, were safe from violence. It began on the night of Australia Day, 26 January 1963. Five people were shot that one night in Cottesloe and Nedlands. Two of the five, John Sturkey and George Walmsley, died and another, Brian Weir, suffered brain damage and died three years later.

Two weeks later, on the night of 9 February 1963, Rosemary Anderson, aged seventeen, was deliberately run down on Stubbs Terrace in the Perth suburb of Shenton Park. She died from her injuries at Royal Perth Hospital later that night.

Police arrested her boyfriend, nineteen year old John Button, the same night. Anderson had left Button's home after they argued. When she left the house, Button had followed in his Simca, repeatedly asking her to get in the car. She refused. He stopped his car as Anderson approached the railway subway on Nicholson Road. After a few minutes, Button started up his vehicle, drove under the subway and turned left into Stubbs Terrace. Then the story gets messy.

Button gave two statements to police, one before and one after he had been told Rosemary had died of her injuries. In the first, he said he drove up and saw Anderson lying on the side of the road. In his second statement, he said that when he saw her walking on Stubbs Terrace he decided to scare her by driving his car as close as possible to her but instead he hit Anderson with the left-hand side of the front of his Simca. Police charged Button with wilful murder.

At his trial on 29 April 1963, the Supreme Court of Western Australia found Button guilty of manslaughter and sentenced him to ten years with hard labour.

In both the Button and Beamish trials, the defence raised concerns about the 'confessions'. Both alleged the confessions were the result of police pressure and in the case of Beamish, was actually the result of police prompting, or suggesting, answers. The allegations carried no weight with the judiciary or the jury in either trial.

On the night of 31 August 1963, the police apprehended a man named Eric Cooke. A husband and father, Cooke was born in 1931 with a harelip and cleft palate, which limited his speech to a peculiar mumble. The police had staked out a site on the banks of the Canning River in Mt Pleasant, where an elderly couple had come across a rifle while out walking. Cooke had hidden the rifle there after committing one of his murders. He made the mistake of coming back to retrieve it.

It did not take long for Cooke to admit to a string of murders. He also claimed that between 1958 and 1963 he was responsible for six hit-and-run attacks against young women (using stolen cars), eight attacks against women asleep in their beds and other shootings. There was more: he claimed responsibility for the deaths of Jillian Brewer and Rosemary Anderson, for which Darryl Beamish and John Button were already serving gaol sentences. How police reacted initially to these claims is unclear. What is clear is that after further questioning he retracted his confessions to the murders of Brewer and Anderson.

Cooke was charged with four wilful murders, an attempted murder and an unlawful wounding. He was tried only for the wilful murder of Sturkey, for which the court found him guilty and sentenced him to death.

After Cooke's conviction, lawyers for both Beamish and

Button visited him on death row where Cooke again confessed to the crimes for which their clients were now serving time. These confessions, made only minutes before he was executed, resulted in further appeals for both Beamish and Button. On 26 October 1964, Cooke was the last person hanged in Western Australia.

The second Beamish appeal commenced on 17 March 1964 in the Supreme Court before Chief Justice Wolff, Senior Puisne Judge Jackson and Justice Virtue. The constitution of the bench illustrated another flaw in the justice system: the chief justice had presided at Beamish's trial and the other judges had sat in judgment on the first Beamish appeal. In a 1966 scholarly critique of the Beamish case Professor Peter Brett of Melbourne University was damning of the constitution of the Supreme Court for this second appeal, pointing out that the bench was being asked to decide on whether a miscarriage of justice might have occurred in their own court. 'It needs no expert knowledge of psychology to realise that any man, however scrupulous, might well be swayed unconsciously by a desire to believe that he had not been a party to such a tragic error.'[299] The well-known principle that justice must not only be done but must manifestly be seen to be done should have precluded a judge sitting in judgment on an appeal against his own decision.[300] Brett also said it was unbelievable that medical evidence held by the Crown and sought by the defence in relation to testing Cooke's veracity was not put to the court. Beamish was unsuccessful with his appeal.[301]

Button likewise failed before the Court of Criminal Appeal.[302] As in the Beamish second appeal, the court held the Crown's case was very strong, and that Cooke's confession to the killing of Anderson lacked credibility and was fabricated. Further, the court did not view the evidence presented by Button's legal team about other similar offences committed by Cooke (hit-and-runs against women on five separate occasions) as compelling.

It would be many years after Beamish and Button had served their prison sentences before justice finally prevailed to correct the tragic errors.

On 20 December 1967, Button was released on parole and in 1968 he married. A chance meeting in 1992 between John's younger brother Jimmy Button and Perth journalist Estelle Blackburn was to prove momentous for John Button. After that meeting,

Blackburn began a long and detailed investigation that led to the publication in 1998 of her book *Broken Lives*, which presents a compelling case that Cooke killed Rosemary Anderson.[303]

In light of Blackburn's revelations, state Attorney-General Peter Foss QC MLC referred the John Button case for reopening. The Court of Criminal Appeal heard the appeal in May 2001 and handed down its decision on 25 February 2002.[304] The court held that if all the evidence that had been presented to this appeal court had been available for the jury's consideration at the original trial, there was a significant possibility a jury acting reasonably would have acquitted Button. They considered the verdict unsafe and unsatisfactory on the ground there had been a miscarriage of justice. There was to be no retrial.

It seems bitterly ironic that Beamish had to wait until April Fools' Day 2004 for the CCA to end the cruel joke the justice system had played on him more than forty years earlier. After a hearing referred to them by the Attorney-General on a petition by Beamish, the Court of Criminal Appeal held that the original 1961 wilful murder conviction should be set aside as there was a substantial miscarriage of justice.[305] The court held the confession of serial killer Eric Cooke to the murder, including his 'gallows confession' fifteen minutes before he was hanged, was decisive.

The court also expressed concern with some aspects of Beamish's alleged confessions to the police. Mainly these related to his inability to communicate adequately, possible prompting by the police to give answers that helped their case and the destruction of a piece of paper by the investigating officer Leitch, on which he recorded questions and answers, including a denial from Beamish that he had killed 'the lady'.

The successful Beamish and Button appeals were not the only cases to rock the public's confidence in the police and judicial system of Western Australia in the new century. One only has to think of the names of Christie,[306] Walsham[307] and Mallard.[308] The Mallard case especially, with its echoes of the Beamish 'confessions', has probably attracted as much attention as the Mickelberg case, and some of the prosecutorial and judicial players in the Mickelberg saga reappeared in Mallard.

In May 1994 an intruder brutally murdered mother-of-two

Pamela Lawrence in her Mosman Park jewellery store, Flora Metallica. The Major Crime Squad and Claremont CIB quickly amassed a list of 136 suspects, including local drug addicts, thieves and psychiatric patients. Andrew Mallard was on this list. Two weeks after the murder, he became the subject of an undercover police investigation.

On 10 June 1994, just hours after his release from Graylands psychiatric hospital, police brought Mallard in for questioning. Detectives David Caporn and Mark Emmett interviewed him for eight hours.[309] One week later, Caporn's colleague John Brandham also questioned Mallard, after which, under advice from DPP John McKechnie QC, they formally charged him with wilful murder.

In 1995, a jury found Mallard guilty of wilful murder. Trial judge Michael Murray showed no mercy, castigating a defiant Mallard as he sentenced him to life imprisonment with a twenty year minimum. The prosecution case had succeeded by relying very heavily on the confessions the police claim Mallard made at these interviews. Mallard had largely spoken in the third person because, he claimed, he was merely responding to police requests to speculate on how the perpetrator might have committed the murder.

Over the next ten years, these alleged confessions were to become the subject of intense scrutiny as Mallard continued to deny vehemently that he had anything to do with the murder of Pamela Lawrence.

On September 1996, Mallard appealed to the Court of Criminal Appeal, led by Chief Justice David Malcolm. Although by this time legislation had mandated the videotaping of police interviews and confessions, the law was not retrospective.[310] Therefore, leading prosecutor McKechnie argued Mallard's conviction was sound. The court agreed and rejected the appeal, confident that there was no miscarriage of justice, although expressing regret the police had not availed themselves of available technology to videotape the interviews.[311] The court did remind the police that, under the new laws, it would expect them to videotape all such interviews in the future.

In 1997 the High Court denied Mallard special leave to appeal and a frustrated Malcolm McCusker QC joined the growing number of people questioning the admissibility of the confessional evidence.[312]

Mallard underwent a polygraph test in 2001, the results supporting his claim of innocence. In July 2003, he passed a second polygraph test. However, the court would not consider the results of either test. Polygraph or lie detector test results are inadmissible as evidence in criminal trials.[313]

In 2002 the stubborn and sometimes testy state Labor politician and former Police Union lawyer John Quigley (earlier involved in Police Union attempts to sue Lovell over *The Mickelberg Stitch*) agreed to review the Mallard case. Mallard could not have done better. Quigley took apart the undercover investigation the police ran on Mallard in 1994. He found the operation gleaned nothing the police could use against Mallard but plenty that could have worked in his favour — except the police and DPP never gave this information to Mallard and his defence team.

Particularly damning was Quigley's discovery that the police failed to disclose evidence[314] demonstrating that, according to the state Chief Forensic Pathologist Clive Cooke, the weapon police claimed Mallard confessed to using could not have caused the injuries that killed Lawrence. The pathologist had carried out extensive tests in which he used the alleged weapon, a large wrench, to inflict wounds on the head of a pig. The experiments conclusively established that such a weapon could not have inflicted the wounds suffered by Lawrence.

As a result of the new evidence, Attorney-General Jim McGinty agreed to refer the case[315] back to the Supreme Court for a new appeal. During the hearing in 2003, McCusker for Mallard suggested that there might be a perception of bias[316] as former DPP John McKechnie, who gave advice on whether to charge Mallard and appeared for the prosecution at his first appeals, was now a Supreme Court judge. However, McKechnie's colleagues on the bench held his submissions had no basis and the rehearing went ahead.

The three justices hearing the case, Justices Kevin Parker, Christine Wheeler and Len Roberts-Smith, were unimpressed by the new evidence and, after a long and drawn-out hearing, refused Mallard's appeal.[317] They concluded there was no miscarriage of justice and that there was plenty of evidence to support the conviction. As a result, Mallard remained in gaol.

In October 2004, Mallard again applied for special leave to appeal to the High Court.[318] This time he was successful and in November 2005 the High Court unanimously overturned the WA Supreme Court's decision to deny Mallard's appeal.[319] In a judgment critical of the state's Supreme Court, prosecution office and police, the High Court quashed Mallard's conviction. They ordered a retrial but suggested the DPP might decide not to proceed on the evidence, given its doubtfulness and the fact that Mallard had already spent considerable time in gaol.

Following the High Court's decision, the Corruption and Crime Commission announced it would hold an inquiry once the retrial question was resolved.

Robert Cock QC, the Director of Public Prosecutions, decided not to retry Mallard, due to a lack of evidence. However, he reiterated, somewhat obdurately, that Mallard was still the 'prime suspect' and described the High Court decision as a 'tragedy'.

In May 2006, WA Police Commissioner Karl O'Callaghan announced a cold case review of the Lawrence murder and suspended a number of officers (two of them had risen to assistant police commissioner status) involved in the original investigations. The cold case review found a palm print left at the scene of the crime in Lawrence's shop matched that of a man already in gaol in Western Australia for murder. The man, Simon Rochford, a British backpacker, also matched the description of the person seen in the shop at the time of the murder. The CCC requested that the details of the review be kept secret from both the suspended officers and the public, 'for operational reasons'.

In October 2006, Commissioner O'Callaghan reinstated the five suspended officers (saying he had seen no evidence of misconduct) and announced that Mallard was no longer a suspect. Unfortunately, Rochford committed suicide in prison a week after the cold case team interviewed him and following a journalist's unsanctioned, but not expressly forbidden, airing of his name on a news program in Perth as the new prime suspect. Thus, officially, Pamela Lawrence's murderer remains untried.

Both O'Callaghan and Robert Cock publicly apologised to Mallard for the twelve years he spent in prison, and in November 2006 Mallard received an interim compensation payment of

$200,000, with the state government raising the possibility of more to follow after the CCC inquiry.

The CCC report was released on 7 October 2008.[320] The report cleared some police officers, the Chief Forensic Pathologist and Cock. But it opinioned a combined six charges of misconduct against Assistant Commissioners Mal Shervill and David Caporn, including withholding information from the defence and causing witnesses to change their statements. The inquiry made two opinions of misconduct against prosecutor Ken Bates, including the non-disclosure of significant forensic test results to the defence.

While many of the overturned cases involved murders, not all did. The Karpa fraud, like the Mickelberg case, concerned that precious Western Australian mineral — gold. The Karpa Springs story involved allegations of falsifying gold deposit results, insider trading, share market scams and impenetrable Swiss bank accounts.

In September 1988 three prospectors, Clark Easterday and brothers Dean and Len Ireland, began sample drilling on their mining tenement near Mt Gibson, Western Australia. The results suggested there was no gold in the area. Disappointed but still hopeful, the trio tried again in March 1990, using a more advanced drilling method. This time, the samples revealed apparently huge concentrations of gold within the ore, indicating, the men estimated, deposits worth around $2 billion.

Excited by their apparent strike, the men swore to secrecy the drilling company they used. However, the drilling company had a secret agreement with a local mining company, Perilya, to tip them off when particularly lucrative test samples were found. Perilya contacted the men and arranged a third drilling at the site to confirm the recent results.

On 1 June 1990, Perilya and the men reached an agreement giving Perilya the option to buy the tenement if the results confirmed the earlier samples. Perilya's directors and geologists, along with the Ireland brothers and an expanded drilling crew, all went to the mine site to witness this third drilling. This was to ensure that the samples were accurate and not tampered with. When the tests confirmed the earlier results, the company exercised its option and purchased the tenement from the prospectors for $6 million.

Not long after the sale, Perilya's shares, which were suspended during the drilling, recommenced trading and their value rose exponentially. On 12 July, the day trading resumed, the leftover drilling samples were stolen from a Perth storage warehouse. As a result, there was no way of retesting the sample that confirmed the find.

While share prices ballooned, Perilya commenced a fourth test drilling. This one, on 28 July, indicated no trace of gold. The company contacted the three men and informed them of the 'problem'. The men offered to buy back the tenement for the purchase price but the company did not take up the offer; instead it contacted the police alleging fraud.

The police began investigating the complaint and the Department of Minerals and Energy conducted a fifth drilling program. This test confirmed no gold was present on the site. The original ore samples had been 'salted' with gold from another source.

Salting — in which crushed gold is added to the drill sample before the tests to boost the results — is illegal; it is usually done in quantities sufficient to cause excitement, but not enough to arouse suspicion. The person or persons who salted the Karpa Springs Three find, however, threw caution to the wind, adding far too much gold to the original drilling sample. The test results indicated an ore grading of almost thirty grams of gold per ton, indicating more than eighty tons of gold within the leases and making it the largest deposit in Australia — many times larger than the adjacent Mt Gibson goldmine. Such breathtaking results were bound to attract increased scrutiny and it was only a matter of weeks before the whole charade fell apart.

On 27 February 1991, the three men were arrested and charged on eleven counts — one count of conspiracy to defraud and ten counts of false pretences. The indictment alleged that the men conspired to create the false impression that their mining prospect at Karpa Springs contained a high concentration of naturally occurring gold. The indictment alleged that by doing so, the men had conspired to induce investors to 'deliver money to them'. On 30 July 1993, the men were convicted and each was gaoled for three and a half years.[321] They appealed, but the court dismissed the appeal in May 1994.

In 2003, after they had completed their gaol terms, the men again appealed their original conviction, having being granted the right through the Royal Prerogative of Mercy by Attorney-General Jim McGinty.

In the original trial the men had claimed the samples had not been salted and that the results of the sample test were genuine. They had also suggested that others had motive and opportunity to salt the sample. Now their appeal defence was that 'the convictions were unsafe and unsatisfactory, having regard to evidence that was not disclosed to [them] prior to or at the time of the trial.'[322] The police and the Australian Stock Exchange had investigated Perilya over undisclosed share trading and concerns over the company's involvement in the Karpa Springs find, but did not inform the defence team of their investigations.

During cross-examination in the original trial, Detective-Sergeant Zappa was asked whether he had been in contact with the ASX regarding Perilya's stock market movements. He acknowledged he had been in contact but said the ASX were not concerned by Perilya's share price movements. This was misleading. The ASX had expressed strong concerns over Perilya in a report of which the police were aware. In fact, the Australian Securities Commission had contacted the ASX over possible breaches of the law surrounding Perilya share trading but did not pursue charges because of a lack of clear evidence. Zappa's response effectively meant the defence did not pursue this line of investigation any further.

There also existed fresh evidence indicating the company knew that the samples were probably salted and that the salting had occurred through the drilling rig. The mining company bought the find from the three men for $6 million, despite the fact that they had already secretly investigated the site and their geologist had concluded there was no gold to be found there. One employee summed up the position by saying, 'If it's real we can't afford not to be part of it, and if it's fake we can at least talk our way out of it.'[323]

The original Crown case failed to establish how or when the prospectors salted the sample and rested on the assumption it must have been them because no one else had the motive. The Court of Criminal Appeal held the prosecution should have disclosed the ASX report as it provided a lead on evidence relating to motive. If the defence had pursued this path, they may have investigated whether there were opportunities for other parties to salt the sample. The court also held that the new evidence fully demonstrated that Perilya knew the gold in the samples from Karpa Springs might well have been salted. This combined with the withheld evidence indicated the existence of other parties with a motive to salt the mine.

The WA Court of Criminal Appeal overturned the conviction on the basis that police and DPP had unfairly withheld evidence from the defence lawyers during the original trial.[324] The court also accepted new evidence that indicated the men may have been collateral victims of a classic pump and dump share scam. This is a scheme in which fraudsters artificially inflate a share price by issuing false and misleading glowing assessments of a company's future performance. They then dump their overvalued shares in the marketplace, or sell their lowly valued shares into the falsely inflated market.

All three appeal justices unanimously agreed the original verdict should be quashed, though Justice Graeme Scott had reservations due to the strong circumstantial evidence implicating the men. The evidence produced at appeal provided an alternative to the Crown case and through that a possible defence for the accused. However, it did not establish that the men did not commit, or could not have committed, the fraud.

Arguably however, more money was to be made through the speculative trading of mining company shares than the prospectors could ever make by profiting from a false claim. Robert Cock QC agreed people might have been involved in a massive insider trading scam that benefited from the salting of the mine. Whether those people perpetrated the fraud themselves or simply were aware of it and took advantage of the knowledge is unclear. These questions will probably never be answered as the names of those who profited from the share run are hidden behind Swiss bank accounts and offshore companies.

Cock agreed that the incompetent oversight by the prosecution, in failing to disclose evidence, effectively cost the taxpayer hundreds of thousands of dollars in bringing the case to court.

With the justice system under such attack, the Mickelbergs were champing at the bit to have what they hoped would be their final day in court.

CHAPTER 16
THE FINAL APPEAL

1 December 2003. It had been a long wait. But now, as Ray, Peter and their legal teams filed into the Supreme Court they were hoping that this, the first day of summer, would signal the end of a winter of discontent, endured for more than twenty years.

Fourteen months after hearing Lewandowski's confession, the Court of Criminal Appeal reconvened.[325] Once again, Malcolm McCusker QC was there to represent Ray, and the high-profile and tenacious Martin Bennett was appearing for Peter. On the other side, Simon Stone would again present the Crown case, assisted by Joe Randazzo, although illness and hospitalisation was to curtail his involvement. The makeup of the bench was troubling Ray and Peter. Although they were comfortable with South African–born Justice Steytler, the other two justices made them nervous. Chief Justice David Malcolm had ruled against them in their 1998 appeal, although it was well known that he was very conscious of his obligations. Their anxiety about the third member of the bench was more justified.

Justice Michael Murray had joined the bench in 1990 after twenty-six years in the Crown Law Department where he appeared in many cases as the Crown prosecutor. This was no bar to him hearing the appeal, but Murray had also acted for the state in opposing appeals by the brothers in 1984 and 1987, and was thus sitting in judgment on a case in which he had previously been so involved. Ray and Peter could not believe Murray did not disqualify himself. McCusker and Bennett were also surprised. Surely, they thought, Murray and his judicial colleagues could see the concerns. How could the community be confident the bench hearing this high-profile case had come to the appeal without any bias?

As recently as 2000, the High Court commented on the legal principle of independent and impartial tribunal and the test for 'reasonable apprehension of bias'. In the case of *Ebner v Official Trustee in Bankruptcy*[326] it had held that 'fundamental to the common law system of adversarial trial is that it is conducted by an independent and impartial tribunal.' Furthermore, in that case, the court held that a judge is disqualified if a fair-minded lay observer might reasonably apprehend that the judge might not bring an impartial mind to the resolution of the question the judge is required to decide.

The important concern is not whether a judge is *actually* biased, but whether a fair-minded or reasonable person might doubt that, for whatever reason, the judge would be even-handed, or bring a fair and unprejudiced mind to the case. It is so important that justice be seen to be done, that even the possibility — not the probability — of a failure of impartiality is enough to disqualify a judge from sitting. As Murray had prosecuted in an earlier hearing of the Perth Mint swindle case against the Mickelbergs, even the most benign bystander might have raised an eyebrow at his appointment to the bench for this appeal.

However, the Mickelbergs' legal teams decided not to object for fear of putting the whole bench offside. Ray later said, 'It wasn't for us to remind the court of what its responsibility was in this very serious case for our justice system. They are supposed to be the experts. We shouldn't have to tell them how to run the court.'[327]

Justice Steytler had, in another case, made it clear that he thought 'the prudent course would, in my opinion, ordinarily be one of self-disqualification in such cases' where judges had previously dealt with the parties involved. That case dealt with Murray standing in judgment in a case where he had prosecuted the appellant eleven years previously, but in a different matter to that on appeal.[328] Murray had chosen not to disqualify himself, on the ground that he had no recollection of his involvement as prosecutor of the appellant.

Here in the Mickelberg appeal, Murray had again refused to disqualify himself even though he had represented the Crown in the matter now before the appellate court. Malcolm and Steytler had not forced the issue. The Chief Justice might have brought some pressure to bear on Murray but there was nothing much he and Steytler could do about it, apart from refusing to sit on the appeal (which would have been an unusual course in circumstances where the Mickelbergs had not themselves chosen to object).

Although it might seem that the Mickelbergs were unnecessarily adopting the high moral ground and thereby jeopardising their appeal, there is another possible reason for them not wanting to rock the boat. The *Guide to Judicial Conduct*[329] warns judges to be careful to avoid giving encouragement to attempts by a party to use procedures for disqualification illegitimately, such as in an attempt to influence the composition of the bench or to cause delay. Had they pushed too hard, that may have persuaded the whole bench that they were trying to influence its composition, which might well have upset all members, not just Murray.

They could not afford to throw away what was surely their last chance to clear their names. It would be their final opportunity to prove as fact the idea that Crown Prosecutor Davies had dismissed as so fanciful in 1983: that 'there is something vile and rotten in the whole of this group of officers who paraded themselves before you in such a brazen fashion and carried it off so well.'

McCusker made it clear in his opening comments to the bench that the Perth Mint swindle trial was fatally flawed. There had been 'a fundamental miscarriage of justice.' He submitted that in view of the fresh evidence from Lewandowski, the Crown should show cause as to why the appeals should not be allowed. McCusker argued that even if the Crown were to argue that they had sufficient evidence to convict without the police verbals, the only question should be whether the appellants 'have demonstrated that there has not been a fair trial.'

Peter's counsel Martin Bennett agreed. He said the court could save countless days of hearings if they dealt with the threshold issue; that being whether 'such a radical departure from the constitutional right to a fair trial before a jury that conviction should be set aside.'

However, the court held that the Attorney-General had referred the matter to the appeal court under section 140(1)(a) of the *Sentencing Act* and it was required to consider the case in its entirety, subject to the normal procedures of an appeal. To win the appeal, Ray and Peter needed to show there was a realistic possibility that, in light of all the admissible evidence including that given at trial, a jury acting reasonably might have acquitted them.[330]

Peter had six separate grounds of appeal but, as Justice Steytler said, the most serious claim was Lewandowski's fresh evidence that police had fabricated the principal evidence, which rendered it so unreliable as to cast grave doubts on the whole of police evidence, sufficient to show a serious miscarriage of justice. His Honour also winnowed Ray's several grounds of appeal to their kernel, which was that Lewandowski's fresh evidence raised serious doubts about the veracity of police claims that Peter had incriminated Ray and 'casts further doubt on the veracity of the fingerprint evidence.' Both Peter and Ray also challenged the truth of the incriminating evidence that Brigitte Holz gave at the 1998 appeal.

The Mickelbergs sought leave to recall for further cross-examination a number of police officers who gave evidence at the trial. The court refused, holding that although it was required to review the whole case, the appeal was not a 'retrial of the whole action'. In other words, Steytler said, Lewandowski's fresh evidence did not give the brothers the right to cross-examine 'the same people on precisely the same grounds as had previously been done in the hope that, on this occasion, something more might be produced.' Stone, for the respondents, tried the same tactic and failed just as ingloriously.

Nor did he fare any better when he tried, as he had done fourteen months earlier, to discredit Lewandowski's confession. Justice Steytler said it was 'a big ask to suggest that [Lewandowski's] evidence was such that when viewed in conjunction with all of the other things which have previously been raised and which are raised again in this appeal such that it would have been given no weight at all by a jury.'

With the tactical skirmishing over, counsel for Ray and Peter introduced three key witnesses. First was Robert Goff, part-owner of a bar in Bali in which Lewandowski held an interest. He testified Lewandowski had told him in November 1987 he had fabricated evidence to convict the Mickelbergs.

Peter Broad followed, telling the court that while on a chartered flight from Carnarvon to Perth, an intoxicated Lewandowski 'openly said "they" had "done a job" on the Mickelberg brothers.' Broad added it was clear the brothers had been framed and Lewandowski was proud of it.

The third witness, Kenneth Gordon, presented his evidence by affidavit because he was medically unfit to attend court in person. He swore Lewandowski visited his home in the mid 1980s with a view to buying some fishing equipment. According to Gordon, Lewandowski 'big-noted' himself as one of the detectives who 'got the Mickelbergs' and boasted that they (presumably Hancock and Lewandowski) 'beat the shit out of' Peter. Gordon said Lewandowski expressed surprise that Peter 'held out, as it usually did not take long to get a confession and statement from anyone we did this to.'

Stone cross-examined Goff and Broad but could not discredit their evidence. Two other witnesses, John Flint and Frank Perry, each tendered their evidence by affidavit. But Stone chose not to cross-examine them — with good reason. Their evidence concerned Brigitte Holz's affidavit given at the 1998 appeal, and it was damning.

Flint, an investigative journalist with the *Sunday Times*, swore in his affidavit that Holz had told him the police 'had applied some pressure to her to make the affidavit that she eventually signed in relation to the Mickelberg matter' and on which the Crown relied so heavily in the 1998 appeal.

That was the build-up. Counsel for the brothers then passed the ball to Perry, a business proprietor and supporter of the Mickelbergs, to execute the slam-dunk. In his affidavit, he said Holz told him the police visited her five times trying to persuade her to sign an affidavit but she wanted nothing to do with the matter. They left messages on her answering machine to which she did not respond and left her in no peace until finally, in desperation, she agreed to sign, just 'to get rid of them as she had felt harassed.' She did not write the affidavit, the police did. And she only glanced at it before signing it 'because she left it up to the police to get it right.'

Stone was desperate. Considering the weight given to Holz's affidavit and oral evidence at the 1998 appeal, he really had no choice but to call Holz — a woman emotionally and physically drained by her son's death from AIDS in 1996 and by the after-effects of injuries she suffered in an earlier car accident.

She was to get no compassion from the forensically skilled and aggressive Martin Bennett when the time came for his cross-examination. When Bennett played an audio recording of a conversation she had with Perry, Holz admitted the police wrote the affidavit and that she only flicked through it before swearing it before a justice of the peace, and that she did not tell the truth at the 1998 appeal when she told the court the police had not pressured her to sign it.

Back in 1998, Holz gave no indication that she viewed what Peter said to her and what she overheard him saying about the brothers' involvement in the Mint swindle as being said in a joking way. Now she did. When Bennett asked why she did not say this to the court in 1998, she replied that no one asked her.

Stone argued Holz never said she actually heard Peter and Ray say they perpetrated the Mint swindle. However, Justice Steytler refuted the argument by pointing to the court judgment in the 1998 appeal, which said, 'Mrs Holz testified that after the Mickelbergs had been charged with offences in relation to the theft from the Perth Mint they participated in several discussions at the workshop. She said that on several occasions Peter boasted that the police would never be able to prove that they had stolen the gold ...' Moreover, his Honour said, if Flint's evidence was true, then it was clear Holz perjured herself at the 1998 appeal hearing. Stone could see he was facing an uphill battle on the issue and said he would not pursue the matter any further. But he added, 'The Crown sees it, as I say, as an expression of an opinion by her. Her opinion as to whether or not they were guilty or not is really beside the point.'

But the misery was not over for Stone. After the lunch adjournment on 9 December 2003, Bennett asked Holz if she had discussed with anyone over lunch that day the evidence she was giving in court. Holz replied 'No.' Bennett followed up, 'You had lunch by yourself, did you?' Holz said she had lunch with a friend. And there the matter rested — until the next morning.

When the hearing began on the morning of December 10, Bennett reminded Holz she was still under oath before asking whether the friend with whom she had lunch was Sandra De Maio. Holz confirmed she had lunched with De Maio but said she was not a friend.

Bennett: 'You know her to be a senior prosecutor with the office of the Director of Public Prosecutions?'

Holz: 'Yes.'

Bennett: 'Did Ms De Maio pick you up in the morning and bring you to court yesterday?'

Holz: 'No, I came here mit [sic] a taxi.'

Bennett: 'You came in a taxi and she met with you?'

Holz: 'Yes.'

Bennett: 'Then she met with you over lunch?'

Holz: 'Yes. She took me ...'

Bennett: 'And met with you after court yesterday?'

Holz: 'Yes.'

Bennett: 'And discussed with you ...?'

Holz: 'But just to get the taxi for me that I can go home.'

Bennett: 'A senior prosecutor waited to organise a taxi for you?'

Holz: 'Yes.'

Bennett: 'Why didn't you say to their Honours yesterday, "I had lunch with a senior prosecutor from the office of the Director of Public Prosecutions"?'

Holz: 'I didn't even know she was a senior prosecutor.'

Bennett: 'She didn't tell you that she worked for Mr Stone's office?'

Holz: 'I know that she works there but I thought she was just the secretary or doing things for him. I didn't even know she was a senior ...'

Bennett: 'Prosecutor?'

Holz: 'Prosecutor.'

Bennett: 'You had no discussion at all with Ms De Maio over lunch concerning your evidence?'

Holz: 'No.'

Bennett: 'That's your evidence?'

Holz: 'I didn't talk to her about the evidence.'

Bennett: 'Or about what was happening in court?'

Holz: 'No. I didn't talk to her.'

Bennett: 'Why did you say to their Honours yesterday you had lunch with a friend?'

Holz: 'Well, I consider her as a friend. I mean, it's a friendly face but ...'

Bennett: 'She's got a friendly face?'

Holz: 'Yes, she's nice.'

Bennett did not take the matter any further. He had achieved his objective. He had further dented Holz's already battered credibility. And he had exposed the impropriety of a senior prosecutor from the Director of the Office of Public Prosecutions meeting a witness on more than one occasion during her breaks from giving evidence in court; an impropriety Stone did not even attempt to explain.

What was the DPP thinking? Were the meetings between Holz and De Maio an attempt by the DPP to help Holz say the 'right thing' but not necessarily the truth? If so, this was most inappropriate and contrary to the long-established legal position that 'the proper motivation of a prosecutor is to secure the result to which, on his view, the evidence fairly leads.'[331] Its role is not to secure a conviction at all costs. The DPP must curb 'the "over-zealous" police officer who sets out to secure a conviction on the strength of his own investigation, regardless of the sufficiency of evidence or any consideration of public interest.' Even in the heat of battle in the adversarial court arena, the public prosecutor must maintain this neutrality and furnish all relevant evidence which may be probative to proving the innocence or guilt of an accused.[332]

Having barely survived Bennett's relentless barrage Holz still had to endure questioning from McCusker before she could escape her tormentors. Displaying a bit of black humour, McCusker's junior, Dr James Edelman, turned to Bennett and whispered that if he rose to pretend to cross-examine Holz, it would probably traumatise her beyond recovery. Edelman spared Holz the experience.

Things did not improve for the Crown when it called District Inspector John Gillespie. At the time of the Mint swindle investigation, Gillespie was a junior probationary detective, a fact he was keen to reinforce in giving his evidence to the court. Moreover, he had not worked with Hancock before and recalled that he was a very forceful leader. Gillespie too was to endure a relentless grilling during cross-examination.

Earlier in the hearing Carolyn Edwards, a neighbour of Gillespie, had testified that he had given her a copy of *The Mickelberg Stitch* in 1985. Gillespie said he could not remember that, and emphatically rejected her testimony that he had told her the Mickelbergs had been 'set up'. Bennett asked why she might have said this. Gillespie replied that she was rude to many of the neighbours and, in fact, she had at one time told Gillespie's wife 'to eff off.'

Bennett asked Gillespie to explain inconsistencies in the evidence he gave at trial about his conversation with Sheryl Mickelberg at the Whitford City Shopping Centre on 26 July 1982.[333] Gillespie and Detective Round had testified, and Sheryl had denied, that she asked, 'Who were the two detectives who went to Penang anyway?' However, as police officers Hancock and Billing did not go to Malaysia until 11 August 1982, and the police department only acknowledged the trip publicly on 26 August 1982, this testimony did not ring true. When Bennett pressed for an answer, all Gillespie offered was, 'I would say if that was said at the time, that's what was written down there and that's what was said at the time. That's the only explanation I can give.'

Ray and Peter had reason to feel happy with the way things were going. But Ray was also particularly keen to vindicate his claim that the police had forged his fingerprint 'crime mark' on the WABS cheque.

Buoyed by the fresh evidence of police fabrication, McCusker submitted that three fingerprint marks on the back of the WABS cheque, all at the same angle, supported the case for forgery. The court did not have this information at either the 1983 trial or the 1987 appeal; it only came to light at the 1998 appeal. McCusker directed their Honours to the Crown expert witness evidence at the 1987 appeal who, he said, 'gave evidence to the court that one of the indicia to him that the print was not a forgery was that he would have expected there to be at least two prints if there was a forgery because he said he would expect the forger to have more than one attempt.' Furthermore, McCusker added, if the defence expert witness had found the angle of the single print peculiar, how much more peculiar would he have found three prints all at this same peculiar angle? He answered his own question: 'Three times more peculiar.'

McCusker also distanced Ray from the speculation of defence counsel Ron Cannon at the 1983 trial that Hancock might have tricked Ray into placing his fingerprints on the cheque during the police interview in 1982. He reminded the court Ray had never suggested such a thing and directed their Honours to Ray's affidavit for this current appeal in which he swore Cannon acted without any instruction to advance this defence.

Justice Steytler then pointed out to McCusker the defence had not suggested at the trial that someone had used the silicone rubber finger to forge the prints. McCusker replied, 'I will tell you what happened at the trial, your Honour. It has a rather unhappy history. A Mr Bardwell was engaged by those representing Raymond Mickelberg as, it was believed, a fingerprint expert. A rubber silicone finger was made so he could carry out an experiment.

'In order to produce a print, and showing incidentally that he was no expert, he applied the finger to an ink pad and that was doomed — even I think the lay person could appreciate that wouldn't produce a good print. What he should have done, and the accepted way of doing it, would be to get the silicone rubber finger and rub it against some part of the skin, your own skin, and then apply it.

'The problem was that because of Mr Bardwell's unsuccessful attempt it wasn't suggested that that's what had occurred, but it was strongly suggested at the '87 appeal and experts were called from around the world to say that prints could be forged.'

Stone counterattacked. The truth, he said, was the defence abandoned the silicone hand theory at trial because Bardwell's test did not assist them. Moreover, the conclusion one could draw from Cannon's line of questioning of Ray during the trial was that he was acting on instructions from Ray.

McCusker had the last word on this issue. 'The question of course is — it's remarkable if Raymond was the fraudster doing the typing, as has been suggested. What did he do, wear gloves while using the typewriter for the other two cheques, the PBS cheques, and take them off and put his finger on the cheque three times to type the WABS cheque? Again we say these are all circumstantial points but commonsense tells us ... that that's extremely unlikely.'

Earlier in the hearing, McCusker had recapitulated the arguments about the Peter Gulley account at Perth Building Society and asked rhetorically why, if Ray had perpetrated the swindle, would he have unnecessarily put an account number on each of the cheques if he knew it was not required? He reminded their Honours of evidence that Ray had reported the loss of his PBS passbook. However, this was very much a side issue now in view of the Lewandowski revelation of police fabrication. The appeal would succeed or fail on this issue.

And so, twelve days after it began, the hearing ended — not with a bang, but a whimper, as Chief Justice David Malcolm declared, 'The Court will reserve its decision.' Deep down, the brothers thought they had won. However, they had been disappointed too many times to truly believe their twenty year ordeal was coming to an end. Once more, all they could do was wait, and wait, until somebody told them once and for all, 'it's over.'

CHAPTER 17
THE VERDICT

Friday 2 July 2004 was a typical winter's day in Perth, a mid-morning temperature around thirteen degrees centigrade and a thunderstorm threatening. The front page of the *West Australian* led with a story of a very big trial; not the Mickelbergs but Saddam Hussein, who was refusing to sign his charge sheet when he appeared before a judge to face war crimes charges. It would be different tomorrow, when the Mickelbergs would be front page again.

For Ray and Peter this was the day on which, surely, their seemingly interminable battle with the Western Australian justice system would end. Twenty-two years, one trial and eight appeals in which the brothers had been the star performers was about to culminate in — what? Defeat was barely imaginable. Victory would be sweet — but bittersweet. Each brother had paid a big price: loss of freedom, family, friends, reputation, and Brian, the brother they still mourned.

Yet, surprisingly, as the legal teams, media and public filed into the Court of Criminal Appeal at 10 a.m. to hear the final verdict, the two 'stars' — the focus of every act in the twenty-two year drama — were missing. Ray and Peter had decided not to attend.

The brothers claimed they had formed the view the media was hostile towards them and that they were tired of media scrums thrusting cameras and microphones in their faces. A strange claim, considering that, since Lewandowski's revelations, the media had been anything but hostile. Moreover, for twenty-one years, the pair had courted the media vigorously.

More likely, they were acting on the instructions of promoter and publicity veteran Harry M. Miller, whom the brothers, sensing victory, had engaged to manage their media interests.

Miller, long-time manager of legendary TV celebrity Graham Kennedy and, later, court 'celebrity' Lindy Chamberlain,[334] was a skilled and entrepreneurial publicity agent. If there was money to be made out of an event or incident which titillated the public, Harry M. was the man to make it. In many ways, he was also a contemporary of the brothers. On 30 April 1982, a court found Miller guilty of fraud following the collapse of Computicket, an operation he started in 1978. He spent ten months in prison at Long Bay and Cessnock.

The absence of the stars did not deter Mickelberg supporters, media and interested onlookers, who packed the courtroom to hear the decisions and reasons of the Court of Criminal Appeal as it reconvened after a seven-month adjournment to deliver its verdict.

Lewandowski's mother, Irene Burns, frail and wearied by the suffering of her much maligned dead son, was there. So was Lewandowski's friend, private detective Mick Buckley. Irene knew her son had done wrong but she was proud he had blown the whistle on police abuse and corruption. He had paid a big price for his misdeeds but he was her son and she felt she owed it to him to be in court as the curtain fell on the last act of the Mickelberg drama.

It was quiet — an anticipatory holding of the collective breath — as Chief Justice Malcolm leaned slightly towards the microphone and gave his verdict: appeal upheld. There was a momentary sigh of satisfaction as Mickelberg supporters expelled their bated breath. Then, silence again.

The Chief Justice continued. 'Justice (Michael) Murray is of a different opinion,' he said. 'He is of the opinion that the appeals should be dismissed on the grounds that no miscarriage of justice occurred.'

A slightly ragged intake of breath passed through the room as the prize that only seconds before had been so tantalisingly close now threatened to move tauntingly out of reach.

Finally, the agony ended. 'Justice Steytler allowed both appeals.' The brothers had won. It was only a two-one victory but, as Meatloaf was singing way back when this whole drama started, 'two out of three ain't bad!'[335]

There was no raucous, joyous outpouring when the final

verdict arrived. The wait, the tension, and the emotional battering that the brothers and their supporters had endured since that first trial in 1983 were too raw for that. There was instead a stillness, a muted exhilaration that justice at last had been done. But only just.

The reasons behind their Honours' decisions make interesting reading, especially those of Justice Murray.

Malcolm's judgment was relatively brief, adding only a few comments to the reasons for the decision of Justice Steytler. The Chief Justice thought the case against Ray remained strong. However, if the jury had been presented with all the evidence of the original trial and that available before the current appeal, there was a significant possibility that, acting reasonably, they would have acquitted both brothers. He also believed the jury might have been misled into reaching their guilty verdict, resulting in a substantial miscarriage of justice. Therefore, the convictions could not be allowed to stand.

Murray's judgment was perplexing; in parts, it was extraordinary. He began in the customary manner by expressing gratitude to his brother judge, Christopher Steytler, for his exemplary scholarship and analysis of evidence. Then he moved on to disagree with some essential parts of it.

He was decidedly unimpressed with Lewandowski's demeanour and was not 'prepared to accept anything he had to say as the truth.' Reluctantly, it seems, his Honour nevertheless agreed there could be some truth in Lewandowski's recantation, even though his presentation of evidence supporting it lacked 'cogency and persuasive power'. Even more reluctantly, therefore, he 'inevitably' had to disregard Hancock's evidence at trial. He was unhappy about having to do this because he thought it was 'unfair' and he stressed that this did not mean he was prepared to accept as true Lewandowski's recantation, because he had 'zero credibility'.[336]

There seems little doubt Lewandowski was emotionally unwell when he gave his evidence at appeal, which clearly affected his demeanour: it does not follow axiomatically that he did not tell the truth. Moreover, a layperson might be forgiven for questioning Murray's intuitive leap from rejecting Lewandowski's credibility to refusing to accept that other police evidence was tainted, especially that of Gillespie and Round concerning the 'Penang issue' and the evidence of Edwards.

Murray's analysis is curious, seeming to lead him to his preferred outcome by some illogical reasoning. He starts his analysis from the position that 'what Raymond and Sheryl were told, if anything, is a matter entirely of speculation.' From here, he takes an extraordinarily speculative journey himself, arguing Sheryl might have been merely surmising police had been in Penang when Ray and she had visited there recently. 'Why,' he said, 'may Sheryl not have supposed that at some stage she saw such officers?' This seems to be adding speculation upon speculation in an extraordinary fashion.

One might regard this kind of reasoning as bizarre but possible among those predisposed and prejudiced members of the public who had already made up their minds that the brothers were guilty. But it does seem out of place in an appeal court justice's reasons for judgment.

Next, Murray considered the evidence of Edwards lacked 'the necessary degree of cogency.' On the other hand, he defended her vagueness at the 2002 appeal because the conversation took place thirteen years before she revealed it to an investigator acting for the Mickelbergs. Murray also said it was unclear what the expressions 'set up' or 'rigged' meant. Having regard to the content of the conversation Edwards was recalling, one would hardly think it necessary to exhaustively examine alternative dictionary meanings to arrive at the conclusion the words mean to behave dishonestly, to cause somebody to be blamed for an act.

Finally, in accepting the probity of Gillespie's evidence and rejecting that of Edwards, his Honour's reasoning is curious. On the one hand, he acknowledges there had been 'one or more conversations' about the book *The Mickelberg Stitch*, but then says it is unlikely Gillespie would have made any 'specific confession' because the pair's relationship was only social and sometimes uncordial. Yet, later, as we shall see, he was prepared to countenance the possibility that the Mickelbergs were likely to have committed a similar type of indiscretion in admitting complicity in the Mint swindle to Peter Holz in the presence of Mrs Holz, with whom their relationship was merely incidental to their dealing with her husband.

In attempting to account for Brigitte Holz's 'unimpressive' performance at this appeal, and her 'most impressive' evidence at the 1998 appeal, Murray went to some lengths to excuse her performance at this appeal because of her fragile health and the uncompromising cross-examination by Bennett and McCusker. In doing so, he showed a predisposition to prefer her 1998 evidence. 'Had she given the evidence previously given to this court and maintained it under cross-examination, her evidence would have strengthened considerably the prosecution case against both Peter and Raymond.' Maybe it would have. However, that evidence was false. It has to be said, the cross-examination by Bennett and McCusker had been reasonable. What's more, Murray chose not to comment on the police acts of dubious integrity in drawing up the affidavit Brigitte Holz signed in 1996.

In the end, Murray decided that if one removed the 'tainted evidence', particularly that of Lewandowski, Hancock and Holz, the remaining evidence meant it would still be open for a jury to conclude beyond reasonable doubt that Peter and Ray were guilty of the Perth Mint swindle and arson offences.

There were no public claims that Justice Murray's decision was biased or that he had allowed his predispositions to consciously affect his decision. It might have been different had the appeal gone one–two against the Mickelbergs. However, on reading his reasons for judgment and having regard to his past association with the Mickelberg case, it seems that, because justice must be seen to be done, it might have been better had he withdrawn from the final appeal.

In the event, there was to be no controversy, because Justice Steytler came down on the side of the Mickelbergs.

Steytler agreed with Murray and Malcolm that in many respects Lewandowski was an unsatisfactory witness. 'His oral evidence was replete with inconsistencies' and 'much of his evidence bore the hallmarks of reconstruction.' Nevertheless, he thought it quite probable a jury would have accepted his evidence as truth, especially when the evidence of independent witnesses Robert Goff, Peter Broad and Kenneth Gordon supported Lewandowski's confession of fabrication. It was, he said, 'very probable that a jury would accept that evidence.'[337]

What may have helped the Mickelbergs avoid a one–two

defeat was Steytler's decision not to disregard Lewandowski's 'tainted' evidence,[338] as Murray had done. 'Rather,' he said, 'it seems to me to be a matter of some significance for this court to consider what the jury might have done if it had had the contradictory evidence from Lewandowski to the effect not only that he was a perjurer but also to the effect that Hancock ... was a perjurer and someone who was prepared to manufacture evidence against the petitioners,' as well as other evidence used to convict the brothers.

Of the witnesses for Peter and Ray at the 2002 appeal who were cross-examined by the Crown (Goff, Broad and Edwards), Steytler was of the view that nothing said in the cross-examinations was likely to cause a reasonable jury to doubt their evidence.

He was not so generous in his assessment of the evidence of Holz and Gillespie. Holz's evidence in the 2002 appeal was 'unimpressive' and unlikely to persuade a reasonable jury. In contrast, her evidence in the 1998 appeal converted a matter, which at that time — without the additional knowledge of evidence fabrication — was finely balanced, into one in which there was 'no possibility that a reasonable jury, on hearing her evidence, and all the other evidence in the case ... would come to a verdict other than guilty.'

His assessment of Gillespie was scathing. 'In my opinion, Gillespie's evidence in respect of his and Round's conversation with Sheryl Mickelberg and the evidence in respect of his conversation with Edwards plainly raise questions of credibility ... which are fit to go to a jury. It would undoubtedly be open to a jury ... to accept the evidence of Edwards ahead of that of Gillespie or to regard it as creating a reasonable doubt as to the reliability of his testimony.' For Gillespie, who was by this time a District Inspector, Steytler's comments were particularly damaging. In stark contrast to Murray's tortured reasoning, Steytler left no doubt that a jury would prefer Sheryl Mickelberg's account of the conversation than that of Gillespie and Round.

Turning to the specifics of the cases against the brothers, Steytler emphasised that Crown Prosecutor Ron Davies, in both his opening and closing addresses to the jury in the 1983 trial, made it plain that the prosecution regarded 'confessional evidence' as one of the 'most important tools of criminal investigation.'

He told the jury in his opening address the 'clear admissions of involvement in the general scheme' of the Mint swindle was 'all important to the Crown case and to the jury's consideration' and 'the police conversations with the three accused (Ray, Brian and Peter) cannot be underestimated.'

Then there were the allegations of police fabrications, of noble cause corruption, and the Crown's response to that. Steytler viewed it important enough to quote Davies' response to the allegations: 'It is an attempt to get away from what it is that the jury is being asked to accept. We will return to it, but what they are asked to accept is that there has been disgusting, vile, outrageous, concerted behaviour on the part of a large group of police officers who in a bald-faced way present themselves before you and brave it out — perjury, a concoction of evidence, fabrication of evidence, cheating with documents, cheating with fingerprints ...'

Steytler quoted more from Davies' rejection of the Mickelberg allegations where the Crown Prosecutor said it would be 'rotten' for the police to engage in the alleged corrupt behaviour even if they thought the Mickelbergs were guilty of the Perth Mint swindle. 'It is rotten, Mr Foreman, ladies and gentlemen, if any such thing or any hint of it has occurred. We will not stomach it for a moment, because it is obviously not what has happened. It is the other side who are pulling the wool over your eyes.'

Steytler also noted the comments of the trial judge in summing up to the jury. Judge Heenan had also emphasised the police confessions, saying to the jury, 'If you accept the police officers as to what the accused Peter Mickelberg said and as to how he behaved on those occasions, you would be entitled to find that he was deeply involved in the Mint swindle.'

Steytler also referred to Heenan's comments to the jury that if Peter's allegation of maltreatment by Lewandowski and Hancock was true, and if his denial of making any admissions to the police officers was true, 'then the police officers behaved in disgraceful fashion — there is no two ways about it — and their evidence should be rejected out of hand.'

Unlike Murray, Steytler believed the flow-on effect of Lewandowski and Hancock possibly having lied would be significant. A reasonable jury would certainly entertain doubts about the truth of Gillespie and Round's evidence about the 'Penang issue' and Carolyn Edwards' evidence. A reasonable jury would also be uneasy about the reliability of Hooft's and Henley's accounts of their interview with Peter on 26 July 1982. And they would likely be sceptical of Detectives Tovey and Allen's claim that Peter expressed a reluctance to tell them where the gold was because Ray would 'kill' him.

Steytler then turned to some of the circumstantial evidence. First, there was the matter of the white Ford Falcon car. The principal evidence connecting Peter to the purchase of the car was the Talbot note, which police expert evidence at the trial showed Peter wrote. The defence did not challenge that evidence at trial but did so for the first time at the 1987 appeal, where the court criticised the evidence of their expert witness, saying it lacked competence and objectivity. On the other hand, they found the rebutting evidence of John Gregory for the Crown credible. Especially telling was the revelation that the defence had abandoned a plan to introduce Gregory as *their* expert witness in 1983, because Gregory even then had concluded Peter wrote the note.

Equally strong circumstantial evidence placed Peter at the rear of Barker House 'acting suspiciously at the vehicle, using gloves to wipe the boot lock and door handle,' although, Steytler noted, no one had positively identified Peter. Added to this was the circumstantial evidence of Peter's claimed knowledge of Otto Kleiger, which was in fact an alias Ray used; there was his occupation of the Rupert Street premises and his involvement in prior bullion purchases from the Perth Mint using a false name.

However, Steytler was not convinced the circumstantial evidence inevitably would lead to a guilty verdict. He concluded: 'I agree, in this respect, with the 1998 court's conclusion ... that the circumstantial evidence against Peter raised "serious suspicions" against him but did "not establish the case against ... [him] beyond reasonable doubt."'

Unlike Murray, Steytler chose not to assume that Lewandowski had not given evidence. He concluded that, considering all the evidence now available, there was 'a substantial possibility that the jury reached its verdict in reliance upon false evidence and was consequently misled in the manner in which it reached its conclusion.' He continued, 'Once that point is reached, and taking into account that ours is a system of trial by jury and that it is not for this court to usurp the function of a jury, it seems to me that there has, on this basis also, been a substantial miscarriage of justice such that Peter's conviction cannot stand.'

Turning to Ray's appeal, Steytler noted that the 1998 court had said Ray's grounds of appeal in relation to the police evidence were linked to those of his younger brother and logically, 'if Peter should succeed, serious questions would arise in regard to the credibility of the police evidence against Raymond.'

This left the contentious fingerprint evidence as the key difference between Ray's appeal and that of his younger brother. The arguments advanced for and against the allegations the police had forged the fingerprints on the WABS cheque had been contentious enough in the past trial and appeals. Now, the discrediting of police evidence in other aspects of the case introduced an element of doubt that clearly influenced Steytler.

Steytler meticulously set out Ray's arguments at the 1987 and 1998 appeals and noted that McCusker, for Ray, urged the court to view their contentions in a new light, given the evidence of police fabrication. His Honour now did so, drawing a number of conclusions.

First, it would be open for a jury to find that the police removed silicone rubber hands from Ray's home on 15 July 1982, even though there 'was no evidence that any such hand was capable of providing a reasonable quality fingerprint (and it should be remembered that the "crime mark" was not a fingerprint of good quality).' However, Steytler referred to the statement of Justices Toohey and Gaudron in the 1989 High Court appeal, where their Honours said the possibility of forgery could not be 'answered by pointing to the failure of the evidence adduced on behalf of Raymond and Peter to establish positively that as at 15 July there existed a mould capable of making a print.'[339]

Second, while expert evidence suggested it was difficult to produce a forged fingerprint of acceptable quality using the silicone rubber finger and even more difficult using the so-called 'lifting' technique, there was evidence that, though difficult, it was nevertheless possible to produce a fingerprint that did look genuine. His Honour noted that Sergeant Henning of the fingerprint section of the police force had said such a technique was common knowledge.

Third, there were a number of significant anomalies in the fingerprint evidence. For example, 'the failure, contrary to accepted practice, to photograph the "crime mark" (notwithstanding its propensity to fade or even disappear), or otherwise to record its existence when first it was said to have been discovered.' Then, there was the police failure to compare fingerprints still on the files from Ray's 1976 conviction with the 'crime mark' prints on the WABS cheque. In fact, the police had not even taken the fingerprints of any of the Mickelberg brothers when they first became suspects. Moreover, when they did get around to it, on 15 July 1982, they only took Ray's. Finally, there was the unexplained anomaly of the second and third fingerprints, which were at an unusual angle, leading Steytler to conclude, contrary to the view of the 1998 appeal court, that a forger would make more than one attempt at forgery, 'not wanting attention to be given to the less successful attempt.'

Importantly, Steytler said that when the 1998 court had reached their conclusions they thought Hancock and Lewandowski's evidence was cogent and credible. Now, 'it seems to me that a reasonable jury, taking into account the evidence of gross dishonesty on the part of Hancock and Lewandowski, and the other defects in the police evidence ... might well look at the various anomalies in the fingerprint evidence with considerably more suspicion than might otherwise have been the case.'

Finally, after his detailed and meticulous examination of all evidence — factual and circumstantial — that was available at the 1983 trial and the appeals of 1987, 1998 and 2002, Steytler concluded the case against Ray was still strong, even without considering the police evidence of alleged confession and disregarding Brigitte Holz's testimony. He thought there was a strong likelihood a jury would prefer the expert evidence of the prosecution to that of the defence, to conclude Ray had left the fingerprint on the WABS cheque. Nor did Ray's testimony that he had lost his PBS passbook impress his Honour. Indeed, he said, Ray's 'evidence of the loss of the passbook leaves an impression of dissembling.' Added to this is the undisputed fact 'that the account was kept in a false name, with an address that had only a tenuous connection to him, and he may have believed that it would not be traced to him.'

Steytler's analysis at this point suggests a leaning towards dismissing the appeal. But, and this is the crux of his decision, the duty of the appeal court does not imply a power to usurp the role of a jury. Its role is to consider what a reasonable jury might decide based on all the evidence before it. Therefore, Steytler was not prepared simply to treat the Lewandowski evidence as non-existent. Had he done so, the final court verdict might well have been one–two, or perhaps even zero–three.

In the event, his Honour said, 'Given that a reasonable jury might well not be prepared to rely upon the police evidence of admissions made by or concerning Raymond (and, indeed, would inevitably share the feelings of abhorrence which any decent-minded citizen would feel for conduct of the kind described by Lewandowski, being conduct which undermines the integrity of, and public confidence in, the justice system), given, also, that it is now open to a jury to conclude that there is a reasonable doubt as to the genuineness of the fingerprint and given that Raymond, does, at least, offer an explanation for the circumstantial evidence which is not incapable of acceptance, I am unable to conclude that the case against Raymond remains so strong that it must inevitably result in his conviction by a reasonable jury. Rather, it seems to me that there is a significant possibility that, in the light of all of the admissible evidence, including that given at the trial, a reasonable jury would acquit Raymond. It follows that, in my opinion, there has been a substantial miscarriage of justice.'

As was the case for Peter, and for the same reasons, Steytler also concluded that 'there was a substantial possibility that the jury reached its verdict in reliance upon false evidence and was consequently misled in the manner in which it reached its conclusion.' Thus also on this basis, there had been a substantial miscarriage of justice such that Ray's conviction could not stand.

In the game of golf, there is an old saying that, at the end of the round, the scorer asks not 'how' but 'how many'. So too, in this appeal, no matter how ambivalent the judges' reasoning, the duty of the judicial scorer was to look at the scorecard and declare 'it's over.'

Outside the Supreme Court building, the usual media pack

was there. Malcolm McCusker was there. Irene Burns was there. Ray and Peter were not. McCusker covered for his missing stars, declaring this 'a great day for WA justice.'[340] Irene Burns wished her son could have borne his anguish long enough to hear the verdict for which he had paid so dearly. As a grieving mother, she had, since the death of her son, formed a close relationship with Peggy Mickelberg, grieving with her at the loss of her son, Brian, and sharing her frustrations and anxiety as she waited for the court to announce its decision. With a mother's zeal, Irene defended her son to the assembled journalists. 'Other detectives could have spoken out but they just didn't have the guts to do it. He tried to do the right thing and has done it, and I hope that he can rest in peace at last.'[341]

Meanwhile, the brothers were waiting anxiously at their respective homes for the verdict. McCusker phoned Ray; Bennett called Peter. Each greeted the news with joy and relief, tinged, as they gathered at a friend's home to celebrate with family and supporters, with residual anger that their battle to expose the corrupt police officers had taken so long.

But one senior police officer was neither contrite not conciliatory. Standing before a phalanx of microphones and cameras, Assistant Commissioner (Crime) Mel Hay assailed the assembled journalists with a defiant and aggressive repudiation of the decision. He questioned whether Lewandowski's recanting would have altered the decision of the jury at the 1983 trial and he speculated that the final appeal might have been different if Hancock had been alive to refute Lewandowski's allegations.[342]

He defended Hancock as a good officer who had locked up many criminals. What's more, he said, officially the police force still believed the Mickelbergs were guilty. All evidence pointed to the brothers and the police force did not intend to apologise to them. 'We don't apologise to criminals when they get acquitted at a trial,' he said. 'We do our job. The WA Police Service arrests people because we believe the person has committed a crime. You don't arrest people if you don't believe they've committed a crime.' He concluded by asserting that, as far as he was concerned, the Mickelbergs' victory did not mean the case was unresolved. 'It's a case of not proved.' Ironically, while the appeal court was overturning the brothers' convictions, the District Court was hearing evidence from a bar worker at the Ora Banda pub that Hancock 'went for his gun after a row' on the night Billy Grierson was shot dead.

But Australia's adversarial justice system is based on the presumption of innocence. It is often difficult for an accused to prove beyond reasonable doubt that they are innocent. As prominent criminal barrister Chester Porter QC noted in his slim but powerful volume, *The Conviction of the Innocent: How the law can let us down*, 'It is unusual for a person accused to be able to prove quite clearly that he or she is innocent in the strict sense that that person simply did not commit the crime. Even a waterproof alibi only removes the accused person from the scene of the crime. In many cases, that person could have acted through another person.'[343] Still, many of the public would have shared Hay's views.

Clearly, Hay was angry and disappointed. However, the result of the appeal did not indicate a failure of the judicial system to deliver justice. Rather, it illustrated, dramatically, the outcome when police engage in behaviour that is corrupt, either in the mistaken morality of a 'noble cause' or the less worthy motive of getting the job done at any cost.

Chief Bob Harrison of the Vacaville Police Department in California has said, 'If the law represents an expression of moral sentiment, then police officers stand as instruments of that morality.'[344] Police officers are society's protectors. It is imperative for a civil society, for a just society, that the police do not deny members, all members of the society, their basic human rights and engage in behaviour that is corrupt and an abuse of processes. To do so, runs the real risk of eroding public confidence in the policing institution necessary for a functioning civil society and for the proper and effective operation of the judiciary and government.

Justice Steytler displayed the same sentiment in his reasoning when he said that corrupt behaviour, as described by Lewandowski, violates what decent-minded citizens would see as appropriate and undermines the integrity of, and public confidence in, the justice system.

Many people will ask themselves the question members of jury must never ask: 'If you didn't do it, who did?'[345] It is human to ask this, but it is not the jury's responsibility, nor their right, to nominate or suggest an alternative perpetrator.

The police divers never did find the gold on the seabed off Kalbarri. The gold deposited at Channel Seven premises appears unlikely to have originated from the Perth Mint. The Mint gold remains missing.

The justice system has decided the Mickelberg convictions were 'unsafe'. Moreover, because the brothers had already served the sentences that the court imposed on them in 1983, the appeal court had decided that the question of a retrial did not arise. While the verdict might well be a point of contention forever, one thing is beyond doubt — the lives and reputations of many of the players in the Mickelberg saga have been wrecked. Some have taken their own lives; others have died by murder or misadventure. Families have been torn apart; children have suffered the consequences. And the integrity of the policing, judicial and political system of Western Australia has suffered.

The Mickelberg story is just one of a series of cases that have recently brought into focus police corruption and incompetence. It has also revealed an apparent readiness by many in the political and judicial system to disregard the voices of protest of those caught up in the web and intrigue of police investigation. At the time, there seemed to be a too-ready willingness to prefer the official views and claims of the police rather than accept that not all those who raise their voices in protest have personal axes to grind. Perhaps, however, the appeals of the Mickelbergs, Beamish, Button and Mallard have changed that.

Without doubt, the Mickelberg story is a morality tale — and the moral is clear. Police officers, and prosecutors, who contemplate immoral and corrupt shortcuts to get the job done must remember the reason why, in criminal trials, our system of justice demands juries be satisfied beyond all reasonable doubt that the accused is guilty. It makes this demand because our system recognises and honours Blackstone's famous dictum that it is better ten guilty persons go free than one innocent person be found guilty.

EPILOGUE

Five years after what was supposed to be their final victory and twenty-five years after the battle began, I ask the brothers if they are enjoying their triumph. Ray answers emphatically, 'No, it shouldn't have taken that long, and it's not finished. It won't be finished until we win the court case against the cops or the state government gives us a more reasonable offer.'

Peter shows only slightly less bitterness. Underlying the momentary feelings of satisfaction that Ray and he finally convinced the court they were right is the bitter memory of the battles they had to fight to win their war, in the course of which they lost their brother Brian.

Release from the tension of battle has not brought them peace of mind while the police force remain unrepentant and the state government refuses to accept that the outcome of the appeal warrants compassionate consideration of a more generous ex gratia award — a payment 'made by the government to an individual who has suffered harm at their hands without any strict legal obligation to do so.'[346]

Assistant Commissioner Mel Hay's public outburst after the verdict had fired the desire for retribution. 'We didn't start this. The Assistant Commissioner Melvyn Hay started it and we never give in,' Ray thunders.[347] No one who had followed the Mickelberg saga could doubt that Ray meant every word.

Only four days after their Supreme Court triumph, Ray and Peter were spoiling for another fight. They were angry about Justice Murray's dissenting judgment, but they could do nothing about that. Assistant Commissioner Hay was a different matter.

They served a writ on him, claiming he defamed them when he said there was still sufficient evidence linking the Mickelbergs to the Perth Mint swindle. Ray and Peter accompanied their lawyer, Martin Bennett, to police headquarters to serve the writ papers on Hay. The writ, which had been filed in the Supreme Court, claimed Hay's statements were false and defamatory of the brothers, causing them substantial damage and distress.

Then they faced the media and the inevitable question: why after fighting their case for nearly twenty-two years were they prepared for another battle in court? The fighting Ray said, 'He started. We'll finish it. He's on notice. Put up or shut up. We challenge him now. Bring it on. Bring it on fast. We're happy to take the challenge.'[348]

Peter told reporters that Hay's statement 'definitely soured the win. Ill-informed comments from someone who had no involvement in the case ever.' He added, 'At the end of the day, Ray and I are innocent of these crimes and police commissioner Melvyn Hay decided to back up the crimes committed by (detectives) Hancock, Lewandowski, Tovey, Cvijic, Gillespie, Round, Hooft — all named in the Supreme Court judgment.'[349]

Peter also questioned why the police were not following up media reports of a deceased criminal who was supposedly involved in the Mint swindle. According to Peter, his counsel at trial, Brian Singleton, had relayed to him that a man with a criminal past told Singleton he had been recruited by another criminal to defraud the Perth Mint of gold in a manner identical to what actually happened with the Mint swindle. But Singleton told the story differently: he told the *West Australian* he was approached by a man who said he recalled another plot, which he believed to be similar to the Mint swindle.[350] Singleton added, 'He was not involved. He doesn't know whether it took place or didn't take place. He just finds it surprising that way back then there was a plan which was very similar to the Mint swindle plan.'

Ray and Peter were also seeking substantial damages from the state for wrongful conviction and imprisonment. As well, they were pursuing a civil action, commenced in 2003, against a number of the officers who were part of the initial investigation team. They had also joined the state to this civil action as a necessary and proper party to the resolution of their dispute.[351] Although joined to the defendants in the dispute, the state refused to cover the legal costs for the defence for the officers, former officers and the families of Hancock and Lewandowski. The Police Union stepped into the breach for all except Lewandowski

— the union's revenge for crossing the blue line.

The Mickelbergs[352] faced an uphill battle in their quest for compensation. Ray and Peter could only sue the police officers who had behaved corruptly; they could not sue the state.[353] The law is clear on this — police officers, while public officers, are not employees or agents of the government and nor, therefore, of the state, the police force or the commissioner of police. Police officers are independent of the state 'with independent discretion to carry out particular tasks under statute and therefore not an employee of the state.'[354] Thus, the state cannot be held to be vicariously liable or jointly or severally liable for the acts of police officers.

The Mickelberg brothers were prepared to discontinue any civil action if the state came good with an acceptable ex gratia payment. They believed they were entitled to around $13.6 million in damages but claimed that would never come close to compensating them for the pain and suffering they had endured since they were charged with the fraud back in 1982. They based this claim on the assets they owned when sentenced to gaol, which included abalone licences, diving income and real estate (including a share of a farm in New Zealand). Martin Bennett told the media they were not asking the government to put a value on the period they wrongfully spent in prison, or even 'a value on the destruction of Ray's marriage, the loss of the ability to watch his three children grow up. We are just saying these were assets the Mickelbergs owned when they were wrongly sent to gaol and ought to be given back to them.'[355]

John Button, who had received the state's highest ex gratia payment of $460,000 for his wrongful conviction for the murder of his girlfriend, supported the Mickelbergs in their claim for $13.6 million. But the man who had responsibility for the matter in state Cabinet, Attorney-General Jim McGinty, scoffed at the amount saying it was 'out of the ballpark of anything that the state government would contemplate.'

However, within days of McGinty's knock-back, Ray did have a financial win of sorts — even if it only meant getting back what was rightfully his in the first place.

On 9 May 1983, not long after the brothers had started their gaol sentences in the notorious Fremantle Prison, Don Hancock had raided Ray's home, still looking for the Mint swindle gold. He took away 152 ounces of gold and 900 ounces of silver Ray had legitimately purchased from the Mint. Hancock said he needed to see if it matched the stolen gold (why he took the silver is unknown) and if it did not, he would return the precious metals to Ray. He never did so. The Perth Mint had held it since 1995 after the Mint and the Mickelberg brothers reached an agreement in which the Mint ended its civil action against the brothers to recover the losses it suffered due to the Mint swindle.[356] The Mint also agreed it would return the gold and silver to Ray if he were ever acquitted of the fraud. When the Court of Criminal Appeal quashed Ray's convictions, he demanded the return of the precious metals. The Mint agreed to do so but seemed to be dragging its feet on the matter, so Ray decided to make things happen.

Around lunchtime on Friday 13 August 2004, Ray drove his utility to the Mint. His eighty-two year old mother was in the passenger seat. He walked into the Mint and asked to see Chief Executive Officer Edward Harbuz. After a brief wait, Harbuz appeared and Ray requested the return of his gold and silver. Harbuz was taken aback by the request (why is not clear) but it seems the Mint had made a decision that morning that the metals should be returned, so the CEO did not see a problem with acceding to the request.

When a Mint official brought the gold and silver to Ray in a steel box, he checked its contents, signed a release form and drove home, from where he invited the media to photograph and film him with $100,000 of precious metal, favouring them with a rare smile as they did so. However, the smile vanished as he told the media he would need to sell the gold and silver to finance the legal suit against the state. In the meantime, he would secure it in a bank safety deposit box.

In late June 2007, Master Newnes of the Supreme Court of Western Australia struck out the Mickelbergs' civil action.[357] The law was clear that the state was not legally liable for the damages sustained by the brothers; there was no 'cause of action' against the state and the claim against it was therefore struck out. As the actions against the former police officers or their estates (by now they had all retired and, of course, Hancock and Lewandowski were dead) were joined with the action against the state, these actions were doomed too. The Mickelbergs were at liberty to commence a new action against the former officers or their estates, but not against the state.

The loss in the Supreme Court led to renewed negotiations between the Mickelbergs and Attorney-General McGinty.[358] At a meeting in Jim McGinty's Fremantle electorate office in November 2007, he tabled an offer from the state of $400,000 each. The brothers rejected it, pointing out that it stacked up badly compared to the $460,000 awarded to John Button in 2003 and the $163,000 for Vincent Narkle, whose conviction for sexual assault (rape) was overturned by the Court of Appeal in April 2006.[359] Narkle spent eighteen months in gaol, and Button served approximately sixty months. Ray spent 98.5 months in gaol and Peter 82.5 months. The payouts for Narkle and Button worked out in both instances to $9000 for each month of incarceration. Had the state applied the same formula, Ray and Peter could have expected $886,500 and $742,500 respectively.[360]

Also, the degree of misconduct or criminality of state public officers was much greater in the Mickelberg case. In the Narkle case, the police failed to disclose to Narkle that the investigating detectives had shown the complainant photographs, including one of Narkle. The DPP conceded that this may have affected the reliability of the complainant's subsequent formal identification of Narkle on a photo board. While this was unacceptable behaviour by the police, it was not conduct of a serious criminal nature. Button confessed to the police that he had run over his girlfriend. Although he later retracted it, there was no allegation that the police had fabricated the confession.

The conduct of some police officers involved in the Mickelberg case was criminal, including perjury. As McCusker wrote in a letter to the Attorney-General dated 21 November 2007, 'The Court of Criminal Appeal expressly found that it was that criminal conduct by police officers which made the convictions unsafe or unsatisfactory, and a substantial miscarriage of justice.' He also emphasised that the brothers had been diagnosed as suffering from post-traumatic stress disorder; they had lost all their assets; and they now had no means of earning a livelihood. Ray's marriage was destroyed and with it his family life with his children. 'The impact on each of them, personally, of imprisonment has been devastating. Lesser men would have completely cracked.'

McGinty was unmoved, even provocative. He claimed that some lawyers retained lingering doubts that the Mickelbergs were innocent of the Mint swindle, notwithstanding the quashing of their convictions. As the state's senior law officer, McGinty would have known that the opinion — whether his or that of unnamed lawyers — was irrelevant. The onus to prove guilt beyond reasonable doubt lay with the prosecution; this it had failed to do. The highest court in the state had quashed the Mickelbergs' convictions. The brothers were not required to do more.

As the Mickelbergs and McGinty haggled over the ex gratia payments, the police force finally faced the music when, on 15 December 2005, Police Commissioner Karl O'Callaghan apologised for the now retired Assistant Commissioner Mel Hay's defamatory remarks. He said, 'The WA Police Service acknowledges that Raymond and Peter Mickelberg were, and remain, entitled to the presumption of innocence for the Mint swindle offences and should therefore be apologised to.' He also said, 'Mel Hay acknowledges that his statements caused distress to Raymond and Peter Mickelberg and sincerely apologises.'[361]

Anxious to bury the matter once and for all, the Attorney-General made another offer to the Mickelbergs. In a letter to McCusker dated 19 December 2007, he said Cabinet had agreed to make payment of $500,000 to each brother on the condition they discontinue their civil action against the former police officers or their estate. Additionally, they were to release and indemnify 'the State, its officers, employees or agents (including any present or former police officer), as well as their estates.'

The Mickelbergs were only prepared to cease all civil actions against the former officers or their estates if the ex gratia payment came to a total of $1.6 million, although even this amount was far less than the millions they believed they deserved. In the new year McGinty came back with a new offer: still $500,000 per brother, but he had dropped the condition that they must cease the civil actions or agree to the indemnity stipulation.[362] The brothers were still unhappy and angry but felt they had no choice but to accept the offer; they needed the money to continue their civil actions.

The secretary of the WA Police Union, Mick Dean, was also unhappy. He was annoyed McGinty had left the door open for the Mickelbergs to continue the civil action. He could not understand why the Attorney-General had allowed the litigation barrier to be removed, or why the government would not pay the extra $600,000 to settle the matter once and for all. Dean said, '[McGinty] hasn't settled this at all ... The government thinks this is the end of the matter, well it's a long way from the end.'[363] Later, on evening news broadcasts, he added, 'The Mickelberg case is a cancerous sore on the police force.' He was to get no argument from the brothers on that score.

Never far from the headlines, in January 2009 it was widely reported that Ray had been charged with stealing a fan and a roll of tape to seal the open box containing the fan from a Bunnings store. Police alleged that Ray went into the store and attempted to exchange a cheaper fan for a more expensive one without notifying staff. Ray said it was all just a big misunderstanding. 'I can't see how I could be deemed to have stolen it when I was actually there to pay for it.'[364] Ray said he would defend the charges.

Finally in May 2009 the WA Police Union agreed to settle the Mickelbergs' civil action by making a confidential monetary payout.[365] At around the same time the state government offered Andrew Mallard $3.25 million 'compensation' for his twelve years of wrongful imprisonment. He rejected the offer, naming his price at $7.5 million. Some weeks later, Mallard accepted the government's 'gift' but on the condition that he could still proceed with his civil action against the government and police officers involved. Any sum awarded in that action would be reduced by $3.25 million.[366] However, Mallard eventually opted out of taking the matter further.

Andrew Mallard received more than four times as much compensation as each Mickelberg brother. While not begrudging Mallard of a cent, Peter describes his feelings as 'frustrated and perplexed.' Similarly, John Button claims to be struggling financially as a result of his wrongful incarceration and has recently written to Attorney-General Christian Porter seeking additional funds to the $400,000 he received in 2002.[367] The Attorney-General refused the request. These types of ongoing disputes and concerns have led some to call for an independent body to be responsible for the making of ex gratia payments.[368]

In one more twist of fate, only days after the Mickelberg settlement was announced, it turned out that another battle had already begun. Cancer was threatening Ray's life.[369] Suffering bowel cancer which had spread to his lymph glands, Ray underwent surgery and an intense six-month schedule of chemotherapy. He says that if he recovers he will retire to Denmark and put the last twenty-eight years behind him.

But before retiring to Denmark, Ray had the little matter of the Bunnings charges to deal with. In August 2010, representing himself in the Magistrates Court, he successfully defended the charge of stealing the fan but was found guilty of stealing the tape. The Magistrate said the Crown had failed to prove beyond reasonable doubt that Mickelberg had intended to steal the fan but at the time Mickelberg took the three strips of tape, the tape was still the property of Bunnings. Ray was sentenced to a $200 conditional release order for six months. Representing himself, he successfully appealed the conviction to the Supreme Court of Western Australia. On 15 April 2011 Commissioner Kevin Sleight stated that Ray had an 'honest claim of right' over the tape.

Failing something like a deathbed confession from the real perpetrator, the truth about the Perth Mint swindle is likely to remain a mystery that will continue to intrigue and divide the public into those who believe and those who do not believe the Mickelberg brothers are innocent. A topic for enduring speculation upon which, for those who speculate, nothing rests.

But for Ray and Peter, the consequences are not only enduring, but also probably irresolvable. Sensitive to a real or perceived current of lingering suspicion among strangers, they find it difficult to form new relationships. They find it difficult to trust. They carry the bitterness of their long struggle.

As I end this account of the Perth Mint swindle, I cannot tell you on which side you should stand; I never intended to do that. What I did intend, and I hope I have achieved, is to emphasise that, even in a so-called noble cause, corruption is never acceptable. When corruption prevails, not only do innocent people suffer when they should not and even guilty people suffer more than they should, but our whole system of justice upon which the coherence and stability of our society depends is subjected to sometimes intolerable stress.

BIBLIOGRAPHY

This is a selective bibliography, listing only books and journal articles. For other reference material such as newspaper articles, reports, law cases and legislation refer to citations in the endnotes.

Books

Anonymous, *Guide to Judicial Conduct* (2nd ed. Melbourne: The Australasian Institute of Judicial Administration Incorporated (published for The Council of Chief Justices of Australia), 2007).

J. Almog, 'Fingerprint Development by Ninhydrin and Its Analogues' in H. Lee and R. Gaensslen (eds), *Advances in Fingerprint Technology* (2nd ed. Boca Raton: CRC Press, 2001), 177.

S. Arrowsmith, *Civil Liability and Public Authorities* (Winteringham: Earlsgate, 1992).

C. Ayris, *Fremantle Prison: A Brief History* (West Perth: Cyril Ayris Freelance, 1995).

P. Barry, *The Rise and Fall of Alan Bond* (Sydney: Bantam Books, 1991).

E. Blackburn, *Broken Lives* (Claremont: Stellar Publishing, 1998).

W. Blackstone, *Commentaries* (1966 reprint. London: Dawsons of Pall Mall, 1769).

G. Bolton and G. Byrne, *May it Please Your Honour: A History of the Supreme Court of Western Australia 1861–2005* (Perth: Supreme Court of Western Australia, 2005).

P. Brett, *The Beamish Case* (Melbourne: Melbourne University Press, 1966).

A. Buti, *A Matter of Conscience: Sir Ronald Wilson* (Crawley: University of Western Australia Press, 2007).

Butterworths Concise Australian Legal Dictionary (2nd ed. Chatswood: LexisNexis, 1998).

C. Egan, *Murderer No More: Andrew Mallard and the Epic Fight that Proved his Innocence* (Sydney: Allen and Unwin, 2010).

D. Ellen, *Scientific Examination of Documents Methods and Techniques* (3rd ed. Boca Raton: Taylor & Francis, 2006).

D. Elliott, 'Lie Detector Evidence: Lessons from the American Experience' in E. Campbell and L. Waller (eds), *Well and Truly Tried* (Sydney: Law Book Co., 1982), 100.

J. Fionda, *Public Prosecutors and Discretion: A Comparative Study* (Oxford: Clarendon Press, 1995).

I. Freckleton and H. Selby, *Expert Evidence* (Sydney: Lawbook Co., 2005).

S. Gageler, 'Jurisdiction' in T. Blackshield, M. Coper and G. Williams (eds), *The Oxford Companion to the High Court of Australia* (South Melbourne: Oxford University Press, 2001), 383.

P. Grabowsky, *Wayward Governance: Illegality and its Control in the Public Sector* (Canberra: Australian Institute of Criminology, 1989).

A. Lovell, *Split Image: International Mystery of the Mickelberg Affair* (Perth: Creative Research, 1990).

A. Lovell, *The Mickelberg Stitch* (Perth: Creative Research, 1985).

D. Marshall, *The Devil's Garden: The Claremont Serial Killings* (Sydney: Random House, 2007).

P. O'Brien and M. Webb, *The Executive State: WA Inc & The Constitution* (Perth: Constitutional Publishing Company, 1991).

C. Porter, *The Conviction of the Innocent: How the law can let us down* (North Sydney: Random House, 2007).

P. Williams et al., *The Cost of Civil Litigation before Intermediate Courts in Australia* (Melbourne: The Australian Institute of Judicial Administration Incorporated, 1992).

A. Zuckerman and R. Cranston, *Reform of Civil Procedure: Essays on 'Access to Justice'* (Oxford: Clarendon Press, 1995).

Journal Articles

A. Ashworth, 'Prosecution and Procedure in Criminal Justice' [1979] *Criminal Law Review* 81–492.

G. Eames, 'Towards a Better Direction — Better Communication with Jurors' (2003) 24 *Australian Bar Review* 35.

J. Edelman, 'Admissibility of polygraph (lie detector) examinations' (2005) 29 *Crim Law Journal* 2.

P. Fairall, 'Unravelling the Golden Thread — Woolmington in the High Court of Australia' (1993) 5 *Bond Law Review* 229.

J. Furedy and J. Liss, 'Countering Confessions Induced by the Polygraph: Of Confessionals and Psychological Rubber Hoses' (1986) 29 *Criminal Law Quarterly* 91.

B. Harrison, 'Noble Cause Corruption and the Police Ethic' (1999) 68(8) *FBI Law Enforcement* 1.

S. Henchliffe, 'How much is enough? The common law and statutory limitations on collateral and credibility evidence' (2009) 32 *Australian Bar Review* 24.

M. Kirby, 'Controls over Investigation of Offences and Pre-Trial Treatment of Suspects' (1979) 53 *Australian Law Journal* 626.

G. Lyon and B. Walmsley, 'Consciousness of Guilt — The Use of Lies Told by the Accused' (1997) 71(11) *Law Institute Journal* 50.

K. Mack, 'Challenging Assumptions about Credibility' (2001) 21(4) *Proctor* 16.

E. Magner, 'Exclusion of Polygraph Evidence: Can It Be Justified?' (1988) 30 *Criminal Law Quarterly* 412.

S. Major, 'Am I Special Enough? The Payment of Ex Gratia Compensation by the Commonwealth' (1995) 6 *Australian Institute of Administrative Law Forum* 14.

S. Miller, 'Corruption for a Cause — Police Corruption' (1986) 49(1) *IPA Review (Institute of Public Affairs)* 17.

J. Mnookin, 'Scripting Expertise: The History of Handwriting Identification Evidence and the Judicial Construction of Reliability' (2001) 87(8) *Virginia Law Review* 1723.

A. Palmer, 'Guilt & the Consciousness of Guilt '(1997) 21 *Melbourne University Law Review* 95.

D. Payne, 'Book Reviews: The Beamish Case' (1965–66) 7 *University of Western Australia Law Journal* 576.

T. Percy, 'Despised outsiders: compensation for wrongful convictions' (2007) 81 *Precedent* 20.

W. Pizzi, and L. Marafioti, 'The New Italian Code of Criminal Procedure: the Difficulties of Building an Adversarial Trial System on a Civil Law Foundation' (1992) 17 *Yale Journal of International Law* 1.

L. Porter and C. Warrender, 'A Multivariate Model of Police Deviance: Examining the Nature of Corruption, Crime and Misconduct' (2009) 19(1) *Policing & Society* 79.

P. Priest, 'Credibility of Accused' (1991) 65 *Law Institute Journal* 1142.

P. Ryan, 'Ripe Justice' (2005) 49(5) *Quadrant Magazine* 95.

M. Smithson, S. Deady and L. Gracik, 'Guilty, Not Guilty, or ... ? Multiple Options in Jury Verdict Choices' (2007) 20 *Journal of Behavioral Decision Making* 481.

R. Tailby, 'The Illicit Market in Diamonds' (2002) 218 *The Australian Institute of Criminology* 4.

G. Taylor, 'Judicial Reflections on the Defence Case in the Summing Up' (2005) 26 *Australian Bar Review* 70.

G. Walsh, 'Injury by Justice: Inadequacy of Ex-Gratia Compensation for Wrongful Conviction' (1994) 32(5) *Law Society Journal* 32.

G. Wells, A. Memon and S. Penrod, 'Eyewitness Evidence: Improving its Probative Value' (2006) 7 *Psychological Science in the Public Interest* 2.

J. Widgery, 'The Balance of the Criminal Law Trial' [1972] *NZLR* 688.

C. William, 'Lies as Evidence' (2005) 26 *Australian Bar Review* 313.

P. Williams and R. Williams, 'Access to Justice and the Cost of Litigation' (1992) 8(3) *Policy* 22.

P. Young, 'Criminal Law — Use of Lies by the Accused' (1997) 71 *Australian Law Journal* 682.

ENDNOTES

CHAPTER I

1 **Chief Crown Prosecutor**: A 'Crown Prosecutor' is responsible for the prosecution of persons alleged to have committed criminal offences. They represent the Crown, against whom, it is said, all criminal offences are committed (traditionally conceived as a breach of the King's Peace and an attack on public order — see Review of the Criminal and Civil Justice System in WA, Project 92, *West Australian Law Reform Commission*, 1999 at 6.9 'Victims'; 'Where do they belong? Giving victims a place in the criminal justice process,' J. Wemmers, a paper presented at the National Victims of Crime Conference, 23 and 24 September 2008, Adelaide, SA, 2, available at http://www.cicc.umontreal.ca/recherche/victimologie/adelaide_paper.pdf).

2 **QC**: Abbreviation for 'Queen's Counsel'. The title QC is an 'honorary rank bestowed on a barrister or legal practitioner practising in the style of a barrister ... a mark and recognition by the Sovereign of the professional eminence of the counsel upon whom it is conferred.' (*Butterworths Concise Australian Legal Dictionary* (2nd ed. Chatswood: LexisNexis, 1998)). In Western Australia, the title 'QC' is gradually being phased out by the title 'Senior Counsel' (*Abbr.* SC).

3 **Chairman of the District Court**: The Mint swindle trial was heard in the District Court of Western Australia, in Perth, an intermediate court in the Western Australian judicial hierarchy. Like most courts the District Court has a head judge, in the District Court's case, the 'Chairman', who has some additional roles especially in procedural rule-making and general administration.

4 **'... his opening address to the jury ...'**: Under current Western Australian law, ss.143(1) of the *Criminal Procedure Act 2004* (WA) provides that 'before any evidence is given in a trial the prosecutor is entitled to give an opening address to the court about the prosecutor's case.' The defence is then provided an opportunity to make an opening address after the prosecution (subsections 143(2) and (3)). At the time of the Mint swindle trial, the law was essentially the same (*Criminal Code* (WA) s. 637 [now repealed]).

5 **'... indicted'**: An indictment is the written document that is presented to a superior court that triggers the exercise of its jurisdiction to hear the prosecution of an offence. The indictment process was at the time of the Mint swindle dealt with under Chapter LXII of the *Criminal Code* (WA).

6 **'... eight counts'**: An accused (or accuseds) may be tried for more than one offence at the same trial in some circumstances. Under the now-repealed

s.585 of the *Criminal Code* (WA) distinct and separate offences could be tried together if the 'offences were alleged to be constituted by the same acts or omissions, or by a series of acts done or omitted to be done in the prosecution of a single purpose.' Now see *Criminal Procedure Act 2004* (WA) schedule 1 clause 7.

7 **Conspiracy to defraud**: Section 412 (now repealed) of the *Criminal Code* (WA) provided that 'any person who conspires with another by deceit or any fraudulent means to ... defraud the public ... or to extort any property from any person, is guilty of a crime, and is liable to imprisonment with hard labour for seven years.'

8 **Burglary**: Section 403 (now repealed) of the *Criminal Code* (WA) provided that 'any person who ... (1) Breaks and enters a schoolhouse, shop, warehouse, or counting-house, or a building which is adjacent to a dwelling-house and occupied with it but is not part of it, and commits a crime therein ... is liable to imprisonment with hard labour for fourteen years.'

9 **Arson**: Section 444 (now repealed) of the *Criminal Code* (WA) provided that 'any person who wilfully and unlawfully sets fire to ... (a) any building or structure whatever ... is guilty of a crime, and is liable to imprisonment with hard labour for life.'

10 **'... falsely claimed to an employee of the director of the Perth Mint that three cheques presented in payment for the bullion were genuine'**: Another three charges of fraud (see note 7 above), one for each cheque.

11 **'Circumstantial and scientific evidence'**: Evidence can be categorised in various ways. 'Circumstantial' evidence refers to evidence brought to establish facts which are not directly relevant to establishing the commission of an offence, but that may give rise to an inference of facts which may be relevant in such a manner. The classic example is where someone claims to have seen an alleged murderer leaving the scene carrying a bloodied murder weapon. It is not direct evidence of guilt, but the jury is invited to make that inference based on that fact. Circumstantial evidence raised in the Mint swindle case for instance included Peter's prior purchases of gold bullion from the Mint using a false name, his knowledge of Otto Kleiger, and his occupation of Unit 7, 112 Rupert Street, Subiaco. 'Scientific' evidence is a loose term used here to refer to various forensic evidence such as fingerprints and handwriting analysis.

12 **'Day after day, the Crown introduced its witnesses'**: After the prosecution (and the accused if they choose to) have completed their opening addresses, the prosecution presents its case. A prosecution case is made up of oral testimony from those who observed matters relevant to the offence (witnesses), and the introduction of material evidence (exhibits).

13 **'They withstood cross-examinations from three defence lawyers'**: Each witness called by the prosecution first gives their 'evidence-in-chief' by answering questions put to them by the prosecution (called 'examination in chief'). The defence (in this case each defence lawyer), is then entitled to 'cross-examine' each witness after they have given their evidence, usually aimed at shedding their answers to the prosecution's questions in a different light or by attacking their credibility.

14 **Admissions**: An admission is some representation made by the accused adverse or contrary to their interest in the outcome of the proceedings. Technically, a confession is broader, connoting a *full* acknowledgement by the accused of the commission of the offence. Both have a special legal consequence. Whereas prior statements made by an accused are generally not admissible evidence (hearsay), any admission or confession made by an accused is admissible. Admissions and particularly confessions are given significant weight by juries and the judiciary, but particular caution must be taken where they are unsigned or uncorroborated — see note 19 below; *McKay v R* (1935) 54 CLR 1.

15 **'... the detectives took the opportunity to question Peter'**: In carrying out investigations, the police have all the powers of a citizen, to do anything that is not unlawful, which includes interviewing and questioning suspects (both under common law — *Marshall v Western Australia* (Unreported, Supreme Court of Western Australia, McKechnie J, 9 May 2008), [26] and enshrined in section 8 of the *Criminal Investigation Act 2006* (WA)). The suspect may refuse to answer any questions or participate in any interview, an aspect of their 'right to silence' (*Petty v R* (1991) 173 CLR 95; *Weissensteiner v R* (1993) 178 CLR 217; *Azzopardi v R* (2001) 205 CLR 50; *Tofilau v R* (2007) 231 CLR 396).

16 **Search warrant**: A document, approved by a judge, magistrate or justice of the peace, that authorises police to do a search and seizure of things 'in relation to an offence.' At the time of the Mint swindle investigation, this was carried out by police under section 504 of the *Criminal Code* (WA). Now see *Criminal Procedure Act 2004* (WA) Part 5 Division 3 (ss.41–45).

17 **'... he agreed to accompany them'**: See note 15 above.

18 **Handwriting experts**: Prosecution witnesses may include both those who observed events relevant to the offence, and expert witnesses – experts in a 'specialised field' of knowledge who are called upon to give their learned opinions based on their expertise. For a good treatment on handwriting analysis generally see D. Ellen, *Scientific Examination of Documents Methods and Techniques* (3rd ed. Boca Raton: Taylor & Francis, 2006). For handwriting evidence in a legal context see J. Mnookin, 'Scripting Expertise: The History of Handwriting Identification Evidence and the Judicial Construction of Reliability' (2001) 87(8) *Virginia Law Review* 1723; *R v Leroy* (1984) 55 ALR 338; *R v Doney* (2001) 126 A Crim R 271.

19 **'Lewandowski said at the trial that he made notes during the interview. He claimed to have read these notes back to Peter who agreed they were accurate but would not sign them'**: The importance of these events is that the notes made in the police interview were said to contain confessions or admissions (see note 14 above). While there has always been a requirement that confessions or admissions be 'voluntary' (see the summary in *R v Swaffield; Pavic v R* (1998) 192 CLR 159, 189 (Toohey, Gaudron and Gummow JJ)), at the time of the Mint swindle investigation in 1982, there was no specific requirement that confessions be signed or independently corroborated. Eventually, and to combat actual and alleged cases of police fraud, such as in the Mint swindle, special legislative provision has been introduced to govern the admissibility of confessions and admissions.

Currently, under section 118 of the *Criminal Investigation Act 2006* (WA) an admission not recorded by audio-visual means without reasonable excuse is inadmissible unless (see s.155) the court is 'satisfied that the desirability of admitting the evidence outweighs the undesirability of admitting the evidence.'

20 '... **Brian went to police headquarters'**: Much of this supposed interview is quoted verbatim and considered in *Brian Mickelberg v R* [1984] WAR 191, 200–201 (Burt CJ), Brian's successful 1983 appeal against conviction.

21 '"**... if you were part of the whole plan and knew about it, then under the law you are equally guilty"'**: Hancock is correct. Under Western Australian law, in addition to the person who actually does an act constituting an offence, every person who aids, counsels or procures a person to commit an offence may be charged and convicted of it (section 7 of the *Criminal Code* (WA)). Further, under section 8, where two or more persons have a 'common intention to prosecute an unlawful purpose,' and in prosecution of that purpose an offence is committed that is a probable consequence of that purpose, each is deemed to have committed that offence.

CHAPTER 2

22 '... **[Bond] was gaoled for corporate fraud in the 1990s'**: For a good coverage see the Bond appeal judgments: *Bond v R* (Unreported, Supreme Court of Western Australia Court of Criminal Appeal, Franklyn J, 12 June 1992); *Bond v R* (2000) 201 CLR 213.

23 '... **fraud in that they had manufactured the nugget with the intention of deceiving prospective buyers'**: Like the charges for the Mint swindle. Conspiracy to defraud under the now-repealed s.412 of the *Criminal Code* (WA): '[a]ny person who conspires with another by deceit or any fraudulent means to ... defraud the public ... or to extort any property from any person, is guilty of a crime, and is liable to imprisonment with hard labour for seven years.'

24 **The admissibility of evidence of prior criminal activity**: See section 8 *Evidence Act 1906* (WA); *Maxwell v Director of Public Prosecutions* [1935] AC 309, 317; *Attorney-General (NSW) v Willesee* [1980] 2 NSWLR 143, 149; *Hinch v Attorney-General (Vic)* (1987) 164 CLR 15.

25 '... **Ron Cannon ... who let the cat out of the bag'**: The significance here is that as explained in the text and in note 24 above, prior criminal activity is primarily not admissible by the prosecution as evidence of guilt. However, the prosecution can use any evidence, including that of past criminal activity (i.e. The Yellow Rose of Texas affair), already raised by the defence. As Cannon raised the Yellow Rose of Texas in his examination in chief of Raymond, the prosecution were free to question on that matter and use it to attack his credibility. It no doubt would have had a broader, latent effect.

26 '"**It like to broke my heart"'**: From the song 'Yellow Rose of Texas' by Mitch Miller, Columbia Records (1955).

27 '... **the jury, the arbiter of fact'**: The role of a jury is to determine facts. This is to be contrasted with the judge's role who determines all matters of law.

28 '... **damaged his credibility as a truthful witness'**: The adversarial tradition of common law criminal justice places great weight on oral testimony, largely

because of the reality that demeanour informs 'believability' based upon ordinary experience and impression. Put simply, the particular witnesses and therefore versions of events, that emerge from rigorous cross-examination as more 'credible' will likely be that preferred by the jury. This is an entirely legitimate approach, and is in fact central to the proper functioning of the adversarial system. See generally P. Priest, 'Credibility of Accused' (1991) 65 *Law Institute Journal* 1142; S. Henchliffe, 'How much is enough? The common law and statutory limitations on collateral and credibility evidence' (2009) 32 *Australian Bar Review* 24; K. Mack, 'Challenging Assumptions about Credibility' (2001) 21(4) *Proctor* 16.

29 '**... he was taken away and fingerprinted**': Under section 50AA of the *Police Act 1892* (WA) (inserted by s.2 of the *Police Amendment Act 1974* (WA), as it then was): 'Where any person is in lawful custody for any offence punishable on indictment or summary conviction, any officer or constable of the Police Force may take or cause to be taken all such particulars as he may think necessary or desirable for the identification of that person, including his photograph, measurements, fingerprints, and palm-prints.' Now see *Criminal Investigation (Identifying People) Act 2002* (WA).

30 '**... verbally identifying themselves but refusing to present documented identification or a search warrant**': For search warrants see Chapter 1 note 16. At the time of the Mint swindle, police had little to no powers allowing the entry of premises for the purposes of a search without a warrant. If a search warrant is required to enter and search premises, and is not obtained, any evidence acquired by virtue of that search will be necessarily unlawfully obtained. However, under the common law, there is no blanket prohibition on the admission of evidence obtained by unlawful means. Where evidence has been unlawfully obtained, it is a matter for the discretion of the trial judge to decide whether to admit the evidence. This involves a balancing of the interests of justice. For this issue see *Bunning v Cross* (1978) 141 CLR 54; *Foster v R* (1993) 113 ALR 1; *R v Swaffield; Pavic v R* (1998) 192 CLR 159; *Ridgeway v R* (1995) 129 ALR 41. For the current position, see *Criminal Investigation Act 2006* (WA), especially section 155. The relevance of 'documented identification' is that when a search warrant is executed, generally the police must show some means of identification to verify the lawfulness of the search pursuant to the relevant search warrant. Currently, see *Criminal Investigation Act 2006* (WA) sections 31 and 45. For other examples of legislative provision to this effect see *Crimes Act 1914* (Cth) subsection 3H(4); *Police Integrity Act 2008* (Vic) paragraph 94(3)(a); *Police Regulation Act 1958* (Vic) subsection 100C(a).

31 '**Peter telephoned Cannon who informed Peter that he didn't need to go unless they charged him**': Under the common law, and at the time of the Mint swindle, the police never had the power to forcibly detain or 'arrest' a person for 'investigative questioning' (*Williams v R* (1986) 161 CLR 278; *Norton v R* (2001) 24 WAR 488). Also see section 570 of the *Criminal Code* (WA) (as it then was) and the later *Bail Act 1982* (WA) section 6. Although the practical reality may have seemed otherwise, strictly, Peter could have refused to go with the detectives unless charged. Even if charged, police could only detain him for the purpose of his being formally charged and appearing before a justice of the peace to have his bail heard. Peter's alleged 'agreement' to accompany police essentially made their taking of him, albeit

veiled by intimidation and a holding-out of greater authority, in strict legal terms, lawful. This position concerning 'investigative arrest' has now been modified in Western Australia where it is now allowed in some instances under Part XII Division 5 of the *Criminal Investigation Act 2006* (WA) (esp. ss.139–140).

32 '**... Hooft and Henley undertook a thorough search, although they had no search warrant**': For acting without a search warrant, see note 30.

33 '**They collected some photographs of Peter, his girlfriend and her family**': Under section 711 of the *Criminal Code* (WA) as it then was, if the officers had a search warrant, they may have seized anything in the house that, on reasonable grounds, might have afforded evidence in the Mint swindle investigation.

34 **Identification parade**: 'A line-up of a sufficient number of similar looking people [either in person or via photographs] to enable a witness to attempt a visual identification of an accused without assistance. A number of common law and statutory rules govern the conduct of proper identification parades.' (*Butterworths Concise Australian Legal Dictionary* (2nd ed. Chatswood: LexisNexis, 1998)). See particularly the discussion by the High Court in *Alexander v R* (1981) 145 CLR 395 and *Festa v R* (2001) 208 CLR 593.

35 '**The questioning continued for about three hours**': Under current Western Australian law, not in operation in 1982, there is a time limit on the allowable period of police custody of a person prior to a person being charged. Under the *Criminal Investigation Act 2006* (WA) police custody of a suspect prior to charges being laid can only be for specific purposes (set out in ss.139(2)), for a reasonable period (ss.140(2)(b)) that does not exceed six hours (ss.140(3)(a)). If a longer period is required, special authorisation for another six-hour period must be sought from a 'senior officer' (ss.140(4)–(5)). If a longer period of custody is required, an application to a magistrate is required (ss.140(6)–(7)).

36 '"... if you confess you can go to Wooroloo"': This is an interesting comment. While the prosecution may make submissions concerning sentencing, the police in Western Australia do not, and have never had, any power to influence, or make agreements concerning, the sentence eventually handed out by the sentencing judge. To so interfere would be an inappropriate interference by the executive arm (i.e. the police) in the judicial sphere of government (see *Malvaso v R* (1989) 168 CLR 227). In fact, offering such an 'inducement' may have made any alleged confession involuntary and therefore inadmissible (see *R v Swaffield; Pavic v R* (1998) 192 CLR 159, 167–171 (Brennan CJ), 188–9, 196–8 (Toohey, Gaudron & Gummow JJ), 209 (Kirby J); *Cleland v R* (1982) 151 CLR 1 (esp. Murphy J); *Tofilau v R* (2007) 231 CLR 396).

37 '**... the three brothers were charged**': This refers to a formal allegation by police that a person has committed the particular offence(s) charged, and, after investigation, is the first step in the criminal justice process.

38 '**Peter refused but was bailed and allowed to go, as were Ray and Brian**': Bail refers to the process where an alleged offender charged with an offence is released from custody on the condition that, inter alia, they will appear at court as required in answer to the proceedings. Today in Western Australia, the bail process is governed by the *Bail Act 1982* (WA), but this was not operational until 6 February 1989. At the time of the Mint swindle,

the process was governed by section 115 of the *Justices Act 1902* (WA) and section 537 of the *Criminal Code* (WA).

39 **'"We are taking the wife and kids and you"'**: See note 31.

40 **'Hancock shouted that unless Ray signed a confession Sheryl would be charged and the children would be made wards of state'**: There are two important aspects to this statement. The first is that if this threat was made, it would surely have made any alleged confession 'under inducement' and therefore inadmissible as evidence (see *R v Swaffield; Pavic v R* (1998) 192 CLR 159, 189 (Toohey, Gaudron and Gummow JJ) and note 36). The second is that although not a certain or automatic result of a criminal charge, it is conceivable that if both Ray and Sheryl were charged with serious criminal offences, the children may have been declared a 'child in need of care and protection' under the now-repealed *Child Welfare Act 1947* (WA), making them a 'ward' of the state under that act (see ss.4 [esp. ss.4(2)], 10, 10A and Part IV).

41 **Alibi**: Latin — elsewhere. A claim by an accused that the person was somewhere other than the place where the crime was committed at the relevant time and, therefore, could not be guilty of the offence.

CHAPTER 3

42 **Noble cause corruption**: Described by Seumas Miller as 'the paradox whereby police necessarily use morally problematic methods to secure morally worthy ends,' noble cause corruption is reported by Porter and Warrender as the most frequent source of police misconduct. It is an attempt to justify corruption in some instances where a cause is 'noble,' in light of the apparent 'greater good.' It involves an obvious philosophical dilemma. See L. Porter and C. Warrender, 'A Multivariate Model of Police Deviance: Examining the Nature of Corruption, Crime and Misconduct' (2009) 19(1) *Policing & Society* 79; B. Harrison, 'Noble Cause Corruption and the Police Ethic' (1999) 68(8) *FBI Law Enforcement* 1; S. Miller, 'Corruption for a Cause — Police Corruption' (1986) 49(1) *IPA Review (Institute of Public Affairs)* 17.

43 **Beyond reasonable doubt**: For there to be a conviction in a criminal trial, the jury must be convinced of every element of the offence 'beyond reasonable doubt.' If not convinced beyond reasonable doubt, a verdict of not guilty must be returned. There is much judicial discussion on the phrase 'beyond reasonable doubt'. The most important recent High Court authority is *Darkan v R* (2006) 227 CLR 373.

44 **Adjourned**: An 'adjournment' is a court order that proceedings be postponed, or interrupted, and continued at a different time and/or place.

45 **Prejudice and preconception**: The jury must make their decision on the admissible evidence, unaffected by any prejudice or preconception. Further, an accused has the right not to be tried unfairly (see *Jago v District Court of New South Wales* (1989) 168 CLR 23). While there is a public interest in the reporting of criminal offences, there is a risk that this right may be impinged where there has been significant pre-trial publicity. There are a number of cases that consider both the effects of pre-trial publicity, and also the various ways it can be avoided. These include adjourning proceedings for a period of time or to another location, and/or giving the jury strict directions. The

latter approach was taken in the Mickelberg trial. In some cases this has been held to have been insufficient. Where the issue of pre-trial publicity has not been properly dealt with, a miscarriage of justice may occur. See *R v Long; Ex parte Attorney General (Qld)* (2003) 138 A Crim R 103; *R v Chami* (2002) 128 A Crim R 428; *R v Glennon* (1992) 173 CLR 592.

46 **'Ray had never suggested that possibility'**: Counsel for an accused appearing at trial have a broad discretion: 'parties are bound by the conduct of their counsel, who exercise a wide discretion in deciding what issues to contest, what witnesses to call, what evidence to lead or to seek to have excluded, and what lines of argument to pursue' (*Nudd v R* (2006) 225 ALR 161, 164 (Gleeson CJ)). Courts will not 'second guess' the methods or approach of trial counsel, and a successful appeal for a miscarriage of justice on these grounds is rare (*R v Western Australia* [2008] WASCA 127 (Unreported, Supreme Court Western Australia Court of Criminal Appeal, McLure and Miller JJA and Murray AJA, 18 June 2008); *Rinaldi v R* (1993) 30 NSWLR 605; *R v Birks* (1990) 19 NSWLR 677, 684 (Gleeson CJ); *D'Orta-Ekenaike v Victorian Legal Aid* (2005) 223 CLR 1, 63 (Gleeson CJ)).

47 **'"... all men are presumed innocent until they are found guilty"'**: The traditional 'golden thread' of the criminal justice system, recognised by the High Court in Australia in 1911 in *Peacock v R* (1911) 13 CLR 619 and affirmed and approved ever since. See also P. Fairall, 'Unravelling the Golden Thread — Woolmington in the High Court of Australia' (1993) 5 *Bond Law Review* 229.

48 **'... a foundation judge of the District Court ...'**: The District Court of Western Australia was created by the *District Court of Western Australia Act 1969* (WA) and began operation on 1 April 1970. It was established as an intermediate court to relieve the case-load of the Supreme Court of Western Australia, the highest court in the Western Australian court hierarchy.

49 **'... sum up for the jury matters of law ...'**: At the conclusion of a criminal jury trial the judge 'sums up' and gives 'directions', providing the jury, before they retire to make their decision, with a final summation of the evidence admitted and arguments given by both the crown and the accused(s), and various directions as to the application of the relevant law. 'The function of a summing up is to furnish information which will help a particular jury to carry out its task in the concrete circumstances of the individual case before it and in the light of the trial judge's assessment of how well that jury is handling its task.' — Gleeson CJ, Gummow, Heydon and Crennan JJ (*Darkan v R* (2006) 227 CLR 373, 394). See generally G. Eames, 'Towards a Better Direction — Better Communication with Jurors' (2003) 24 *Australian Bar Review* 35; G. Taylor, 'Judicial Reflections on the Defence Case in the Summing Up' (2005) 26 *Australian Bar Review* 70.

50 **'... the ultimate decision: guilty or innocent'**: In Australia, while there are variations on a 'not guilty' verdict (such as a not guilty verdict by way of mental incapacity), the possible outcomes of a jury trial are essentially limited to a verdict of guilty or not guilty (or unable to reach a verdict). This can be contrasted with some legal developments around the globe. In Italy under their criminal code judges can choose from a range of acquittals: 1) that no crime was committed; 2) that there was a crime, but the defendant did not commit it; 3) that the defendant is innocent of the crime because

of insufficient evidence to convict him; 4) that there was no crime, because the defendant had a justification for his action (such as self-defence or necessity); or 5) that it was not possible to decide the case due to a procedural fault. A defendant can even appeal one acquittal to seek a stronger form of acquittal. *See* W. Pizzi, and L. Marafioti, 'The New Italian Code of Criminal Procedure: the Difficulties of Building an Adversarial Trial System on a Civil Law Foundation' (1992) 17 *Yale Journal of International Law* 1. A similar but less complex system exists in Scotland where verdicts include guilty, not guilty, and 'not proven'. See M. Smithson, S. Deady and L. Gracik, 'Guilty, Not Guilty, or ... ? Multiple Options in Jury Verdict Choices' (2007) 20 *Journal of Behavioral Decision Making* 481.

51 **'"... it is better that ten guilty persons escape than that one innocent suffers ..."'**: W. Blackstone, *Commentaries* (1966 reprint. London: Dawsons of Pall Mall, 1769), Book 4, Chapter 27, 352. Also see J. Widgery, 'The Balance of the Criminal Law Trial' [1972] NZLR 688.

52 **A conspiracy**: A conspiracy to commit an offence is itself an offence under section 558 of the *Criminal Code* (WA). There are also other specific conspiracy offences in the *Criminal Code*, such as conspiracy to defraud under section 412 (now repealed) and others such as sections 134, 338C.

53 **'... any oral or written statement made by one ... accused could not be admissible against the other ... "unless confirmed or adopted from the witness box by the maker of the statement"'**: The 'best evidence' rule provides in general terms that where available, oral testimony must be preferred to prior written statements (*Browne v Dunn* (1893) 6 R 67 (HL); *Jones v Dunkel* (1959) 101 CLR 298; *Butera v Director of Public Prosecutions (Vic)* (1987) 164 CLR 18). The adversarial context of the Australian criminal justice system is fundamentally based on the discovery of truth through examination and cross-examination of witnesses by opposing counsel. Similarly, the hearsay rule would also dictate that a prior statement made out of court could not be admitted as evidence to support the truth of the matters stated therein. See *Pollitt v R* (1992) 174 CLR 558; *Kamleh v R* (2005) 213 ALR 97; *Walton v R* (1989) 166 CLR 283. For a recent High Court decision on the issue of co-accuseds see *Bannon v R* (1995) 185 CLR 1.

54 **'... the judge warned the jury such evidence could not be used to show a propensity to commit the crimes ... but only as showing "some familiarity with the procedures that applied at the Mint when bullion was sold"'**: This was because of the operation of the evidentiary rule concerning 'similar fact evidence.' The rule states that the prosecution cannot adduce evidence of particular previous misconduct of the accused if that evidence shows that the accused had a tendency or propensity to engage in conduct of the kind in issue. See *Thompson v R* (1989) 169 CLR 1, 15 (Mason CJ and Dawson J). However, if the material is relevant in establishing an inference of the existence of another fact relevant in the proceedings (i.e. their 'familiarity with the procedures that applied at the Mint'), then it will be admissible and allowable as evidence to that extent (*Martin v Osborne* (1936) 55 CLR 367, 375; *Perry v R* (1982) 150 CLR 580; *Pfennig v R* (1995) 182 CLR 461).

55 '... **jury members "will ... be influenced ... by the impression that particular witness left upon you when giving evidence in the witness box"'**: In other words, credibility. See Chapter 2 note 28.

56 **The test for circumstantial evidence**: *McKinney v R* (1991) 171 CLR 468; *Plomp v R* (1963) 110 CLR 234.

57 '... **if the jury found that "the accused have told lies ... what weight can you give to the [accused's evidence] ... in relation to other matters?"'**: So-called 'Edwards lies' (from *Edwards v R* (1993) 178 CLR 193). Where the accused tells lies concerning important matters about an offence, it can be used as evidence to demonstrate an implied admission of a consciousness of guilt. See also G. Lyon and B. Walmsley, 'Consciousness of Guilt — The Use of Lies Told by the Accused' (1997) 71(11) *Law Institute Journal* 50; P. Young, 'Criminal Law — Use of Lies by the Accused' (1997) 71 *Australian Law Journal* 682; A. Palmer, 'Guilt & the Consciousness of Guilt' (1997) 21 *Melbourne University Law Review* 95; C. William, 'Lies as Evidence' (2005) 26 *Australian Bar Review* 313.

58 **Truthfulness of police officers**: See M. Kirby, 'Controls over Investigation of Offences and Pre-Trial Treatment of Suspects' (1979) 53 *Australian Law Journal* 626, 635; P. Grabowsky, *Wayward Governance: Illegality and its Control in the Public Sector* (Canberra: Australian Institute of Criminology, 1989), 284.

59 '... **they must treat eyewitness identification evidence carefully; frequently it is wrong and often has resulted in miscarriages of justices'**: See the discussion from the High Court in *Alexander v R* (1981) 145 CLR 395 and *Festa v R* (2001) 208 CLR 593. For a more extensive treatment of the subject, see G. Wells, A. Memon and S. Penrod, 'Eyewitness Evidence: Improving its Probative Value' (2006) 7 *Psychological Science in the Public Interest* 2.

60 '**This would be treating the identification evidence in the same way as circumstantial evidence, but due to the unreliability of identification evidence, this cannot be done'**: The leading High Court authority on this issue is *Festa v R* (2001) 208 CLR 593, an unsuccessful appeal claiming that breach of this rule had resulted in a miscarriage of justice. See also *AK v Western Australia* (2008) 232 CLR 438, 484 (Heydon J).

61 '**"... a fingerprint is, in effect, an unforgeable signature"'**: The traditional belief, and the belief at the time of the Mint swindle trial, was that a fingerprint was impossible to forge. This is typified by the statement of Griffith CJ in *Parker v R* (1912) 14 CLR 681, 683: 'Signatures have been accepted as evidence of identity as long as they have been used. The fact of the individuality of the corrugations of the skin on the fingers of the human hand is now so generally recognised as to require very little, if any, evidence of it, although it seems to be still the practice to offer some expert evidence on the point. A finger print is therefore in reality an unforgeable signature.' Today, the possibility of fingerprint forgery using modern techniques is an acceptable conceivability. See generally I. Freckleton and H. Selby, *Expert Evidence* (Sydney: Lawbook Co., 2005), Chapter 16 'Fingerprinting Evidence', 583–96.

62 '**"... are you agreed upon your verdicts?"'**: The jury's verdict must generally be unanimous. Currently in Western Australia, however, section 114 of the *Criminal Procedure Act 2004* (WA) modifies this procedure. A unanimous

verdict is still generally required, but in any case other than murder trials, if after three hours the jury has not arrived at a verdict, a decision of ten or more jurors will be sufficient for a conviction.

63 **Sentencing**: Once a guilty verdict has been reached, the accused is sentenced according to law. Currently in Western Australia, this is carried out under the *Sentencing Act 1995* (WA). Prior to this, sentencing was dealt with very generally under s.656 of the *Criminal Code* (WA). In general terms, within each relevant *Criminal Code* offence provision is included a statutory penalty (usually a set term of imprisonment). The trial judge then acts via a principled discretion to sentence the offender to any punishment up to that statutory period. Various factors would inform this discretion, these now set out more extensively in the *Sentencing Act 1995* (WA). Where an offender is convicted for multiple offences (such as in the Mint swindle), the judge may order that the respective sentences for each be served concurrently (together) or consecutively (added together). In this situation the overriding consideration is to impose a sentence which adequately reflects the 'true criminality' of the accused's misconduct (see *R v Nguyen* [2000] NSWSC 1177 (Unreported, Supreme Court of New South Wales, Whealy J, 15 December 2000), [43]; *R v Daley* (Unreported, Supreme Court of Victorian Court of Appeal, Winneke P, 20 February 1997), [5]; *Pearce v R* (1998) 194 CLR 610; *R v Crofts* [1999] 1 Qd R 356 cited by Steytler P in *Hapke v Western Australia* [2006] WASCA 188 (Unreported, Supreme Court Western Australia Court of Criminal Appeal, Steytler P, Roberts-Smith JA, Murray AJA, 25 September 2006), [2]. Also now see section 88 of the *Sentencing Act 1995* (WA)).

64 **The contemporary reaction to the Mickelberg sentences:** J. Odgers, 'Mickelberg terms "questioned"', *West Australian*, 26 March 1983, 5.

65 **'... he would have imposed lighter sentences if the Mickelbergs had revealed where the missing gold bullion was'**: See note 63. Matters influencing the exercise of the sentencing judge's discretion include any remorse shown by the accused (lack of which may indicate a greater need for deterrence: *Neal v R* (1982) 149 CLR 305, 315; *R v Pinder* (1992) 8 WAR 19, 37 (Murray J)) and the effect of the criminal misconduct on other parties, especially the victim (the Mint) (see *R v P* (1992) 39 FCR 276, *R v Webb* [1971] VR 147). The Mickelbergs' failure to reveal the location of the missing gold and/or return it to the Mint, would have (to the court) indicated a contempt for the justice system and have perpetuated the loss and damage sustained by the Mint (for the specific issue of reparation and its effect on sentence, see *R v Tran* (1998) 96 A Crim R 53; *R v Rowe* (1982) 7 A Crim R 39; and now section 110 of the *Sentencing Act 1995* (WA)). This is certainly correct in law, but the obvious problem is that if the Mickelbergs did not commit the crime, then returning the gold or revealing its location would have been impossible, and their sentence would have been increased, largely by reason of the wrongful conviction. Somewhat of a contradiction.

CHAPTER 4

66 **'... who loathed weakness':** During his initial interview with Hancock, Ray told him, 'I hate weakness. I loathe it. you know. I'd rather die than be treated weak.'

67 **'"... This has never deterred us nor shall it now"'**: A. Lovell, *The Mickelberg Stitch* (Perth: Creative Research, 1985) 262.

68 **Fremantle Prison**: See C. Ayris, *Fremantle Prison: A Brief History* (West Perth: Cyril Ayris Freelance, 1995).

69 **The Mickelbergs and Robert Walker**: See the actual conclusions reached by the commission in Commissioner L. F. Wyvill QC, 'Report of the Inquiry into the Death of Robert Joseph Walker', *Royal Commission into Aboriginal Deaths in Custody*, Australian Government Publishing Service, Canberra, 30 March 1991.

70 **'Ray and Peter had already commenced private prosecutions against several police officers ...'**: A private prosecution is a prosecution commenced by a private person, rather than the State Director of Public Prosecutions or other government bodies initiating the action. Currently, under sections 20, 80 and 83 of the *Civil Procedure Act 2004* (WA) a prosecution cannot be commenced by a private individual unless that person is specially appointed to do so by the Governor under section 182 of that act.

71 **Shirley Finn**: See for example a two-part special in the late 80s: H. Schmitt, '13-year riddle over slain vice queen', *Daily News,* 23 June 1988, 6–7; or more recently M. Ambrose, 'Cold Case', *Sunday Times (STM* section), 23 April 2006, 10–12.

72 **Royal commission**: An enquiry established under the *Royal Commissions Act 1968* (WA) empowering a commission with special powers to inquire into and report on a specific contentious matter.

73 **The 1975 Royal Commission Into Matters Surrounding the Administration of the Law Relating to Prostitution**: Commissioner J.G. Norris, *Report of the Royal Commission Into Matters Surrounding the Administration of the Law Relating to Prostitution*, Western Australian state government, Perth, June 1976 (the '1975 Royal Commission Report').

74 **Spike Daniels**: 1975 Royal Commission Report, 98.

75 **'The police did not allow working girls with criminal records and strictly enforced the rule that excluded men or criminal syndicates from the industry'**: 1975 Royal Commission Report, 18–22.

76 **'The Royal Commission also found Daniels' claims of police impropriety were unjustified'**: 1975 Royal Commission Report, 163–4.

77 **'However, the Commissioner was sceptical and made no adverse findings about the police'**: 1975 Royal Commission Report, 117–8.

78 **'... the 2004 Police Royal Commission'**: Commissioner G. Kennedy, *Final Report of the Royal Commission Into Whether There Has Been Corrupt Or Criminal Conduct By Any Western Australian Police Officer*, Volumes I and II, Western Australian state government, Perth, January 2004.

79 **'The 1982 report ...'**: O. Dixon, *The Report of O.F. Dixon on the Action Taken by the Police Regarding Allegations of Graft and Corruption within the Police Force and What Further Action is Necessary Regarding such Allegations*, Western Australian state government, Perth, 24 March 1982 (the '1982 Report').

80 **'... the article reported that "two senior policemen have resigned after inquiries into allegations of protection payments by prostitutes"'**: The article was front-page of the *Western Mail* on 24 December 1981 in an article titled: 'Police Quit after Claims of Payoffs'. These allegations were reported in the 1982 Report, 25.

81 '**... both men resigned immediately'**: 1982 Report, 27–9.

82 '**... including two made by Tangney and Butler:** 1982 Report, 33.

83 ibid., 74–5.

84 ibid., 22.

85 ibid., 75.

86 ibid., 40–41.

87 '**... the Dixon report ... could not reach any positive conclusion about corruption'**: The 1982 Report, 78–9.

88 '**It concluded that the Police Commissioner ... had not attempted to "cover up" anything'**: The 1982 Report, 83.

89 '**In 2005 the police announced they would reopen the Shirley Finn case'**: J. Kelly, '"No Hope" in Finn Case', *Sunday Times,* 26 June 2005, 29.

90 **Sir Francis 'Red' Burt**: The Constitutional Centre of Western Australia, 'Sir Francis Theodore Page Burt 1990–1993' available at http://www.ccentre. wa.gov.au/index.cfm?event=governorsFrancisburt.

91 **Sir Ronald Wilson**: See A. Buti, *A Matter of Conscience: Sir Ronald Wilson* (Crawley: University of Western Australia Press, 2007).

92 **Peter's 1983 appeal**: *Peter Mickelberg v R* (Unreported, Western Australian Court of Criminal Appeal, Burt CJ, Brinsden and Smith JJ, 4 November 1983).

93 '**"... ought not result in a duplication of penalty"'**: See Chapter 3 note 63. Duplication of penalty essentially connotes double punishment for the same offence. To reflect the true criminality of criminal misconduct the court must avoid doubly punishing an offender, which may be an issue where convictions are made for multiple offences. Similar considerations inform the rule against 'double jeopardy' – see *Pearce v R* (1998) 194 CLR 610.

94 '**This ... sentence ... the Chief Justice did not view as "excessive ..."'**: The appeal against sentence was pursuant to section 689 *Criminal Code* (WA). To appeal against a sentence, the appellant must show that the sentence imposed by the trial judge was 'manifestly excessive' (*Ryan v R* (2001) 206 CLR 267; *Lowe v R* (1984) 154 CLR 606; *AB v R* (1999) 198 CLR 111; *Urquhart v R* (Unreported, Western Australian Court of Criminal Appeal, Malcolm CJ, Franklyn and Walsh JJ, 13 September 1995). Now see ss.23(1)(b) and 31(4) of the *Criminal Appeals Act 2004* (WA)).

95 '**Ray ... lodged his appeal against his conviction out of time'**: Under the *Criminal Code* (WA) section 695 as amended by section 5 of the *Criminal Code Amendment Act 1975* (WA), Ray was required to lodge his appeal within twenty-one days of conviction.

96 '**The CCA did hear [Ray's] appeal against the length of his sentence ... but ... he was unsuccessful'**: *Raymond Mickelberg v R* (Unreported, Western Australian Court of Criminal Appeal, Burt CJ, Brinsden and Smith JJ, 4 November 1983).

97 '**... a two–one decision'**: Under section 62 of the *Supreme Court Act 1935* (WA) where proceedings are heard by more than one justice, the question is decided according to the decision of the majority.

98 **Brian's appeal**: *Brian Mickelberg v R* [1984] WAR 191.

99 *Tumahole Bereng v R*: [1949] AC 253, 270. For more on the effect of out-of-court lies ('Edwards lies') see Chapter 3 note 57.

100 **'The transfer was never registered. This means that ... Brian's interest in the family home had not legally transferred to his wife'**: The Torrens system of land registration was established in Western Australia by the *Transfer of Land Act 1893* (WA).

101 **Chief Justice Burt on the trial judge's directions**: For directions and summing-up see Chapter 3 note 49. Chief Justice Burt at 203 referred to the following passage from Justice Dixon in *Mckay v R* (1935) 54 CLR 1, 10: 'Even if confessional evidence might appear sufficient to submit to a jury, yet a conviction would doubtless be quashed if it appeared that the jury had been allowed or encouraged to act upon views of it which are unsafe. It is conceivable that a direction to a jury that they might convict, although they were unable to find confirmatory evidence, or to accept it, might in some circumstances have this result.'

102 **'... quashed the conviction'**: Where a guilty verdict is set aside by a superior court on appeal, nullifying the conviction.

103 **'dissenting judgment'**: A 'dissenting judgment' is a judge's decision that is in the minority (and therefore not to be followed).

104 *Plomp v R*: (1963) 110 CLR 234, 247.

105 **Brian's release**: R. Gibson, 'Prisoners Cheer One of their Departed', *West Australian*, 5 November 1983, 1.

106 **'... Ray and Peter stood a far better chance of securing release through a retrial than by relying on an appeal ...'**: This is because the evidential and procedural rules are different in an appeal to a retrial. In an appeal, the court decides simply whether the trial judge made a mistake on a question of law, the jury's decision could not be supported by the evidence, or whether the sentence was manifestly excessive or inadequate. It does not 're-try' the matter, which can cause difficulty for appellants where the allegations of misconduct infect significant aspects of the original trial. In a retrial the court retries the matter, taking the evidence again (including oral evidence) and a new judge or jury decides the matter. In a retrial, unfairness arising from defects in the original trial can be avoided. See for example section 39 of the *Criminal Appeals Act 2004* (WA).

CHAPTER 5

107 **Peter's 1984 appeal:** *Peter Mickelberg v R* (Unreported, Western Australian Court of Criminal Appeal, Wallace, Smith and Rowland JJ, 2 April 1984).

108 **The Yellow Rose of Texas**: For an extensive coverage of these events see A. Lovell, *The Mickelberg Stitch* (Perth: Creative Research, 1985), Chapter 15 'The Yellow Rose of Texas', 169–78.

109 **'... 31 August 1984, the CCA in a two–one majority decision reduced the sentences of Ray, Peter and Pozzi'**: *Raymond John Mickelberg, Peter Mickelberg and Brian Ronald Pozzi v R* (1984) 13 A Crim R 365.

110 **'[The]** *West Australian* **... was running a major news feature'**: See B. Howlett, 'Book Questions Key Evidence: Police Launch Inquiry into Mickelberg Trial', *West Australian*, 2 March 1985, 3.

111 '... "one of the slickest operations I'd ever heard of in the book industry"': A. Lovell, *Split Image: International Mystery of the Mickelberg Affair* (Perth: Creative Research, 1990), 61.

112 **The Mickelberg Stitch:** A. Lovell, *The Mickelberg Stitch* (Perth: Creative Research, 1985).

113 **'Book on Mickelbergs removed from sale':** R. Wainright and S. Faull, 'Book on Mickelbergs removed from sale', *West Australian*, 9 March 1985, 1.

114 **'Some booksellers continued to sell it by ingenious methods':** A. Lovell, *Split Image: International Mystery of the Mickelberg Affair* (Perth: Creative Research, 1990), 66.

115 **'... Quigley served the injunction on Lovell':** For this anecdote see A. Lovell, *Split Image: International Mystery of the Mickelberg Affair* (Perth: Creative Research, 1990), 70. An injunction is a court order obtained upon an application by a party restraining them from doing, or forcing them to do, a particular act. A failure to comply with the terms of an injunction is a contempt of court.

116 **The April 1985 injunction**: A. Lovell, *Split Image: International Mystery of the Mickelberg Affair* (Perth: Creative Research, 1990), 75.

117 **'The injunction remained in force until October 1985 when, after Lovell appealed to the court, Justices Olney and Kennedy, with Justice Wallace dissenting ... lifted it'**: *Lovell v Lewandowski* [1987] WAR 81. The majority held that there were no exceptional circumstances before them that would justify a continuation of the injunction and that the issues of whether the material was defamatory or whether the defences of justification and fair comment applied were to be determined at trial. In dissenting, Justice Wallace held exceptional circumstances were present because on the facts a jury had already made a determination of the appellant's arguments beyond reasonable doubt (at the 1983 Mickelberg trial) 'and that it was not in the public interest that a convicted person should be able to make serious allegations against his investigators to the effect that they fabricated evidence or committed perjury in order to have another trial when all those matters had received a jury's prior attention.'

118 **'Police officers filed defamation suits against Lovell, Thomas and some of the retailers':** For the litany of litigation during this period, see A. Lovell, *Split Image: International Mystery of the Mickelberg Affair* (Perth: Creative Research, 1990), 63–83 and Chapter 25 'Litany of Lies', 325–329. Also see *Billing v Lovell* (Unreported, Supreme Court of Western Australia, Nicholson J, 1 December 1988); *Lovell v McKechnie* (Unreported, Supreme Court of Western Australia, 3 August 1989, Ipp J); *Lewandowski v Myer WA Stores Ltd* (Unreported, Supreme Court of Western Australia, Staples M, 8 September 1989); *Lovell v Parker and Parker, Sunday Times, Kenneth Martin and Donald Smith* (Unreported, Supreme Court of Western Australia, Staples M, 21 December 1989); *Billing v Thomas* (Unreported, Supreme Court of Western Australia, Ng M, 19 January 1990); *Lovell v Western Australian Police Union of Workers* (Unreported, Supreme Court of Western Australia, White M, 20 December 1990); *Lewandowski v Lovell* (Unreported, Supreme Court of Western Australia, Adams M, 11 February 1992); *Lewandowski v Lovell* (Unreported, Supreme Court of Western

Australia, Adams M, 13 May 1992); *Lewandowski v Lovell* (Unreported, Supreme Court of Western Australia, Adams M, 19 June 1992); *Lewandowski v Lovell* (Unreported, Supreme Court of Western Australia, Walsh, Murray and Owen JJ, 23 July 1992); *Lovell v Western Australian Police Union of Workers* (Unreported, Supreme Court of Western Australia, Hawkins M, 20 November 1992); *Lewandowski v Lovell* (Unreported, Supreme Court of Western Australia, Kennedy J, 8 March 1993); *Lewandowski v Lovell* (Unreported, Supreme Court of Western Australia, Adams M, 29 November 1993); *Lovell v Hancock* (Unreported, Supreme Court of Western Australia, Adams M, 21 December 1993); *Lewandowski v Lovell* (Unreported, Supreme Court of Western Australia, Kennedy J, 8 March 1994); *Lewandowski v Lovell* (1994) 11 WAR 124; *Lewandowski v Lovell* (Unreported, Supreme Court of Western Australia, 22 April 1994, Bredmeyer M); *Lovell v Western Australian Police Union of Workers* (Unreported, Supreme Court of Western Australia, Adams M, 19 August 1994); *Lewandowski v Lovell* (1995) 13 WAR 468; *Lewandowski v Lovell* (Unreported, Supreme Court of Western Australia, Adams M, 14 April 1995; *Lewandowski v Lovell* (Unreported, Supreme Court of Western Australia, Steytler J, 27 May 1996); *Lewandowski v Lovell (No 2)* (Unreported, Supreme Court of Western Australia, Kennedy, Murray and White JJ, 14 June 1996); *Lewandowski v Lovell* (Unreported, Supreme Court of Western Australia, Murray J, 9 August 1996); *Lovell v Western Australian Police Union of Workers* [2004] WASC 19 (Unreported, Supreme Court of Western Australia, Sanderson M, 17 February 2004); *Lewandowski v Lovell* [2006] WASCA 54 (Unreported, Supreme Court Western Australia Court of Criminal Appeal, Wheeler, Roberts-Smith and Pullin JJA, 31 March 2006); *Lovell v Western Australian Police Union of Workers* [2009] WASCA 34 (Unreported, Supreme Court Western Australia Court of Criminal Appeal, Steytler P, Owen and Pullin JJA, 9 December 2008).

The *Lovell v Lewandowski* [1987] WAR 81 decision has become a particularly important precedent in the context of interlocutory injunctions. An interlocutory injunction is a court order requiring a person either do or refrain from doing a certain thing. Failure to do so can be contempt of court. *Lovell v Lewandowski* stands for the proposition that where an interlocutory injunction is sought in the context of an alleged defamatory statement, it will not succeed if the defendant (i.e. Lovell here) can show a case for justification (here, a claim of truth). This proposition has been extrapolated generally to provide that in all contexts the power of a court to grant an interlocutory injunction will only be exercised with caution and in clear cases. In the defamatory context for example, only where the words are clearly defamatory and where irreparable injury would result. The court cited and approved *Church of Scientology of California Inc v Reader's Digest Services Pty Ltd* [1980] 1 NSWLR 344, 349–50 (Hunt J). See also *Chappell v TCN Channel Nine Pty Ltd* (1988) 14 NSWLR 153; *Australian Broadcasting Corporation v O'Neill* (2006) 227 CLR 57; *Edith Cowan University Student Guild v Edith Cowan University* [2004] WASC 83 (Unreported, Supreme Court of Western Australia, McKechnie J, 3 May 2004).

119 **'The Police Union bankrolled the legal action by imposing a special levy of $1 per pay from union members':** See for instance *Lovell v Western Australian Police Union of Workers* (Unreported, Supreme Court of Western Australia, White M, 20 December 1990); *Lovell v Western Australian Police*

Union of Workers [2004] WASC 19 (Unreported, Supreme Court of Western Australia, Sanderson M, 17 February 2004); *Lovell v Western Australian Police Union of Workers* [2009] WASCA 34 (Unreported, Supreme Court Western Australia Court of Criminal Appeal, Steytler P, Owen and Pullin JJA, 9 December 2008).

120 **'The police announced they would conduct an inquiry not only into the allegations Lovell made in *The Mickelberg Stitch*, but also into those made by other people involved in producing and distributing the book'**: B. Howlett, 'Police Launch Inquiry into Mickelberg Trial', *West Australian*, 2 March 1985, 3.

121 **'Police Commissioner Brian Bull even publicly announced the police were contemplating bringing criminal charges against Lovell'**: A. Lovell, *Split Image: International Mystery of the Mickelberg Affair* (Perth: Creative Research, 1990), 78–80.

122 **'... the *West Australian* reported that state government inquiries (led by the Crown Law Department) had found no substance in the allegation of forged fingerprints'**: P. McGeough, 'Mickelberg Prints Case Rejected', *West Australian*, 5 July 1985, 1.

123 **The CIB in Moorine Rock**: For this anecdote see J. Hammond, 'Letter to MP Precipitates a Call from CIB', *Merredin Telegraph*, 19 June 1985.

124 **Brian's death:** For a detailed coverage see A. Lovell, *Split Image: International Mystery of the Mickelberg Affair* (Perth: Creative Research, 1990) Chapter 17 'The Death of Brian Mickelberg', 201–209. Another informative source on this tragic event can be found in *Mickelberg v Aerodata Holding Ltd* [2002] WASCA 80 (Unreported, Supreme Court Western Australia Court of Criminal Appeal, Malcolm CJ, Anderson and Steytler JJ, 10 April 2002). After the accident, Faye Mickelberg instigated civil action, under the *Fatal Accidents Act 1959* (WA) against Brian's employer, Aerodata Holdings Ltd, and AGA, the company that serviced the aircraft. She argued that the crash was caused by their negligence and breach of statutory duty. She was unsuccessful at trial in the District Court but on appeal to the Supreme Court sixteen years later she was partly successful, with the court holding that AGA were partially to blame for the accident (along with Brian). The Court held that sixty per cent of the responsibility for the crash should rest with Brian and forty per cent with AGA. The Court found that the Chief Engineer of AGA should not have issued a maintenance release because the fuel gauge was faulty but that Brian was also contributory negligent for his own death because he should not have relied solely on the maintenance release. He 'should have taken other steps, or been more careful in taking other steps, to ensure that the aircraft had adequate fuel for his intended flight, that having been his personal responsibility.'

CHAPTER 6

125 **Desmond Dawson and the Mint swindle gold**: Scottish fingerprint expert Malcolm Thompson, who had been contacted by the Mickelberg committee to provide expert evidence in the 1987 appeals, had been approached by Douglas while attending a conference in Los Angeles in September 1985. Thompson then wrote to Boase about the approach by Douglas. See further

A. Lovell, *Split Image: International Mystery of the Mickelberg Affair* (Perth: Creative Research, 1990), 210–6.

126 '**... section 21 of the *Criminal Code 1913* (WA)'**: An application to the Attorney-General's prerogative of mercy. That provision gave the Attorney-General the discretion to refer an entire case or a particular issue to the Supreme Court Western Australia Court of Criminal Appeal for determination. Now see Part 19 of the *Sentencing Act 1995* (WA).

127 **Ray and Peter's grounds of appeal**: Ray had eight grounds of appeal. Peter's appeal practically repeated seven of these and added another seven grounds, making fourteen grounds of appeal for Peter. They are set out at length in Olney J's judgment at 3–10.

The Fingerprint Evidence: Ray's first six grounds, and Peter's first five, concerned the alleged fingerprint evidence incriminating Ray (the 'crime mark'). Ray and Peter alleged that the trial judge erred both when telling the jury that a 'fingerprint is, in effect, an unforgeable signature' and that there was no evidence that Raymond's fingerprint was available to the police officers on the 24 June 1982. Ray and Peter also raised fresh evidence showing that a fingerprint is not an unforgeable signature, that the police did have access to Ray's prints prior to the 15 July 1982, that the crime mark was consistent with being implanted via silicone replica, and that it could not be scientifically proven as genuine. Ray and Peter relied upon expert evidence from Reginald King, Malcolm Thomson, George Bonebrake, Harold Tuthill and Robert Olsen.

The Photo-fit Evidence: Peter's grounds six and seven alleged that Exhibit 21 (the photofit drawing) was not constructed by the method alleged but from a passport photograph of Peter. He further argued that it should never have been admitted as evidence because no witness identified Peter as the man depicted in it. Ray's seventh ground similarly raised fresh evidence that 'wholly changed the significance of [the photofit sketch].' Both relied upon expert evidence from Wilfred Ryan, James Proven, Jean Shepherd, Graham Davies and John Domingo.

Inconsistency with Brian's Acquittal: Peter's eighth and ninth grounds of appeal claimed that his conspiracy conviction was 'inconsistent' with Brian's acquittal in *Brian Mickelberg v R* [1984] WAR 191 (see further Chapter 7 note 171).

New Evidence: Peter's tenth ground of appeal identified a preponderance of new evidence (for the distinction between new and fresh evidence see note 134) which established a miscarriage of justice, including:

• Peter's secret tape. See note 148.

• Evidence that Peter's solicitor Ron Cannon had prior to the Mint swindle trial appeared for a possible alternate suspect (Arpad Security Agency Pty Ltd) and an investigating police officer (Andrew Tovey). See note 137.

• Evidence from Pauline Lee, Wendy Baker and Betty Rebakis about Peter's occupancy of Unit 7, 112 Rupert Street, Subiaco.

• Evidence from expert Geoffrey Roberts that the 'Talbot note' could not be proven beyond reasonable doubt to have been written by Peter.

• Evidence from Grant Carroll and Mr and Mrs Stacey confirming Peter's alibi.

Exhibits 23 and 78: Peter's eleventh ground of appeal alleged that the trial judge erred when admitting into evidence Exhibits 23 and 78. Exhibit 23 consisted of three pictures; on the left was a black and white passport photo of Peter Mickelberg and in the centre and on the right was this photo overlaid with pictorial representations of the hair and glasses of the suspect as constructed by police assisted by Mr and Mrs Allen. Exhibit 78 was a single copy of the third picture. Peter argued that this approach was contrary to the best evidence rule which required eyewitnesses give evidence orally (see Chapter 3 note 53).

Peter's Prior Conviction: Peter's twelfth ground of appeal alleged that the judge erred in not discharging the jury when the Crown displayed Peter's prior criminal conviction for possession of an unlicensed firearm (see Chapter 2 note 25).

Police Fabrication: Peter's thirteenth ground of appeal claimed that fresh evidence showed that the police had fabricated evidence. Evidence from Arthur Walsh and Bill Barrett was relied upon.

An Unsafe and Unsatisfactory Verdict: The last ground of appeal for both Ray and Peter was a general catch-all claim that 'in all the circumstances the verdict of the jury was unsafe and unsatisfactory.'

128 **'... the impressive list of forensic experts that Lovell and Boase were able to gather'**: For an extensive coverage on these happenings see A. Lovell, Split Image: International Mystery of the Mickelberg Affair (Perth: Creative Research, 1990), chapters 7–8, 10–11, 13, 19–21.

129 **The affidavits**: An affidavit is sworn evidence given in written form. The issue with Avon Lovell and Tim Boase's practices here is that an affidavit is supposed to be a witness's own statement of what they perceived and believed. Nevertheless, it was and still is a common practice for lawyers to prepare affidavits for their clients and Boase and Lovell's conduct was not illegal or fraudulent.

130 **'The Perth trip was off'**: For this anecdote see A. Lovell, *Split Image: International Mystery of the Mickelberg Affair* (Perth: Creative Research, 1990), 124–33.

131 **The Crown's legal team**: The Crown was also assisted by M. Mischin and other solicitors from the Crown Law Department from time to time.

132 **Justice Wallace**: Justice Wallace was a graduate of the University of Melbourne. When he came to Perth he entered the partnership of Kott Wallace which later became Kott Wallace and Gunning. He was appointed to the Supreme Court of Western Australia in 1972.

133 **'... Peter's 1983 appeal'**: *Peter Mickelberg v R* (Unreported, Western Australian Court of Criminal Appeal, Wallace, Smith and Rowland JJ, 2 April 1984).

134 **Fresh evidence**: Ordinarily an appeal court will only decide an appeal on the basis of evidence already given at trial. The court will decide, in the light of that evidence, whether the decision of the trial court was incorrect. In addition, the appellant can introduce 'fresh', but not merely 'new' evidence, to show that the decision should have been different. The distinction between fresh and new evidence is that while both are types of evidence that were *not* lead at the original trial, fresh evidence is evidence that could not

have been discovered by the appellant with reasonable diligence (*Gallagher v R* (1986) 160 CLR 392). This would be the case where, for example, the evidence either did not exist or had not been disclosed by the prosecution prior to the original trial. 'New' evidence is the corollary of this test, being evidence that could have been discovered with reasonable diligence prior to the original trial (and therefore evidence that was reasonably available to the appellant at trial but whose use was decided against), and cannot be used as evidence in an appeal. This rule is not a 'hard and fast' rule: *Re Knowles* [1984] VR 751; *Green v R* (1938) 61 CLR 167. See generally *Mickelberg v R* (1989) 167 CLR 259; *Mallard v R* (2003) 28 WAR 1, *Mallard v R* (2005) 224 CLR 125.

135 **'Normally the bench decides appeals entirely on legal argument, without witnesses appearing in person'**: Again, the essence of an appeal is the decision of whether the original trial was affected by some error in, or wrongful decision concerning, on behalf of the trial judge on the evidence that was admitted at the original trial. As such, there is usually no need to hear any oral evidence from witnesses. This will only usually occur where the relevant witnesses have some 'fresh' evidence to give with respect to the matter. This special power of the court to take oral evidence on appeal was set out in paragraph 697(b) of the *Criminal Code* (WA). Now see paragraphs 40(1)(b) and (c) of the *Criminal Appeals Act 2004* (WA).

136 **'MINT SWINDLE: SECURITY FIRM ACCUSED'**: G. Williams, 'Mint swindle: Security Firm Accused', *Daily News*, 25 August 1983, 1. Also see *Mickelberg v R* (Unreported, Supreme Court of Western Australia, Wallace, Olney and Pidgeon JJ, 18 November 1987), 47–8 (Wallace J), 58–60 (Olney J).

137 **'It puts "Mr Cannon in a conflict of duty and interest of the most extraordinary degree"'**: One of Peter's original grounds of appeal was that Cannon had been neglectful in the defence of his case at trial. While this original ground of appeal was withdrawn, two of Peter's grounds, grounds 10(b) and (c) still involved Cannon's conduct at trial:

'Ground 10: There is new evidence which establishes that there has been a miscarriage of justice:

Evidence that Mr. Cannon the Petitioner's instructing solicitor appeared for Arpad Security Agency Pty Ltd and Arpad Lazlo Bacskai on or about 20th July 1982 in the Court of Petty Sessions, Perth in relation to charges of exceeding the terms of their security licence in relation to the disappearance of $250,000.00 of gold from a TAA flight on 11th June 1982; and

Evidence that Mr. Cannon was at the time of acting for Peter Mickelberg, acting for one of the police officers (Det. Sgt. Andrew Tovey) involved in the prosecution of the accused and, according to the instructions of the accused Peter Mickelberg, the said Det. Sgt. Tovey lied on his oath and concocted admissions by Peter Mickelberg.'

Lawyers have a duty to their clients not to act with a conflict of interest. Clearly, if Cannon acted on other occasions for a possible alternate suspect, or an investigating police officer, his ongoing interest in the protection of their interests may have been in conflict with his duty to act diligently and most effectively for Peter. If a conflict of interest were established, it may have been a ground for finding that a substantial miscarriage of justice had resulted, requiring the court to set aside the conviction. See *Blackwell v Barroile Pty Ltd* (1994) 51 FCR 347; *Commonwealth Bank of Australia v Smith* (1991) 42 FCR 390; *Stewart v Layton (t/as B M Salmon Layton & Co.)* (1992) 111 ALR 687.

138 **James Proven's evidence**: James Proven's evidence is set out in the transcript of proceedings at 219–351. For the court's opinion of his evidence, see *Raymond Mickelberg v R*; *Peter Mickelberg v R* (Unreported, Supreme Court of Western Australia, Wallace, Olney and Pidgeon JJ, 18 November 1987), 42–3 (Wallace J), 27–9 (Pidgeon J), 43 (Olney J). Proven gave evidence that he had compared an enlargement of the photofit sketch with Peter's passport photograph. He was of the opinion that the strong similarities between them meant that it was 'highly improbable' that the photofit sketch had been based entirely on a verbal description using the Penry photofit facility. The justices found that Exhibit 21 had simply not 'purported to be a photofit construction by the Penry photofit method' and as such Proven's evidence was therefore largely based upon 'incomplete and largely incorrect information.' Olney J also mentioned that Proven's evidence was 'unconvincing and lacked objectivity.' Wallace J considered that Proven, who had no past experience with sketching, had no 'relevant qualification' and that his credibility was 'completely destroyed' when his evidence was compared with the evidence of another Crown witness, Wilfred Ryan. Although Wallace J suggested that the sketch did *not* 'bear a likeness' to Peter, he stated that this was not 'in issue.' The real purpose of the allegation relating to the sketch was, according to Wallace J, to demonstrate police *mala fides* (bad faith) and for this purpose the appellant's arguments failed.

139 **Donald Cherry's Evidence**: Donald Cherry's evidence is set out in the transcript of proceedings at 48–215. For the court's opinion of his evidence, see *Raymond Mickelberg v R*; *Peter Mickelberg v R* (Unreported, Supreme Court of Western Australia, Wallace, Olney and Pidgeon JJ, 18 November 1987), 41–2 (Wallace J), 21–6, 29 (Pidgeon J), 43 (Olney J). Cherry's evidence was very similar to that of James Proven (see note 138). Excerpts from his affidavit outlining his findings are set out in Pidgeon J judgment (at 25–26). The justices treated Cherry's evidence very much like that of Proven's. Wallace J added that Cherry lacked experience with photofit systems and he could not therefore accept Cherry's evidence and emphasised that Henry was 'obviously an observant person.' Pidgeon J emphasised that, according to police, no passport photograph of Peter was ever seized during the investigation.

140 **Kenneth Pierce's evidence**: Kenneth Pierce's evidence is set out in the transcript of proceedings at 357–550. For the court's opinion of his evidence, see *Raymond Mickelberg v R*; *Peter Mickelberg v R* (Unreported, Supreme Court of Western Australia, Wallace, Olney and Pidgeon JJ, 18 November 1987), 40–3 (Wallace J), 18–30 (Pidgeon J), 43–8 (Olney J). Pierce was the police officer who made the photofit sketch as a synthesis of the descriptions given by the Allens and Henry on the 25 and 26 of June 1982. Pierce gave evidence that he had constructed the photofit sketch using the description given by the witnesses and that no photograph was ever present. Henry also gave evidence to this effect. Pidgeon J described Pierce as 'an impressive witness' who was honest and sincere.

141 **George Bonebrake's evidence**: George Bonebrake's evidence is set out in the transcript of proceedings at 1086–1149. For the court's opinion of his evidence, see *Raymond Mickelberg v R*; *Peter Mickelberg v R* (Unreported, Supreme Court of Western Australia, Wallace, Olney and Pidgeon JJ, 18 November 1987), 33–4 (Wallace J). When giving evidence Bonebrake at first expressed an opinion that 'the latent fingerprint on the cheque is consistent with a latent fingerprint made using a silicone finger and is not consistent with the fingerprint made by Raymond John Mickelberg on the fingerprint card, which appears as part of the charted enlargements, or with the series of inked fingerprints furnished by Mr. Boase.' After extensive questioning however Bonebrake recanted: 'on a review of the material made available to me it cannot be determined with any degree of accuracy whether the latent fingerprint on the check was made by the actual finger or a silicone finger.' Wallace J emphasised that the material provided to the witness (and to Olsen, Tuthill, Thomson and King) by the appellants was of inferior quality and that the witness seemed to have been 'influenced by the information provided by the appellants' supporters.' The main issue was that the appellants' experts had failed to 'approach their examination of the document devoid of ... extraneous knowledge as the police's alleged possession of silicone rubber replicas.'

142 **Robert Olsen's evidence**: Robert Olsen's evidence is set out in the transcript of proceedings at 1150–84. For the court's opinion of his evidence, see *Raymond Mickelberg v R*; *Peter Mickelberg v R* (Unreported, Supreme Court of Western Australia, Wallace, Olney and Pidgeon JJ, 18 November 1987), 34 (Wallace J). Olsen gave evidence very much like that of Bonebrake (see note 141 above), suggesting that the crime mark may have been a forgery. Accordingly, the court dealt with Olsen's evidence similarly. They viewed his objectivity as compromised by the appellants' supporters' suggestions of forgery via silicone replica prior to his analysis. Wallace commended Olsen for being 'honest and courageous enough to finally express the opinion that he was unable to tell whether the crime mark was a forgery and therefore it should be viewed as genuine.'

143 **Malcolm Thomson's evidence**: Malcolm Thomson's evidence is set out in the transcript of proceedings at 1003–86. For the court's opinion of his evidence, see *Raymond Mickelberg v R*; *Peter Mickelberg v R* (Unreported, Supreme Court of Western Australia, Wallace, Olney and Pidgeon JJ, 18 November 1987), 32–3 (Wallace J). Thomson gave evidence similar to that of Bonebrake and Olsen (see notes above) and the court treated it similarly.

144 **Harold Tuthill's evidence**: Harold Tuthill's evidence is set out in the transcript of proceedings at 794–860. For the court's opinion of his evidence, see *Raymond Mickelberg v R*; *Peter Mickelberg v R* (Unreported, Supreme Court of Western Australia, Wallace, Olney and Pidgeon JJ, 18 November 1987), 32–3 (Wallace J). Tuthill's evidence was similar to, and was dealt with very much like that of Olsen, Bonebrake and Thomson. However, Tuthill had also expressed the opinion that 'had the cheque come to him without knowledge of the possible use of a rubber finger the only thing that would have led him to be suspicious was the position of the crime mark on the back of the cheque.' The position of the crime mark on the back of the cheque was suspicious, but Wallace J found that the 'position[ing] of the crime mark [itself] cannot be the subject of expert evidence.'

145 **Reginald King's evidence:** Reginald King's evidence is set out in the transcript of proceedings at 860–990. For the court's opinion of his evidence, see *Raymond Mickelberg v R*; *Peter Mickelberg v R* (Unreported, Supreme Court of Western Australia, Wallace, Olney and Pidgeon JJ, 18 November 1987), 31–3 (Wallace J). King's evidence was to the same effect as Olsen, Bonebrake, Thomson and Tuthill (see notes above) and the court was similarly dismissive of his opinion. Like Tuthill, King thought that the position of the crime mark was suspicious, but this could not be the subject of 'expert' evidence.

146 **Arthur Walsh's evidence:** Arthur Walsh's evidence is set out in the transcript of proceedings at 1197–1210. For the court's opinion of his evidence, see *Raymond Mickelberg v R*; *Peter Mickelberg v R* (Unreported, Supreme Court of Western Australia, Wallace, Olney and Pidgeon JJ, 18 November 1987), 51–2 (Wallace J), 70–75 (Olney J). Walsh testified that on 16 July 1987 he met Lewandowski at Ogilvie's Tavern in Applecross and that the latter made statements to the effect that he and Hancock had 'stitched up' the Mickelbergs. Olney J particularly emphasised that Walsh did not impress in the witness box and that his background was questionable.

147 **The Talbot note:** The Talbot note read 'Robert Talbot C/o Meekatharra Post Office, Meekatharra'. This note was admitted into evidence at the Mint swindle trial (Exhibit 20) and opinion was heard from handwriting expert Sergeant Edward Billing to the effect that Peter had written the note and was therefore involved in the Mint swindle. The evidence of Geoffrey Roberts, John Gregory and Edward Billing is set out in the transcript of proceedings at 1346–5, 1992–2000 and 689–772 respectively. For the court's opinion on the Talbot note and the evidence of these experts see *Raymond Mickelberg v R*; *Peter Mickelberg v R* (Unreported, Supreme Court of Western Australia, Wallace, Olney and Pidgeon JJ, 18 November 1987), 49–51 (Wallace J), 36–42 (Olney J), 36–7 (Pidgeon J).

148 **Peter's secret tape:** The court gave little weight to the tape recording because it was not 'fresh evidence'. It was merely 'new evidence' that was available at trial that counsel elected not to use. See *Raymond Mickelberg v R*; *Peter Mickelberg v R* (Unreported, Supreme Court of Western Australia, Wallace, Olney and Pidgeon JJ, 18 November 1987), 46–7 (Wallace J), 57–8 (Olney J). During the brothers' 2003 appeal, the media had a field-day about the 'Hancock Tape', as it would later be known, despite it playing a relatively minor role: see 'Tape key to Mint appeal', *The Australian,* 5 December 2003, cf. *Mickelberg v R* [2004] WASCA 145 (Unreported, Supreme Court of Western Australia Court of Appeal, Malcolm CJ, Murray & Steytler JJ, 2 July 2004).

149 **Legal professional privilege:** Evidence of a confidential communication between a client and legal adviser may be refused to be admitted as evidence in court without the client's consent if the communication was made for the dominant purpose of the client obtaining legal advice or assistance, or with reference to actual or contemplated judicial proceedings. See *Grant v Downs* (1976) 135 CLR 674.

150 **The Queensland royal commission:** Commissioner T. Fitzgerald, *Report of a Commission of Inquiry Pursuant to Orders in Council,* Commission of Inquiry into Possible Illegal Activities and Associated Police Misconduct, Queensland state government, Brisbane, July 1989.

151 **'Faces of dashed hope'**: M. Lang, 'Faces of Dashed Hope', *West Australian*, 19 November 1987, 1, 3.

152 **Brian Bull's statements**: ibid.

CHAPTER 7

153 **'A police officer charged with stealing government stores complained that the officers from the Internal Investigation Unit had verballed him, fabricating a confession to a crime'**: S. Menegola, 'Statement made up: inspector', *West Australian*, 21 April 1988, 9.

154 **'... one of six detectives on trial for assault and conspiracy admitted inventing a statement he attributed to a man who police were questioning about stolen property'**: R. Gibson, 'Crime confession false, says officer', *West Australian*, 24 May 1988, 6.

155 **'... two officers — aka the "Water Torture Cops" — were gaoled for punching and kneeing a suspect, and placing his head and left hand under boiling water from a coffee urn'**: T. Barrass, 'Torture case pair are free', *Sunday Times*, 23 April 1989, 13.

156 **Ray's letter to the *Sunday Times***: Anonymous, 'Gold swindler supports police', *Sunday Times*, 23 April 1989, 13. The letter was published alongside the article on the 'water torture cops' (see note 155).

157 **'A 1989 *Sunday Times* editorial ...'**: Editorial, 'Justice seen to be not done', *Sunday Times*, 28 May 1989, 44.

158 **Chief Justice David Malcolm's appointment**: This was a rare event. Malcolm, born in Bunbury in 1938, and a graduate of UWA and Oxford University, 'was the first Chief Justice for a hundred years appointed directly to the office of Chief Justice from the Bar rather than from the Supreme Court Bench ... '. Refer to G. Bolton and G. Byrne, *May it Please Your Honour: A History of the Supreme Court of Western Australia from 1861–2005* (Perth: Supreme Court of Western Australia, 2005), 271.

159 **'In his role as an advocate, he probably had experienced moments of disappointment with judges' sentencing practices'**: Malcolm CJ's bread and butter was, however, civil rather than criminal litigation.

160 **'In the *Daily News* on 24 May 1989, Ray responded ...'**: R. Mickelberg, 'Truth can't harm a just system', *Daily News*, 24 May 1989, 18.

161 **'... the media has a vital role in a free and open society of informing the public of court proceedings'**: This role of the media is well set out in some of the recent case law with respect to media access to court information and materials. See for example *Re Hogan; Ex parte Channel Seven Perth Pty Ltd* [2008] WASC 113 (Unreported, Supreme Court of Western Australia, Blaxell J, 13 June 2008); *Re Pamela Hogan Magistrate of the Magistrates Court at Perth; Ex parte Western Australian Newspapers Ltd* [2009] WASC 31 (Unreported, Supreme Court of Western Australia, Heenan J, 9 January 2009).

162 **'Peter Fitzpatrick ... wrote in the *Daily News*'**: P. Fitzpatrick, 'Half-Truths Harm Justice', *Daily News*, 31 May 1989, 11.

163 **'In a rejoinder to Fitzpatrick's criticism Ray said ...'**: R. Mickelberg, 'Handicapped needs fair go', Letters to the Editor, *Daily News*, 28 June 1989, 7.

164 **The 1988 High Court decision**: *Peter Mickelberg v R; Raymond Mickelberg v R* (1989) 167 CLR 259.

165 **The Mickelbergs' counsels**: Assisted by Gary Lawton and Peter Searle respectively.

166 **'The majority of the High Court held that they did not have the power to receive fresh evidence ...'**: Under section 73 of the *Commonwealth of Australia Constitution,* the High Court was made a general court of appeal from all federal courts and all State Supreme Courts — it has jurisdiction 'to hear and determine appeals from all judgements, decrees, orders and sentences' from 'any Justice or Justices, exercising the original jurisdiction of the High Court, any other federal court or court exercising federal jurisdiction, and state Supreme Courts.' Refer to S. Gageler, 'Jurisdiction' in T. Blackshield, M. Coper and G. Williams (eds), *The Oxford Companion to the High Court of Australia* (South Melbourne: Oxford University Press, 2001), 383, 384. The court cited and upheld well-established authorities, especially from the United Kingdom, in deciding that the High Court's appellate jurisdiction under section 73 only gave the High Court the power to review a decision of a state court by way of strict appeal ('confined to determining the correctness or otherwise of the decision made by the Court of Criminal Appeal on the material before it' — Toohey and Gaudron JJ at 299). See further *Ronald v Harper* (1910) 11 CLR 63; *Flower v Lloyd* (1877) 6 Ch D 297; *Birch v Birch* [1902] P. 130; *Davies and Cody v R* (1937) 57 CLR 170, 172 and the other cases cited at 265–271 (Mason CJ), 274–5 (Brennan J), 276–89 (Deane J), 297–9 (Toohey and Gaudron JJ).

167 **Justice Deane's decision**: Justice Deane disagreed with his colleagues, saying that the High Court's refusal to receive fresh evidence in the exercise of its appellate jurisdiction in criminal cases rested on 'unstable foundations.' He said: 'In reaching this conclusion, I have been influenced by the fact that, to the extent that a nation's final appellate court is disabled from doing justice in an individual case before it, it is the nation, rather than the court, which is diminished.' See *Peter Mickelberg v R; Raymond Mickelberg v R* (1989) 167 CLR 259, 288.

168 **'"... would not, if placed before the jury at the trial, have affected the outcome of the trial"'**: Justices Toohey and Gaudron (with whom Chief Justice Mason and Justice Brennan agreed) said the Crown's expert witnesses expressed 'that a high degree of luck would be necessary to forge a print of the quality and in the position of the print on the cheque. Luck was a necessary ingredient because a successful forgery on a single application of a mould to a surface which only sometimes accepted a print and in circumstances that the print, if accepted, would not be visible until treated.' The justices also noted the expert witnesses called on behalf of Ray and Peter did not contradict the 'high degree of luck' opinion. Justice Deane did not, however, place the same degree of weight as Justices Toohey and Gaudron did on the 'luck' conclusion.

169 **'The High Court allowed Peter's application for special leave to appeal'**: Under section 35 of the *Judiciary Act 1903* (Cth), an appellant does not have an automatic right to appeal from a decision of a State Supreme Court to the High Court, but must first apply for 'special leave' to appeal. The criteria applied for the granting of special leave to appeal is set out in section 35B of

the *Judiciary Act*. This criteria allows the court to consider 'any matters that it considers relevant' and particularly whether the proceedings involve a question of law of public importance, whether the court is required to resolve differences of judicial opinion, or where the interests of the administration of justice require further consideration of the matter.

170 '**... remitting the matter back to the CCA**': On an appeal, an appeal court will generally have powers to make orders including upholding a verdict, altering a verdict, or quashing a conviction. As the role of an appeal court is limited in receiving new evidence and resolving factual disputes, an appeal court will usually also have the power to make an order remitting certain cases back to a lower court to make a decision guided by the judgment and orders of the court of appeal. For instance, ss.14(1)(e) of the *Criminal Appeals Act 2004* (WA) with respect to appeals from courts of summary jurisdiction states that the appeal court may 'order the case to be dealt with again by the court of summary jurisdiction, with or without orders to that court — (i) as to how or by whom it is to be constituted [or] (ii) as to how it must deal with the case.' Courts of summary jurisdiction, such as Western Australia's Magistrates Court, are lower in the judicial hierarchy than courts of 'superior' jurisdiction such as the Supreme Court of Western Australia and the District Court of Western Australia.

171 '**... whether his conviction for conspiracy was inconsistent with the acquittal of Brian**': Two or more verdicts will be inconsistent if given by a single jury and on the facts of the matter they cannot be reconciled or are technically or legally inconsistent. If different verdicts have been reached where no reasonable jury considering the evidence could have arrived at two different conclusions, the verdicts will also be inconsistent (*R v Nanette* [1982] VR 81; *R v Kirkman* (1987) 44 SASR 591). In cases such as *Mackenzie v R* (1996) 190 CLR 348, an inconsistent guilty verdict has been quashed on appeal. Where, such as in the Mint swindle, two or more accused have been tried together, verdicts are likely to be inconsistent where different verdicts are reached although there is no difference in the evidence against each (*R v Darby* (1982) 148 CLR 668). Peter and Raymond argued that as they had been convicted of a conspiracy involving three persons, a finding of guilt against all three was required to support a conviction for involvement in that alleged conspiracy. As Brian was acquitted on appeal and there was no alternative conspiracy alleged solely between Raymond and Peter, this, they alleged, made their convictions inconsistent with Brian's acquittal. See *Raymond Mickelberg v R*; *Peter Mickelberg v R* (Unreported, Supreme Court of Western Australia, Wallace, Olney and Pidgeon JJ, 18 November 1987), 11–12 (Wallace J).

172 '**They also remitted these matters back to the CCA for consideration**': Apart from Justice Deane, the other justices did not believe any positive outcome for Peter on the conspiracy charge raised doubts in relation to the guilt of Ray.

173 **Peter's 1989 CCA appeal**: Peter was represented by McCusker and Searle.

174 **The 1989 CCA decision**: See *Peter Mickelberg v R (No. 2)* (1989) WAR 497.

CHAPTER 8

175 **Alison Fan and the Channel Seven gold**: See R. Taylor, 'Gold find: call for full immunity', *West Australian*, 1 November 1989, 1–2. For more see R. Taylor, 'Chief denies rort at mint', *West Australian*, 2 November 1989, 2; M. Lang, 'Now a question of who owns the gold', *West Australian*, 2 November 1989, 2.

176 **ICP-MS analysis**: ICP-MS (inductively coupled plasma mass spectrometry) is a type of mass spectrometry capable of ascertaining very precisely the chemical make-up of particular material. By ICP-MS testing (or 'finger-printing') of the gold pellets, their precise make-up could be identified and compared to other samples to assist in establishing their identity.

177 '**... the 1991 Supreme Court hearing in which Avon Lovell was seeking to strike out a libel action against him by eight detectives he named in *The Mickelberg Stitch*'**: Supreme Court action #1331/1995. The case never reached a final judicial determination. See the cases referred to in Chapter 5 note 118 and particularly *Lewandowski v Lovell* (Unreported, Supreme Court of Western Australia, Adams AM, 4 December 1991).

178 '**... Ray and Peter had asked new Attorney-General Cheryl Edwardes to review their case'**: 'The ... Attorney General, Hon Cheryl Edwardes MLA, responded to a petition by the Mickelbergs under section 21 of the Criminal Code (The Royal Prerogative of Mercy). She sought a response to the Petition from the Director of Public Prosecutions, Mr John McKechnie QC, and independent advice from Mr Brian Martin QC. Subsequently, special leave to appeal was granted to Peter Mickelberg. An ex-gratia payment to Peter Mickelberg to help pay for his appeal has been approved.': Chairman D. Tomlinson MLC, *Interim Report of the Select Committee on the Western Australian Police Service*, Term of Reference 3, Western Australia Legislative Council, Perth, 9 June 1996. Peter's case was referred to the Court of Criminal Appeal on 15 November 1994, CCA number 236 of 1994. This litigation was to continue until 1999, see *Peter Mickelberg v R; Raymond John Mickelberg v R* (Unreported, Western Australian Court of Criminal Appeal, Malcolm CJ, Ipp and Wheeler JJ, 12 February 1999).

179 **Hancock's statements to the media**: Hancock also criticised Fan for not going to the police immediately with the gold bar and note but rather using local talkback radio to broadcast the event. Subsequently Fan complained to Police Commissioner Brian Bull about Hancock's remarks saying that she had contacted the offices of the Attorney-General within thirty minutes of receiving the gold bar and Police Commissioner Brian Bull within three hours.

180 **Superintendant Scott's investigation**: See L. Betti, *West Australian*, 2 November 1989, 1.

181 '**... the State Ombudsman's conclusion'**: See E. Freeman, *Annual Report 1988–1989*, WA government Printers, Perth, 1989. An Ombudsman is a statutorily appointed office holder responsible for the investigation of actions taken by government departments or authorities. An Ombudsman investigation can arise as a response to a complaint to the Ombudsman or on the motion of the Ombudsman themselves. Upon completing its investigation, the Ombudsman makes a report which includes the reasons

for his/her opinion. However, an Ombudsman's report is recommendatory and not legally binding. In Western Australia the Ombudsman is called the 'Parliamentary Commissioner', and is established and governed by the *Parliamentary Commissioner Act 1971* (WA).

CHAPTER 9

182 '... **Peter, who had pleaded in vain with authorities to release Ray ...':** J. Bartley, 'Let My Brother Go Free', *Daily News,* 22 December 1989, 3.

183 **'"There was a sense in the business community that you could stretch the envelope"':** 'Alan Bond', *Enough Rope with Andrew Denton,* ABC TV, 3 November 2003.

184 '**[Packer] purchased a piece of price real estate in Perth's CBD, known as Westralia Square ...':** A. Banks, 'How the Red Inc flowed in WA', *The Australian,* 23 July 2005, 33.

185 **'"all West Australians are crooks"':** M. Drummond, 'Deal of the Decade for Packer', *Sydney Morning Herald,* 8 May 2004, 43, 46. It appears the Westralia Square site has finally left its past behind with plans recently revealed for a forty-six storey tower that will be the new headquarters for BHP Billiton — see M. Hawthorne, 'Perth Mayor drops BHP HQ relocation bomb', Business Day, *The Age,* 13 March 2008, 1, 4.

186 '... **the legendary WA Inc scandal':** WA Inc was the common abbreviation for WA Incorporated which referred to the commercial activities of the WA state government during the Burke–Dowding period (Brian Burke was premier in 1983–87 and Peter Dowding in 1987–90). See further P. O'Brien and M. Webb, *The Executive State: WA Inc & The Constitution* (Perth: Constitutional Publishing Company, 1991); Chairman G. Kennedy, *Report of the Royal Commission into the Commercial Activities of government and Other Matters,* Part 1, Western Australia state government, Perth, 20 October 1992; Chairman G. Kennedy, *Report of the Royal Commission into the Commercial Activities of government and Other Matters,* Part 2, Western Australia state government, Perth, 13 November 1992.

187 **Bond's 1992 criminal trial:** See generally *Bond v R* (1992) 62 A Crim R 383 (appeal judgment).

188 '**Bond's house of corporate cards collapsed in 1989':** The sources of information on Alan Bond's 1989 corporate downfall are extensive. Besides the various court judgments handed down during the aftermath, see most usefully P. Barry, *The Rise and Fall of Alan Bond* (Sydney: Bantam Books, 1991).

189 '... **it was 1997 before [Bond's dishonest dealings] earned him a seven-year gaol sentence':** See *R v Bond* (1997) 24 ACSR 518; *Bond v R* (2000) 201 CLR 213.

190 '... **those same laws did not allow the Commonwealth to appeal':** Under section 17 of the *Director of Public Prosecutions Act 1983* (Cth) authority was given to the Commonwealth DPP, where appointed, to 'institute and carry on, in accordance with the terms of the appointment, prosecutions for ... offences [against the laws of the state].' As the court recognised an important distinction between instituting and conducting prosecutions and appealing a decision, and that the authority given only extended to the former, the Commonwealth DPP did not have the jurisdiction to appeal against a

decision made in a State Supreme Court. Therefore, the sentence imposed by the appeal court (the Western Australian Court of Criminal Appeal) could not be upheld.

191 '... the *Sydney Morning Herald* reported on 7 October 2000': I. Verrender, 'Book Review — Going for Broke: How Bond got away with it', *Sydney Morning Herald,* 7 October 2000, 10.

192 'It has become folklore that the horse was drugged ... to ensure victory': M. Presnall, 'A steward's life: from Tamworth to the wild west', Turf Talk, *Sydney Morning Herald,* 24 September 2004, 15.

193 'He died of a heart attack in 1990 at the age of fifty-three – intestate!': A person dies 'intestate' when they die without a will. Following the exit from Bell, Holmes à Court focused on the family company Heytesbury before his death. The empire was successfully run by his wife, Janet, who for many years was the richest woman in Australia.

194 **Brian Burke's convictions**: 'False Pretences' are fraudulent statements. For Burke's unsuccessful appeal against sentence for the 1994 false pretences charge, see *Burke v R* (1994) 75 A Crim R 48. For Burke's unsuccessful appeal against that conviction, see *Burke v R* (Unreported, Western Australian Court of Criminal Appeal, Rowland, Franklyn and Owen JJ, 2 November 1994). The charges against Burke in 1997 were heard before Justice Sadleir in the District Court, see *R v Burke* (Unreported, District Court of Western Australia, Sadleir J, 28 February 1997). For Burke's successful 1997 appeal against this conviction see *R v Burke* (Unreported, Western Australian Court of Criminal Appeal, Malcolm CJ, Pidgeon and Walsh JJ, 23 July 1997).

195 **David Parker's convictions**: For the 1994 stealing conviction, see *Parker v R* (Unreported, Western Australian Court of Criminal Appeal, Malcolm CJ, Ipp and Steytler JJ, 26 May 1995) (unsuccessful appeal to WACCA); *Parker v R* (1997) 186 CLR 494 (successful High Court appeal).

196 **'O'Connor ... was tried in 1995 and gaoled'**: The Constitutional Centre of Western Australia, 'Ray O'Connor Biography' available at http://www.ccentre.wa.gov.au/index.cfm?event=premiersRaymondoconnor.

197 **The Argyle Diamonds affair**: See Chapter 14 'Argyle' in Commissioner G. Kennedy, *Final Report of the Royal Commission Into Whether There Has Been Corrupt Or Criminal Conduct By Any Western Australian Police Officer,* Volume I, Western Australian state government, Perth, January 2004, 391–493. Also see R. Tailby, 'The Illicit Market in Diamonds' (2002) 218 *The Australian Institute of Criminology* 4.

CHAPTER 10

198 **Electro Static Deposition Analysis (ESDA)**: ESDA testing operates on the same principle as a photocopier, in which a fine black powder is attracted to impressions of writing from the overlaid sheet. In many ways it is similar to the schoolboy or detective trick of rubbing a pencil over the top sheet of paper to reveal what has been written on the previous page. For the successful Birmingham Six appeal, see *R v McIlkenney* (1991) 93 Cr App R 287.

199 '... McCusker's argument prevailed and on 1 April 1992 the Chief Justice made detailed orders allowing for the release of the documents': See *Raymond Mickelberg & Peter Mickelberg v R* (1992) 59 A Crim R 288. The

Chief Justice added: 'In the case of Lewandowski's notes the purpose of the test is to determine whether they were written in the page sequence which they appear to have been written in. If they were, that would tend to confirm that they were not a fabrication. If they were not, that would raise questions which may need to be further investigated. If the result is inconclusive, that would be the end of the matter. If Dr Kobus's negatives are examined and found to be what Dr Kobus said they were, that would settle the matter once and for all. If they were not, again, a question would be raised which may need to be investigated. If the result is inconclusive, again that could also be the end of the matter. In the case of the note on Raymond's police file, if the tests were to establish that the note by Detective Sergeant Henning regarding the destruction of Raymond's fingerprints was not written in 1976 that would raise a question to be investigated. If it was written in 1976 or the test is inconclusive that may be the end of the matter.'

200 **'In an interview with *The Bulletin* ...'**: J. Cohen, 'Goldfingered', *The Bulletin*, 5 May 1992, 41.

201 **Radley and Baxendale**: For a detailed coverage of Radley and Baxendale's report and conclusions, see *Peter Mickelberg v R; Raymond Mickelberg v R* (Unreported, Western Australian Court of Criminal Appeal, Malcolm CJ, Ipp and Wheeler JJ, 12 February 1999).

202 **'Ray and Peter held a media conference on the same day'**: Also see D. Humphries, 'Test Prove That Evidence was Fabricated, Court Told', *The Age*, 14 May 1992, 5.

203 **Richard Brunelle**: For a detailed coverage of Brunelle's evidence see *Raymond Mickelberg v R* (Unreported, Western Australian Court of Criminal Appeal, Malcolm CJ, 29 November 1996); *Peter Mickelberg v R; Raymond Mickelberg v R* (Unreported, Western Australian Court of Criminal Appeal, Malcolm CJ, Steytler and Wheeler JJ, 30 October 1997).

204 **Hancock's *Sunday Times* interview**: See J. Pollard, 'Top cop hits back on framing charge', *Sunday Times*, 28 June 1992, 1, 4.

205 **'As early as 1990, in his weekly *Sunday Times* column, Howard Sattler had pressed for Ray's release from prison'**: H. Sattler, 'Time to free Mickelberg', *Sunday Times*, 25 February 1990, 45.

206 **'... a special appeal under section 21 of the *Criminal Code 1913* (WA)'**: See Chapter 6 note 126.

207 **'... while the consent of the Governor of Western Australia was required, the State Attorney-General determined whether the matter should proceed to court'**: For instance the modern provision, section 140 of the *Sentencing Act 1995* (WA), reads: 'A petition for the exercise of the Royal Prerogative of Mercy ... may be referred by the Attorney General to the Court of Appeal ...'.

208 **The *Sunday Times* story (2 August 1992)**: see M. Saxon, 'No rules for police, says top cop on secret tape', *Sunday Times*, 2 August 1992, 7.

209 **The *West Australian* story (14 August 1992)**: see N. Aisbett, 'Mickelberg bombshell', *West Australian*, 14 August 1992, 1, 8–9.

210 **The *Sunday Times* story (16 August 1992)**: M. Saxon and C. Manly, 'Mint man puts appeal on line', *Sunday Times*, 16 August 1992, 2.

211 **The *West Australian* story (14 August 1992)**: N. Aisbett, 'Questions asked of "new" evidence timing', *West Australian*, 14 August 1992, 9.

212 **'... a sympathetic ear in the new Attorney-General Cheryl Edwardes'**: See Chapter 8 note 178.

213 **'McKechnie sought to block the release of his opinion ... [and] ... the Martin report, claiming legal professional privilege and public interest immunity'**: For legal professional privilege see Chapter 6 note 149. McKechnie's claim to this privilege would have been based on the fact that Martin QC's report was obtained for the dominant purpose of obtaining legal advice or assistance, or with reference to actual or contemplated judicial proceedings (i.e. the Mickelberg case).

Public interest immunity is another kind of evidentiary privilege that can exempt the production of documents or information where disclosure would be against the public interest. When considering whether the immunity applies the court weighs the public interest supporting the admissibility of the evidence against the public interest against compelling its production (see *Sankey v Whitlam* (1978) 142 CLR 1). McKechnie's claim to this privilege essentially amounted to a claim that the public interest in disclosure of the Martin report was outweighed by the public interest factors weighing against its production.

214 **Avon Lovell's publications**: Lovell published a follow-up book in 1990, which deals with the action by the police to prevent distribution of *The Mickelberg Stitch* and the 1987 appeal. See A. Lovell, *Split Image: International Mystery of the Mickelberg Affair* (Perth: Creative Research, 1990). On the various defamation proceedings, see Chapter 5 note 118.

215 **The Western Australian Legislative Council Select Committee on the Western Australian Police Service report**: Chairman D. Tomlinson MLC, *Interim Report of the Select Committee on the Western Australian Police Service*, Term of Reference 3, Western Australia Legislative Council. Perth, June 1996. See pages 8–9 especially.

216 **'The government had granted Peter an ex gratia payment to finance the appeal ...'**: An ex gratia (or 'act of grace') payment is a payment ... made by the government to an individual who has suffered harm at their hands without any strict legal obligation to do so.

217 **'It was now late 1995. The appeals were not heard until 1998'**: The legal wrangling from 1995 to 1998 in these proceedings was extensive, with a number of hearings prior to the substantive trial in 1998 concerning the admissibility of evidence, and applications by the Mickelbergs to amend their grounds of appeal and for forensic testing of exhibits. See *Raymond Mickelberg v R* (Unreported, Western Australian Court of Criminal Appeal, Malcolm CJ, 29 November 1996); *Raymond Mickelberg v R* (1996) 90 A. Crim. R. 126; *Raymond Mickelberg v R* (Unreported, Western Australian Court of Criminal Appeal, Malcolm CJ, Murray and Steytler JJ, 1 April 1997); *Raymond Mickelberg v R, Peter Mickelberg v R; Raymond Mickelberg v R* (Unreported, Western Australian Court of Criminal Appeal, Malcolm CJ, Murray and Wheeler JJ, 13 August 1997); *Peter Mickelberg v R; Raymond Mickelberg v R* (Unreported, Western Australian Court of Criminal Appeal, Malcolm CJ, Steytler and Wheeler JJ, 30 October 1997); *Peter Mickelberg*

v R; Raymond Mickelberg v R (Unreported, Western Australian Court of Criminal Appeal, Malcolm CJ, 27 February 1998); *Raymond Mickelberg v R* (Unreported, Western Australian Court of Criminal Appeal, Malcolm CJ, 12 March 1998). The substantive proceedings eventually took place on various dates in May and November 1998: see *Peter Mickelberg v R; Raymond Mickelberg v R* (Unreported, Western Australian Court of Criminal Appeal, Malcolm CJ, Ipp and Wheeler JJ, 12 February 1999).

CHAPTER 11

218 **'The *West Australian* editorial'**: See Editorial, 'State plays politics on corruption', *West Australian*, 20 June 1996, 12.

219 **'The Select Committee ... proposed an independent Police Anti-Corruption Commission with royal commission powers of investigation into allegations of police graft and corruption'**: On the day the Select Committee report was released, Premier Richard Court released his own anti-graft package which included the replacement of the Official Corruption Commission with the Anti-Corruption Commission, which would be able to investigate allegations of corrupt, criminal and serious improper conduct by police and public officials, including members of parliament. The Anti-Corruption Commission was indeed established by the Court government. Police Commissioner Bob Falconer, a Victorian who had been appointed in part to clean up police corruption and bring in a new standard of professionalism to the police force, dismissed the Select Committee's suggestion that if their recommendations were not taken up a royal commission was needed. Falconer said the Select Committee hadn't understood the changes he had instigated through the force's Delta reform process, which the police commissioner argued had brought a new professionalism and ethical culture to the service.

220 **'... institutionalised code of silence'**: 'The blue wall of silence, the code, brotherhood, secrecy, loyalty, solidarity and protecting your mates; these are the constructs upon which traditional assumptions about police culture have been built.': Commissioner G. Kennedy, *Final Report of the Royal Commission Into Whether There Has Been Corrupt Or Criminal Conduct By Any Western Australian Police Officer*, Volume II, Western Australian state government, Perth, January 2004, 31. Also see pp. 35–6, 55–8, 235, 254–6 and Commissioner G. Kennedy, *Final Report of the Royal Commission Into Whether There Has Been Corrupt Or Criminal Conduct By Any Western Australian Police Officer*, Volume I, Western Australian state government, Perth, January 2004, 41–2.

221 **'... an "ideal backdoor for drug importation ..."'**: 'The Ones That Got Away', *Four Corners*, ABC TV, 7 August 2000 (transcript available at http://www.abc.net.au/4corners/s160338.htm).

222 **Corruption and Crime Commission of Western Australia report**: *Report to the Joint Standing Committee on the Corruption and Crime Commission with regard to the Commission's Organised Crime Function and Contempt Powers*, Western Australia government, Perth, December 2005.

223 **Bruno 'The Fox' Romeo**: See *Barbaro v Minister for Immigration and Ethnic Affairs* (Unreported, Federal Court of Australia, Smithers J, 4 August 1982); *Barbaro v Minister for Immigration and Ethnic Affairs* (Unreported, Federal

Court of Australia, Smithers J, 17 December 1982); *Pizzata v R* (Unreported, Supreme Court of Western Australia Court of Criminal Appeal, Malcolm CJ, Rowland and Murray JJ, 29 October 1993); *R v Ex parte The Director of Public Prosecutions for Western Australia (In the matter of R v Romeo)* (Unreported, Supreme Court of Western Australia, Malcolm CJ, Kennedy and Rowland JJ, 26 July 1994).

224 **'... inquest into Bowen's murder'**: An Inquest taken at Adelaide in South Australia, on 6–30 April, 3–7 May, 31 May–18 June, 28–30 June, 1–29 July, 10–13 August, and 17 September, 1999, before Wayne Cromwell Chivell, a Coroner for the said state, concerning the death of Geoffrey Leigh Bowen.

225 **John Kizon**: Over the years, Kizon has invested in restaurants, nightclubs, the automotive industry and mining, though police still believe his primary occupation is the head of a major crime syndicate. Although describing himself as a legitimate businessman, in the mid 90s Kizon had no bank accounts in his own name and his six-year average income to the Australian Taxation Office was $3000. For Kizon's unsuccessful appeal against sentence for the 1990 false bank account charges see *Kizon v R* (Unreported, Supreme Court of Western Australia, Wallace J, 20 January 1990). For the Director of Public Prosecutions application for release of the funds in those accounts in those proceedings see *Director of Public Prosecutions v Kizon* (Unreported, Supreme Court of Western Australia, White AJ, 30 August 1991); *Director of Public Prosecutions v Kizon* (1992) WAR 353. For Kizon's unsuccessful appeal against conviction for the 1985 assault see *Kizon v R* (1985) 18 A Crim R 59. In that appeal, while Wallace and Olney JJ formed the majority, dismissing the appeal, Rowland J delivered a dissenting judgment finding that Kizon's appeal should succeed.

226 **Operation Red Emperor**: See Chapter 17 'Red Emperor' in Commissioner G. Kennedy, *Final Report of the Royal Commission Into Whether There Has Been Corrupt Or Criminal Conduct By Any Western Australian Police Officer*, Volume I, Western Australian state government, Perth, January 2004, 553–63.

227 **Andrew Petrelis**: See Chapter 13 'Andrew Nicholas Petrelis' in Commissioner G. Kennedy, *Final Report of the Royal Commission Into Whether There Has Been Corrupt Or Criminal Conduct By Any Western Australian Police Officer*, Volume I, Western Australian state government, Perth, January 2004, 369–89; 'The Ones That Got Away', *Four Corners*, ABC TV, 7 August 2000 available at http://www.abc.net.au/4corners/s160338. htm; Corruption and Crime Commission of Western Australia, *The Anti-Corruption Commission's Investigation Report into any Involvement by Western Australian Police Officers in the Death of Andrew Petrelis*, Western Australia government, Perth, 17 May 2007; Anonymous, 'No evidence police were involved in Petrelis death: CCC', *AAP General News Wire*, 17 May 2007, 1. For Kizon's 1998 cannabis possession charges, see *R v Kizon* (Unreported, District Court of Western Australia, Hammond CJDC, 2 December 1998).

228 **'... no conclusive evidence linked that disclosure to [Petrelis's] death'**: Corruption and Crime Commission of Western Australia, *The Anti-Corruption Commission's Investigation Report into any Involvement by Western Australian Police Officers in the Death of Andrew Petrelis*, Western Australia government, Perth, 17 May 2007.

CHAPTER 12

229 **'The court would review the whole case ...'**: The reference to the 'whole case' was made in section 21(a) of the then *Criminal Code* (WA). In the earlier 1989 High Court appeal — *Peter Mickelberg v R; Raymond Mickelberg v R* (1989) 167 CLR 259 — Justices Toohey and Gaudron (with whom Chief Justice Mason and Justice Brennan agreed) said: 'Prime facie, the reference of the whole case required the Court of Criminal Appeal to consider the case in its entirety, subject only to the limitation that it "be heard and determined ... as the case of an appeal by a person convicted". That limitation necessitates that the matter be determined by "legal principles appropriate to an appeal".'

230 **'The state government had granted Peter $132,000 ... The government at first rejected [Ray's] pleas outright, eventually relenting to the extent of $60,000 ...'**: The payments were made ex gratia (an act of grace payment). See Chapter 10 note 216 and Epilogue note 369.

231 **'... an appeal in the highest appellate court in the state was still an expensive business'**: See generally P. Williams and R. Williams, 'Access to Justice and the Cost of Litigation' (1992) 8(3) *Policy* 22; Law Reform Commission of Victoria, *Issues Paper: The Cost of Litigation* (1990); A. Zuckerman and R. Cranston, *Reform of Civil Procedure: Essays on 'Access to Justice'* (Oxford: Clarendon Press, 1995); P. Williams et al. *The Cost of Civil Litigation before Intermediate Courts in Australia* (Melbourne: The Australian Institute of Judicial Administration Incorporated, 1992).

232 **The cannabis proceedings**: For Raymond's successful appeal see *Raymond Mickelberg v R* [2000] WASCA 219 (Unreported, Western Australian Court of Criminal Appeal, Kennedy ACJ, Ipp and Anderson JJ, 18 August 2000). For Ray's bail hearing see *Raymond Mickelberg v R* [2000] WASCA 163 (Unreported, Western Australian Court of Criminal Appeal, Scott J, 15 June 2000). Ross also successfully appealed against the amount of the fine imposed against him ($900). It was reduced to $300. See *Ross Mickelberg v R* [2000] WASCA 319 (Unreported, Western Australian Court of Criminal Appeal, Kennedy, Ipp and Murray JJ, 30 October 2000).

233 **Legal representatives at Peter's appeal**: In addition, during Peter's appeal Jack Courtis represented the interests of Ray. But he was not required during Ray's later appeal hearing where McCusker took care of matters.

234 **Justice David Ipp**: Justice Ipp was a major player in reform of civil procedure in the state, who in 2002 moved to Sydney and was appointed to the Court of Appeal in the Supreme Court of New South Wales. Refer further to G. Bolton and G. Byrne, *May it Please Your Honour: A History of the Supreme Court of Western Australia from 1861–2005* (Perth: Supreme Court of Western Australia, 2005), 351.

235 **'Their Honours were to consider whether the fresh evidence would have left a jury with a reasonable doubt as to the guilt of the Mickelbergs'**: The court considered Barwick CJ's judgment in *Ratten v R* (1974) 131 CLR 510: 'His Honour referred firstly to the situation where the court considers whether the verdict of guilty should be set aside outright for the reason that innocence is shown, or the existence of an appropriate doubt established. In that event, "the court will consider all the material itself, forming and acting upon its own belief in, or disbelief of, the evidence, and upon its own view of the facts of the case including the evidence at the trial"

(at 518). If the court is satisfied of innocence or entertains a reasonable doubt as to guilt the verdict of guilty will be quashed and the appellant discharged. Later cases have made it plain that it is the view which a reasonable jury must have reached and not the view of the court, which is to be considered: *Whitehorn v R* (1983) 152 CLR 657, 687 (Dawson J); *Chamberlain v R* (1984) 153 CLR 521; *M v R* (1994) 181 CLR 487.

236 **New and fresh evidence**: See Chapter 6 note 134 and *Peter Mickelberg v R* [1999] WASCA 1003 (Unreported, Supreme Court of Western Australia, Malcolm CJ, Ipp and Wheeler JJ, 12 February 1999).

237 '**... Justices Toohey and Gaudron ... stated the legal position ...**': See *Peter Mickelberg v R; Raymond Mickelberg v R* (1989) 167 CLR 259, 301.

238 *Ratten v The Queen:* See *Ratten v R* (1974) 131 CLR 510, 517. In the later High Court case of *Lawless v R* (1979) 142 CLR 659 at 699, Justice Ninian Stephen held that evidence in a criminal trial should be regarded as fresh if the accused's want of knowledge 'is not so unexplained as to lead to the inference that it was the product of an intentional failure to make inquiries.' Although it should be noted that he was in a minority in this case in holding such a view.

239 **Terry McLernon**: McLernon also testified that Lewandowski had said that he had been at a meeting with a solicitor, in which 'other police were there, Hancock and Billingsworth (sic) to name two. They had worked out that he would sign something admitting that he did change the confession and that there was some sort of story to cover his position, but he would leave Hancock out of it, that Hancock had no knowledge that Tony had done it.'

240 '**McCusker was unable to dent her credibility in cross-examination ...**': Holz was also cross-examined by Jack Courtis for Ray.

241 '**McCusker began his summing up to the court**': After both parties have presented their case, having presented their evidence, each party has an opportunity to 'sum up' their case to the jury. Also called a 'closing' address.

242 '**The Chief Justice ended the proceeding by reserving the appeal court's decision ...**': Generally, apart from short, simple proceedings the court does not decide a matter immediately at the conclusion of a hearing, but will *reserve* its decision until judgment is delivered at a later date.

243 **Ninhydrin**: 2,2-Dihydroxyindane-1,3-dione ($C_9H_6O_4$). When peptides and proteins present in fingerprints are exposed to ninhydrin, a deep blue or purple colour is produced, aiding in the identification and clarity of fingerprints. See J. Almog, 'Fingerprint Development by Ninhydrin and Its Analogues' in H. Lee and R. Gaensslen (eds), *Advances in Fingerprint Technology* (2nd ed. Boca Raton: CRC Press, 2001), 177.

244 '**... the police standard requirement of at least twelve points of identification ...**': This requirement is one of internal police procedure (see *Peter Mickelberg v R; Raymond Mickelberg v R* [1999] WASCA 1003 (Unreported, Supreme Court of Western Australia, Malcolm CJ, Ipp and Wheeler JJ, 12 February 1999), 144–238) and is not a strict legal rule. The fingerprint expert provides evidence of the resemblances between the print obtained and the accused's actual fingerprints through these points of identification, but the jury must decide whether the conclusion made is correct. See *R v O'Callaghan* [1976] VR 676.

245 **'That day, police arrested Ray and searched his home again, seized "metal castings" of hands'**: See Chapter 2 note 33.

246 **'... the court's unanimous decision'**: *Peter Mickelberg v R; Raymond Mickelberg v R* [1999] WASCA 1003 (Unreported, Supreme Court of Western Australia Court of Criminal Appeal, Malcolm CJ, Ipp and Wheeler JJ, 12 February 1999).

247 **'They sought unsuccessfully for leave to appeal to the High Court ...'**: See *Peter Mickelberg v R; Raymond Mickelberg v R* (2000) 21(13) Leg Rep C5c and Chapter 7 note 169.

248 **'New Zealand law prevented Australians from settling in that country if they had been given prison sentences longer than five years'**: Under ss.7(1)(a) of the *Immigration Act 1987* (NZ) no residence permit may be granted to a person 'who, at any time ... has been convicted of any offence for which that person has been sentenced to imprisonment for a term of 5 years or more ... '.

CHAPTER 13

249 **The Ora Banda shooting**: See T. Barrass, 'Ghost town testament to murder shockwaves', *West Australian*, 7 April 2001, 8–9.

250 **Hancock as murder suspect**: See T. Barrass, 'Murder left a Dead Man Walking', *West Australian*, 3 September 2001, 9.

251 **Coronial inquest**: An investigation carried out by the Coroner, a publicly appointed official, into the cause and circumstances surrounding a person's death. In Western Australia see the *Coroner's Act 1996* (WA).

252 **'One of Billy Grierson's sisters was reported as saying ...'**: see L. Eliot, 'Bikie's sister blames gang', *West Australian*, 4 September 2001, 4.

253 **Assistant Commissioner Tim Atherton's media conference**: G. Taylor, 'No reason for alarm', *West Australian*, 3 September 2001, 1.

254 **'"I would not like to be a member of an outlaw motorcycle gang over the next few months"'**: B. Ruse, G. Taylor and L. Eliot, 'Police get tough on gangs', *West Australian*, 3 September 2001, 7.

255 **'The state government ... [offered] a $500,000 reward ...'**: G. Taylor and B. Ruse, 'Bikie Bait', *West Australian*, 4 September 2001, 1.

256 **The Claremont serial murders**: The $500,000 dwarfed the previous biggest reward in the state, which the government had offered for the capture of a serial killer responsible for the deaths of three young women who disappeared after visiting nightclubs in Perth's trendy western suburb of Claremont between 1996 and 1997. The bodies of two of them, Jane Rimmer and Ciara Glennon, were found dumped in bush at southern and northern outskirts of Perth. The third woman, Sarah Spiers, remains missing. The fear that gripped the community after these murders has subsided over the years; the pressure on the police to solve the crimes has not. The criticism the police have faced over the investigation into the Claremont serial killings and other murders is chronicled by Debi Marshall in her book, *The Devil's Garden: The Claremont Serial Killings* (Sydney: Random House, 2007).

257 **Operation Zircon, Sidney Reid and Graeme Slater**: Operation Zircon resulted in many Gypsy Jokers members being charged with various

offences. The most significant was the conviction of former Gypsy Jokers boss Len Kirby on drugs charges for which he was sentenced to ten years imprisonment. On these see D. Darragh, 'Bikie loses appeal against drug sentence', *West Australian*, 27 October 2006, 38; D. Darragh, 'Ex-bikie boss gets 10 years', *West Australian*, 5 October 2002, 5; G. Taylor, 'Terror of the bikie gangs winds up', *West Australian*, 25 June 2002, 7; E. Dortch, 'Another Gypsy Joker is held', *West Australian*, 2 April 2002, 11; B. Martin, 'Bomb haul tied to shot bikie', *West Australian*, 1 February 2002, 5. There has been some criticism of the short length of Reid's sentence (see A. Burns, 'Jail sentence too short — son', *West Australian*, 30 March 2002, 6). It seems to have been reduced in light of Reid's ongoing cooperation with the police (see *Hoddy v Hawes* [2003] WASC 22 (Unreported, Supreme Court of Western Australia, Hasluck J, 31 January 2003); *K v Western Australia* [2005] WASCA 131 (Unreported, Supreme Court of Western Australia, Malcolm CJ, Roberts-Smith and McLure JJA, 13 July 2005); B. Dutter, 'Biker murder trial kept secret', *Daily Telegraph*, 29 March 2002, 20; T. Barrass, B. Martin and C. Manton, 'Supergrass', *West Australian*, 30 March 2002, 1 (further reports on pp. 5–7); S. Cowan, 'Gypsy Jokers not bombers — turncoat', *West Australian*, 8 May 2003, 5). For Graeme Slater's acquittal see D. Darragh, 'Bomb widow cries as Gypsy Joker walks', *West Australian*, 21 October 2003, 1, 18–19. See also *R v Slater* [2004] WADC 17 (Unreported, District Court of Western Australia, Fenbury DCJ, 13 February 2004); *R v Slater* [2003] WASC 171 (Unreported, Supreme Court of Western Australia, Anderson J, 29 August 2003).

258 **Hancock's funeral**: Western Australian Police Union General President's Report, 'Don Hancock A Special Person', *Police News*, October 2001.

259 **The 'Dark Horse'**: T. Barrass and T. Robb, 'Dark Horse', The Big Weekend, *West Australian*, 15 September, 2001, 1–2.

260 **Hancock's policing philosophy**: Quoting T. Barrass and T. Robb, 'Dark Horse', The Big Weekend, *West Australian*, 15 September, 2001, 1.

CHAPTER 14

261 **Lewandowski's limited immunity**: In general terms, the Director of Public Prosecution's decision to prosecute an individual (or not) is entirely discretionary. However, in Western Australia, this decision is to be made in accordance with guidelines published under the *Director of Prosecutions Act 1991* (WA): see Director of Public Prosecutions R. Cox QC, *Statement of Prosecution Policy and Guidelines 2005*, Director of Public Prosecutions for Western Australia, Perth, 3 June 2005. Under sections 45 to 52 of those guidelines, an indemnity against prosecution can be given as a last resort where it is in the interests of justice to do so. Various factors to consider include whether the person's evidence is reasonably necessary to secure the conviction of another accused person, the degree of the person's culpability with respect to the acts, the person's agreement to testify at any trial and answer questions honestly and the significance and reliability of the person's evidence.

262 **McLernon and Lewandowski**: See N. Prior, 'Crooked Cop Was Wooed', *West Australian*, 13 June 2002, 1.

263 **The *Mickelberg Stitch* defamation proceedings**: See Chapter 5 note 118.

264 **'... in 1996 new Police Union secretary Mike Dean thought it best to settle the matter ...'**: This settlement was not the end of the matter. See *Lovell v The Western Australian Police Union of Workers* [2004] WASC 19 (Unreported, Supreme Court of Western Australia, Sanderson M, 17 February 2004) esp. at [10]–[15]; *Lovell v Western Australian Police Union of Workers* [2009] WASCA 34 (Unreported, Supreme Court of Western Australia Court of Criminal Appeal, Steytler P, Owen and Pullin JJA, 9 January 2009) esp. at [10]–[14]. In 1996 Lovell won $11,500 damages from a Federal Police agent who falsely arrested and charged him with divulging one of Hancock's taxation file documents in 1990.

265 **'Law Men Clash'**: See B. Martin and B. Harvey, 'Law Men Clash', *West Australian*, 21 June 2002, 1.

266 **'As *Sunday Times* columnist Gary Adshead wrote'**: see G. Adshead, 'Answers needed from Kucera', *West Australian*, 16 June 2002, 4.

267 **'The Liberal Opposition smelled blood and went on the attack'**: McGinty also gave Kucera a copy of his transcript of evidence before the 1998 Mickelberg appeal.

268 **Former Detective Sergeant Frank Scott's statements**: See L. Morfesse, 'Forced confession "common"', *West Australian*, 13 June 2002, 9.

269 **Peter Duvnjak's statements**: See M. Lang, 'What the courier saw', *West Australian*, 14 June 2002, 8.

270 **Andrew Foster's statements**: See D. Clery, 'Detectives "in threats with knife"', *West Australian*, 17 June 2002, 6.

271 **John Fischer's statements**: See Western Australia, *Parliamentary Debates*, Legislative Council, 18 June 2002, 11475–7 (Hon. John Fischer).

272 **'... Lovell secured exclusive media deals to the tune of $130,000 with Channel Seven and the *Sunday Times*'**: The Mickelbergs — Ray, Peter and mother Peggy – did an interview with *New Idea* which could have breached the exclusive arrangements Lovell had negotiated with Channel Seven and the *Sunday Times*. For the *New Idea* article refer to J. Mayman and K. Davies, 'Behind gold bars', *New Idea*, 6 July 2002, 18.

273 **The *Today Tonight* story**: Other media outlets and journalists also chased the story to Thailand. But Channel Seven had sewn up the accessibility to Lewandowski.

274 **'What he said could be actioned by police and others ...'**: V. Laurie, 'The Bloodhound's Tale', *The Weekend Australian Magazine*, 12–13 October 2002, 28, 32.

275 **'This evidence goes beyond the undertaking that I gave him'**: T. Mendez, 'Come home, witness told', *West Australian*, 24 July 2002, 9.

276 **Tim Boase and Avon Lovell**: The falling out between Lovell and Boase was partly played out in the media when large extracts of their letters to each other were published in the *West Australian* on 14 August 2002, 7.

277 **Subpoena**: A subpoena or witness summons is a court order (or in this case, from the royal commission) issued in proceedings requiring the person to whom it is directed to attend a court at a specified place and time for the purpose of giving evidence, producing documents, or both. Failure to

comply within a reasonable time amounts to contempt of court. For the royal commission's power to require attendance by issuing a witness summons see section 9 of the *Royal Commissions Act 1968* (WA), and for the contempt provisions see ss.12A–15B.

278 **'On [Lovell's] way out, he told the media scrum to "get stuffed" and "get fucked"'**: L. Morfesse, 'Tea lover needs a good lie down', *West Australian*, 18 July 2002, 6.

279 **'Peter told the media ...'**: T. Mendez, 'New blow taken on the chin', *West Australian*, 18 July 2002, 7.

280 **'McGinty said it would be unfair for the Mickelbergs to face further delay because of the antics of others not under their control'**: L. Morfesse, 'Brothers get day in sun', *West Australian*, 18 July 2002, 8. See also Attorney-General Jim McGinty, *Media Statement: Court of Criminal Appeal to hear Mickelberg Appeal* (23 July 2002) available at http://www.mediastatements.wa.gov.au/ArchivedStatements/Pages/GallopLaborgovernmentSearch.aspx?ItemId=115902&minister=McGinty&admin=Gallop&page=4.

281 **Avon Lovell's contempt convictions**: He was found guilty of three charges of contempt and fined $10,000 for each. See *G. Kennedy v Lovell* (2002) 27 WAR 39; *Kennedy v Lovell* [2002] WASCA 226 (Unreported, Supreme Court of Western Australia, Malcolm CJ, Murray and Steytler JJ, 15 August 2002); *R v Lewandowski* [2003] WADC 108 (Unreported, District Court of Western Australia, Hammond CJDC, 20 May 2003).

282 **'... Ray thought this was most unfair'**: T. Mendez, 'Brothers fear for appeal witness', *West Australian*, 27 July 2002, 8.

283 **'... with the Court of Criminal Appeal now to test the affidavit, the commission was no longer investigating the Mickelberg matter'**: Under the terms of reference for the royal commission, it was to investigate possible corrupt and criminal police conduct since 1 January 1985. The Mickelberg investigation occurred in 1982, although issues of continual perjury by police officers after 1985 would technically come under the jurisdiction of the royal commission.

284 **'... the infamous police "blue wall of silence ..."'**: Commissioner G. Kennedy, *Final Report of the Royal Commission Into Whether There Has Been Corrupt Or Criminal Conduct By Any Western Australian Police Officer*, Volume II, Western Australian state government, Perth, January 2004, 31.

285 **'... he was to give his evidence on closed circuit TV from another part of the Supreme Court'**: Section 121 of the *Evidence Act 1906* (WA) allows the Supreme Court to take evidence by video or audio link on its own motion or upon the application of a party to the proceedings, where it is in the interests of justice to do so.

286 **Section 11 of the *Evidence Act 1906* (WA)**: '(1) Whenever ... any person called as a witness ... declines to answer any question ... on the ground that his answer will criminate or tend to criminate him, the judge may, if it appears to him expedient for the ends of justice that such person should be compelled to answer such question ... tell such person that, if he answers ... in a satisfactory manner, he will grant him the certificate hereinafter mentioned ... (2) Thereupon such person shall no longer be entitled to refuse to answer any question ... on [that] ground ... and thereafter if such person

shall have given his evidence to the satisfaction of the judge, the judge shall give such person a certificate to the effect that he was called as a witness ... in the said proceeding and that his evidence was required for the ends of justice, and was given to his satisfaction. (2a) Where in a proceeding a person is given a certificate under subsection (2) in respect of any evidence, a statement made by him, as part of that evidence, in answer to a question ... is not admissible in evidence in criminal proceedings against the person other than on a prosecution for perjury committed in the proceeding.'

287 **Perjury**: Under section 124 of the *Criminal Code* (WA): 'Any person who, in any judicial proceeding, or for the purpose of instituting any judicial proceeding, knowingly gives false testimony touching any matter which is material to any question then depending in that proceeding, or intended to be raised in that proceeding, is guilty of a crime which is called perjury.' Perjury is a serious offence. The maximum penalty for perjury under section 125 of the *Criminal Code* (WA) is fourteen years imprisonment.

288 **Immunity from prosecution**: See Chapter 14 note 261.

289 **'... the undertaking ... did not mean evidence gathered outside the agreed areas could not be used to instigate criminal proceedings against Lewandowski'**: L. Morfesse, 'How a television interview undid an immunity', *West Australian*, 3 October 2002, 9.

290 **Simon Stone draws criticisms**: See T. Mendez and S. Pennells, 'Stone draws fire for arrest', *West Australian*, 3 October 2002, 8.

291 **McCusker's statements**: See R. Gibson and T. Mendez, 'Stone sticks to his guns over arrest', *West Australian*, 4 October 2002, 8.

292 **'"Tony Lewandowski was the first to come forward and will be the last"'**: See G. Taylor, T. Mendez and B. Martin, 'Arrest Fiasco', *West Australian*, 2 October 2002, 1.

293 **Derrick Tomlinson's statements**: See T. Mendez and R. Gibson, 'Indemnity a different word in WA', *West Australian*, 5 October 2002, 53.

294 **'... 4 October 2002 [editorial] titled "Immunity-deal spirit breached"'**: Editorial, 'Immunity-deal Spirit Breached', *West Australian*, 4 October 2002, 18. A number of letters to the editor of the *West Australian* supported the editorial and condemned the arrest of Lewandowski. For examples refer to page 15 of the *West Australian*, 9 October 2002. See also R. Gibson & T. Mendez, 'Stone sticks to his guns over arrest', *West Australian*, 4 October 2002, 8.

295 **'However, after only eleven days, the court relented and granted bail'**: In *Lewandowski v Sherman* (Unreported, Supreme Court of Western Australia, Hasluck J, 14 October 2002).

296 **'Finally, on 20 May 2003, Chief Justice Kevin Hammond of the District Court set Lewandowski free from the fear of a lengthy term in the slammer ...'**: In *R v Lewandowski* [2003] WADC 108 (Unreported, District Court of Western Australia, Hammond CJDC, 20 May 2003).

297 **The death of Anthony Lewandowski**: See V. Laurie and K. Shine, 'Bad cop Lewandowski found dead', *The Australian*, 20 May 2004, 6; L. Morfesse, 'Lewandowski ends it all', *West Australian*, 20 May 2004, 5; S. Cowan, 'Death will not stop saga reaching conclusion', *West Australian*, 20 May 2004, 5.

CHAPTER 15

298 **Darryl Beamish's 1961 appeal**: See *Beamish v R* [1962] WAR 85.

299 **Peter Brett's criticism of the Beamish case**: P. Brett, *The Beamish Case* (Melbourne: Melbourne University Press, 1966), 16. Also see P. Ryan, 'Ripe Justice' (2005) 49(5) *Quadrant Magazine* 95. In contrast, Professor Douglas Payne of the University of Western Australia Law School strongly defended the prosecution and judgment in *Beamish*. Refer to D. Payne, 'Book Reviews: The Beamish Case' (1965–66) 7 *University of Western Australia Law Journal* 576.

300 **'... justice must not only be done but ... be seen to be done should have precluded a judge sitting in judgment on an appeal against his own decision'**: 'A judge should not hear and decide a case [and should disqualify themselves] if either the parties or the public might entertain a reasonable apprehension that the judge might not bring an impartial and unprejudiced mind to the resolution of the issues' (*R v Maxwell* (1998) 217 ALR 452, 464 (Spigelman CJ, Sperling and Hidden JJ)). Such an apprehension is a distinct possibility where a judge sitting on appeal has already expressed views on relevant factual issues or as to credibility of witnesses prior to proceedings (*Grassby v R* (1989) 168 CLR 1; *Livesey v New South Wales Bar Association* (1983) 151 CLR 288) or where the judge has already convicted and sentenced the alleged offender for the same or similar offences (*Rendulic v Bevan* [1971] SASR 340).

301 **Darryl Beamish's 1964 appeal**: See *Beamish v R (No 2)* (Unreported, Western Australian Court of Criminal Appeal, Wolff CJ, Jackson J, Virtue J, 22 May 1964).

302 **John Button**: *Button v R* (Unreported, Western Australian Court of Criminal Appeal, Wolff CJ, Jackson SPJ and Virtue J, 22 May 1964).

303 ***Broken Lives:*** E. Blackburn, *Broken Lives* (Claremont: Stellar Publishing, 1998).

304 **John Button's 2001 appeal**: For Button's successful appeal see *Button v R* (2002) 25 WAR 382.

305 **Darryl Beamish's 2004 appeal**: *Beamish v R* [2005] WASCA 62 (Unreported, Western Australian Court of Criminal Appeal, Steytler, Wheeler and McLure JJ, 1 April 2005).

306 **Rory Christie**: On 15 November 2001, Susan Christie went missing never to be seen again. On 30 November 2001 police commenced a possible murder investigation and ultimately charged Rory Christie with murder. In October 2003 Christie was convicted of murder and sentenced to life imprisonment. In March 2005 the conviction was quashed and a retrial was ordered. The retrial commenced but was wound up before completion due to a lack of evidence. The DPP was forced to defend another successful appeal against the conviction of a serious offence. They applied the now seemingly mandatory technique of stating their belief of guilt in the person but that the evidence is insufficient to satisfy the courts. For the successful appeal quashing the conviction see *Christie v R* [2005] WASCA 55 (Unreported, Supreme Court of Western Australia Court of Appeal, McKechnie, Le Miere and Jenkins JJ, 24 March 2005). Also see *Christie v R* [2002] WASC 256

(Unreported, Supreme Court of Western Australia, McLure J, 6 November 2002) (original bail application); *Christie v R* [2003] WASC 151 (Unreported, Supreme Court of Western Australia, Smith J, 14 August 2003) (objection to admissibility of evidence); *R v Christie* [2005] WASC 262 (Unreported, Supreme Court of Western Australia, McKechnie J, 30 November 2005) (no case to answer submission).

307 **Phillip Walsham**: On 28 February 1998 Phillip Walsham sustained serious injuries after falling from a pedestrian overpass and later died in Sir Charles Gairdner Hospital. Walsham was out drinking that night with friends and was on his way home from the Stirling train station. He was attacked and kicked in the head while sitting on a bench at the end of the overpass. The attack was unprovoked and arose after a car driving on the freeway below had rocks thrown at it. The car stopped and the men inside chased the two people they had seen throwing the rocks. The two men escaped and on returning to the car the men attacked the defenceless Walsham in frustration. In May 1998 Magistrate Con Zempilas fined Salvatore Fazzari and Jose Martinez, two occupants of the car who admitted to kicking Walsham, $1500 each for assault occasioning bodily harm. From that date there was little movement in the case and the men believed that was the end of the matter. Five years later, in January 2003, a Coronial Inquiry began into the death of Walsham. Martinez, Fazzari, Pereiras and a fourth man, unnamed because he was a juvenile at the time, were summonsed to give evidence. Fazzari, Martinez and Pereiras were subsequently charged with Walsham's murder. In April 2006, Fazzari, Martinez and Pereiras were sentenced to life imprisonment for murdering Walsham by throwing or pushing him off the footbridge at Stirling station on 28 February 1998. An appeal commenced in June 2007. The appeal was successful. The judges overturned the three convictions after finding the jury's verdict of guilty was 'unreasonable and cannot be supported on the evidence.' On 6 July 2007 Fazzari, Martinez and Pereiras were released from prison. For the successful appeal see *Martinez v Western Australia* (2007) 172 A Crim R 389. Also see *Fazzari v Western Australia* [2004] WASC 71 (Unreported, Supreme Court of Western Australia, McLure J, 23 April 2004); *Fazzari v Western Australia (No 2)* [2004] WASC 233 (Unreported, Supreme Court of Western Australia, Roberts-Smith J, 12 November 2004) (bail applications); *Western Australia v Martinez* (2006) 159 A Crim R 380 (application for trial by judge alone); *Western Australia v Martinez* [2006] WASC 98 (Unreported, Supreme Court of Western Australia, Em Heenan J, 20 March 2006) (admissibility of evidence and application by accuseds to call witnesses); *Western Australia v Martinez* [2006] WASC 126 (Unreported, Supreme Court of Western Australia, Em Heenan J, 21 June 2006) (sentencing).

308 **Andrew Mallard**: Much of this account of the Mallard story can be accessed from C. Egan, *Murderer No More: Andrew Mallard and the Epic Fight that Proved his Innocence* (Sydney: Allen and Unwin, 2010).

309 **'... interviewed him for eight hours'**: See Chapter 2 note 35.

310 **'Although by this time legislation had mandated the videotaping of police interviews and confessions, the law was not retrospective'**: Currently, section 118 of the *Criminal Investigation Act 2006* (WA) prohibits the admissibility of police interviews and admissions in cases of indictable

offences, where they are not, without some reasonable excuse, recorded audio-visually. Under section 155 the court has a general discretion that allows the admissibility of otherwise inadmissible evidence (i.e. where an admission is not recorded) if the desirability of admission into evidence outweighs the undesirability of admission of the otherwise inadmissible evidence.

A 'retrospective' statute is one that operates before its enactment. It is presumed that Parliament intends all statutes, except those relating to procedure, to operate prospectively — see *Maxwell v Murphy* (1957) 96 CLR 261. Legislation will only operate retrospectively if the statutory provision plainly manifests in express terms or, by clear implication, an intention to operate retrospectively (see *R v Kidman* (1915) 20 CLR 425).

311 **Mallard's 1996 CCA appeal**: See *Mallard v R* (Unreported, Western Australian Court of Criminal Appeal, Malcolm CJ, Ipp and Wallwork JJ, 11 September 1995).

312 **Mallard's 1997 HCA appeal**: See *Mallard v R* [1997] 18 Leg Rep C20a.

313 **The Law's treatment of lie detector tests**: See *Mallard v R* (2003) 28 WAR 1; *R v Murray* (1982) 7 A Crim R 48 (NSW). This is also the position in Canada (see *R v Beland* (1987) 43 DLR (4th) 641, 649 (McIntyre J); *R v Marquard* (1993) 85 CCC (3d) 193, 228–229 (McLachlan J)), but not the case in some jurisdictions of the United States (see *Frye v United States* 293 F 1013, 1014 (1923); *Aetna Insurance Co v Barnett Brothers Inc* 289 F 2d 30 (1961); *People v Monigan* 390 NE 2d 562 (1979)). See also J. Furedy and J. Liss, 'Countering Confessions Induced by the Polygraph: Of Confessionals and Psychological Rubber Hoses' (1986) 29 *Criminal Law Quarterly* 91; E. Magner, 'Exclusion of Polygraph Evidence: Can It Be Justified?' (1988) 30 *Criminal Law Quarterly* 412; D. Elliott, 'Lie Detector Evidence: Lessons from the American Experience' in E. Campbell and L. Waller (eds), *Well and Truly Tried* (Sydney: Law Book Co., 1982), 100; J. Edelman, 'Admissibility of polygraph (lie detector) examinations' (2005) 29 *Crim Law Journal* 2.

314 **'... the police failed to disclose evidence'**: There is a general disclosure rule under the common law that requires the prosecution disclose to the defence its case against the defence, and also any material which could be said to:

• be relevant or possibly relevant to an issue in dispute in the case;

• raise or possibly raise a new issue not apparent from the prosecution's case; or

• hold out a real, as opposed to fanciful, prospect of providing a lead to evidence which goes to either (a) or (b) above.

See *Mallard v R* (2003) 28 WAR 1; *Easterday v R* (2003) 143 A Crim R 154. The common law rule is further complemented by a series of statutory disclosure mechanisms under sections 35, 42 and 95 of the *Civil Procedure Act 2004* (WA).

315 **'... Attorney-General Jim McGinty agreed to refer the case ...'**: See Chapter 6 note 126, Chapter 10 note 207.

316 **'... perception of bias'**: See note 311. For consideration in the Mallard case see *Mallard v R* (2003) 28 WAR 1, 79–80 (Parker, Wheeler and Roberts-Smith JJ).

317 **Mallard's 2003 CCA appeal**: See *Mallard v R* (2003) 28 WAR 1.

318 **Mallard's HCA special leave to appeal**: See Chapter 7 note 169; *Mallard v R* [2004] HCATrans 421.

319 **Mallard's successful HCA appeal**: See *Mallard v R* (2005) 224 CLR 125.

320 **The Corruption and Crime Commission report**: Corruption and Crime Commission of Western Australia, *Report on the Inquiry into Alleged Misconduct by Public Officers in Connection with the Investigation of the Murder of Mrs Pamela Lawrence, The Prosecution and Appeals of Mr Andrew Mark Mallard, and Other Related Matters*, Western Australian government, Perth, 17 October 2008.

321 **The Karpa fraud trial**: See R. Coulthart, 'Karpa Gold Fall Guys', *Sunday*, Nine Network Australia, 18 May 2003 (transcript available at http://sunday.ninemsn.com.au/sunday/cover_stories/transcript_1276.asp). For Ireland and Easterday's original appeal against conviction see *Ireland v R* (Unreported, Western Australian Court of Criminal Appeal, Pidgeon, Rowland and Wallwork JJ, 6 May 1994).

322 **'"the convictions were unsafe and unsatisfactory ..."'**: *Easterday v The Queen* [2003] WASCA 69 (28 March 2003) para 216.

323 **'"If its real we can't afford not to be part of it, and if it's fake we can at least talk our way out of it"'**: R. Coulthart, 'Karpa Gold Fall Guys', *Sunday*, Nine Network Australia, 18 May 2003 (transcript available at http://sunday. ninemsn.com.au/sunday/cover_stories/transcript_1276.asp).

324 **The Karpa fraud appeal**: See *Easterday v R* (2003) 143 A Crim R 154.

CHAPTER 16

325 **'... the Court of Criminal Appeal reconvened'**: The week before, Justice Murray had presided over a hearing by the brothers for access to police running sheets and information notes from the 1982 Mint swindle. See *Raymond Mickelberg v R* [2003] WASCA 292 (Unreported, Supreme Court of Western Australia, Murray J, 28 November 2003).

326 ***Ebner v Official Trustee in Bankruptcy* and judicial bias**: See *Ebner v Official Trustee in Bankruptcy* (2000) 205 CLR 337, 344–5. Somewhat uniquely, it is up to the individual judge to disqualify themselves, or to hear any objection made by the parties against the judge hearing the case. An improper refusal by a judge to disqualify themselves can be a ground of appeal but cannot otherwise be brought into question (*Rajski v Wood* [1977] 1 NSWLR 333). Also see *Laws v Australian Broadcasting Tribunal* (1990) 170 CLR 70, 87 (Mason CJ and Brennan J); *R v Maxwell* (1998) 217 ALR 452. Such an apprehension is a distinct possibility where, such as here, the judge had expressed views on relevant issues of fact or as to the credibility of witnesses in an earlier case (*Grassby v R* (1989) 168 CLR 1), or where the judge has previously appeared as counsel against a party to the proceedings (*Western Australia v Watson* [1990] WAR 248).

327 **Ray's comments on the judiciary**: See J. Flint, 'Judge should not have heard appeal', *The Sunday Times*, 25 July 2004, 7.

328 **'"the prudent course would, in my opinion, ordinarily be one of self-disqualification in such cases"'**: This case was *McCreed v R* (2003) 27 WAR 554. Steytler J dealt with this issue extensively, providing a comprehensive

exposition of Australian cases decided on this issue. *Webb v R* ((1994) 181 CLR 41) was considered particularly important with Deane J in that case (at 74) identifying four overlapping categories for disqualification being 'interest, conduct, association and extraneous information.' An objection will only prevail if a 'substantial ground' can be identified, and while in Australia the fact that a judge has previously prosecuted the defendant will often be sufficient to require a judge disqualify himself (contrary to the US position, see *McCreed*, 560-1 (Steytler J)), this was not such a case. Although the prior offence (murder) was extremely serious, that Murray J had no independent recollection of the prosecution, the extensive period of time that had elapsed (eleven and a half years), the lack of relationship between the present trial and the previous prosecution, and that nothing unusual or untoward occurred in the course of the prosecution meant that Steytler was not satisfied that this was a case where disqualification was necessary (at 561).

329 **Guide to Judicial Conduct**: Anonymous, *Guide to Judicial Conduct*, (2nd ed. Melbourne: The Australasian Institute of Judicial Administration Incorporated (published for The Council of Chief Justices of Australia), 2007).

330 **'... [the court] was required to consider the case in its entirety ...'**: Under ss.140(1)(a) of the *Sentencing Act 1995* (WA) the petition granted in this case was 'for the whole case to be heard and determined as if it were an appeal by the offender against the conviction or against the sentence ... '. This therefore required a hearing of the entire case. See further Chapter 12 note 229.

331 **'"the proper motivation of a prosecutor is to secure the result to which, on his view, the evidence fairly leads"'**: A. Ashworth, 'Prosecution and Procedure in Criminal Justice' [1979] *Criminal Law Review* 81–492, 482.

332 **The prosecutor's role**: J. Fionda, *Public Prosecutors and Discretion: A Comparative Study* (Oxford: Clarendon Press, 1995), 58. Fionda notes the neutrality role was central to the establishment of the Crown Prosecuting Service in 1986 in the United Kingdom, which is the equivalent of the DPP in Australia. In general terms a public prosecutor must act fairly, in the public interest, and only proceed where there is a 'prima facie case.' For an at length coverage of the prosecutor's role see sections 9–14 and appendix 1 (International Association of Prosecutors, *Standards of Professional Responsibility And Statement Of The Essential Duties And Rights of Prosecutors*) of the Director of Public Prosecutions R. Cox QC, *Statement of Prosecution Policy and Guidelines 2005*, Director of Public Prosecutions for Western Australia, Perth, 3 June 2005.

333 **'Bennett asked Gillespie to explain inconsistencies in the evidence he gave at trial about his conversation with Sheryl Mickelberg at the Whitford City Shopping Centre'**: Detective Round had also taken part in this conversation. A third officer, Porter, was there but apparently did not participate in the conversation.

CHAPTER 17

334 **Alice Lynne (Lindy) Chamberlain**: On the night of 17 August 1980, while on a camping trip to Uluru in the Northern Territory, Chamberlain reported that her two month old daughter Azaria had been taken from her tent by a dingo. On 29 October 1982 Lindy was convicted of her murder. The most

important evidence against Lindy (and her husband Michael, convicted as an accessory) were tests that indicated the presence of blood in the Chamberlains' car. Lindy's subsequent appeals against conviction were unsuccessful (*Chamberlain v R* (1983) 72 FLR 1 (Full Federal Court Appeal); *Chamberlain v R* (1983) 153 CLR 514 (High Court Appeal); *Chamberlain v R (No 2)* (1984) 153 CLR 521 (Full High Court Appeal)). On 2 February 1986 some of Azaria's clothing was found near a dingo lair suggesting innocence and it later emerged under new DNA technology that the 'blood' could have been another substance. Lindy was released on 7 February 1986 and the convictions were quashed on 15 September 1988 (see *Reference under s.433A of the Criminal Code by the Attorney-General for the Northern Territory of Australia of convictions of Alice Lynne Chamberlain and Michael Leigh Chamberlain* [1988] NTSC 64 (Unreported, Supreme Court of the Northern Territory of Australia, Asche CJ, Nader and Kearney JJ, 15 September 1988)).

335 **The final appeal judgment**: See *Peter Mickelberg v R; Raymond Mickelberg v R* (2004) 29 WAR 13.

336 **Recanting witnesses**: Complex evidential issues arise where a witness recants on earlier evidence given in proceedings. The credibility of a witness who confesses to having lied to and misled the court on previous occasions cannot be great. Justice Steytler set out the approach in Western Australia for recanting witnesses comprehensively in his judgment in the final appeal judgment (see the heading 'Recanting Witnesses' in *Peter Mickelberg v R; Raymond Mickelberg v R* (2004) 29 WAR 13, 132–137 (Steytler J)). Steytler cited cases such as *Davies and Cody v R* (1937) 57 CLR 170; *R v Bryer* (1994) 75 A Crim R 456; *R v Gale* [1970] VR 669; *R v Geesing* (1985) 38 SASR 226; *Bourne v Ellis* [2001] WASCA 290 (Unreported, Supreme Court of Western Australia, Malcolm CJ, Miller and Roberts-Smith JJ, 27 September 2001), and concluded that while a recantation of evidence given by a witness will undoubtedly affect that witness's credibility, it cannot itself be grounds for setting aside a verdict on appeal. Such evidence will, however, usually be considered to be 'fresh evidence' and admissible on appeal.

337 **'It was, [Steytler J] said, "very probable that a jury would accept that evidence"'**: Lewandowski denied making the confessions to Goff, Broad and Gordon but Justice Steytler said these denials 'may be explicable upon the basis that in almost every case they were said to have been made while he was in an inebriated condition.'

338 **'... Steytler's decision not to disregard Lewandowski's "tainted" evidence ...'**: Noteworthily, Justice Steytler repeated what was said in *Davies and Cody v R* (1937) 57 CLR 203 and *M v R* (1994) 181 CLR 487, 493 (Mason CJ, Deane, Toohey and Dawson JJ): 'The duty imposed on a court of appeal to quash a conviction when it thinks that on any ground there was a miscarriage of justice covers: "not only cases where there is affirmative reason to suppose that the appellant is innocent, but also cases of quite another description. For it will set aside a conviction whenever it appears unjust or unsafe to allow the verdict to stand because some failure has occurred in observing the conditions which, in the court's view, are essential to a satisfactory trial, or because there is some feature of the case raising possibility that, either in the conclusion itself, or in the manner in which it had been reached, the jury may have been mistaken or misled."'

339 **Toohey and Gaudron JJ**: *Peter Mickelberg v R; Raymond Mickelberg v R* (1989) 167 CLR 259, 303.

340 '... **"a great day for WA justice"'**: A. Mayes and D. King, 'Mickelberg verdicts quashed', *The Weekend Australian*, 3–4 July 2004, 8.

341 **Irene Burns' statement to the media**: T. Mendez, 'Stars miss finale of long-running drama', *West Australian*, 3 July 2004, 8.

342 **Mel Hay's statement to the media**: L. Eliot, 'Police say evidence still strong', *West Australian*, 3 July 2004, 7. See further Epilogue note 364.

343 **'"It is unusual for a person accused to be able to prove quite clearly that he or she is innocent ..."'**: C. Porter, *The Conviction of the Innocent: How the law can let us down* (North Sydney: Random House, 2007), 3–4.

344 **'"If the law represents an expression of moral sentiment, then police officers stand as instruments of that morality"'**: B. Harrison, 'Noble Cause Corruption and the Police Ethic' (1999) 68(8) *Law Enforcement Bulletin* 1, 2.

345 **'"If you didn't do it, who did?"'**: ibid.

EPILOGUE

346 '... **payments "made by the government to an individual who has suffered harm at their hands without any strict legal obligation to do so"'**: D. Varne, *The Civil Liability of the State of Western Australia for the Torts of Members of the Western Australian Police*, Unpublished Honours Thesis, Law School, The University of Western Australia, 2008, 13 (the 'Varne Thesis').

347 **'"We didn't start this. The assistant commissioner Melvyn Hay started it and we never give in"'**: D. King, '"Distressed" Mickelbergs to sue senior officer', *The Australian*, 7 July 2004, 6.

348 **'The fighting Ray said ...'**: T. Mendez, 'Writ and challenge for top cop', *West Australian*, 7 July 2004, 9.

349 **'Peter told reporters ...'**: D. King, '"Distressed" Mickelbergs to sue senior officer', *The Australian*, 7 July 2004, 6.

350 **Brian Singleton and the other Mint plan**: T. Mendez, 'Brothers back with a vengeance', *West Australian*, 7 July 2004, 9.

351 **'As well, they were pursuing a civil action ... against a number of the officers involved in the initial investigation team. They had also joined the state to this civil action ...'**: Supreme Court CIV 1628 of 2003.

352 **The Mickelbergs**: Ray and Peter had also joined the estate of their deceased brother Brian as a plaintiff.

353 **Tortious liability of the state for police misconduct**: *Enever v R* (1906) 3 CLR 969; *Attorney-General (UK) v Goddard* (1929) 98 LJKB 743; *Grimwade v Victoria* (1997) 90 A Crim R 562, 570. See further, Varne Thesis.

354 **'"with independent discretion to carry out particular tasks under statute and therefore not an employee of the State"'**: Varne Thesis, 6. Other officers with an independent discretion include magistrates (*Thompson v Williams* (1914) 32 WN (NSW) 27), legal aid officers (*Field v Nott* (1939) 62 CLR 660), the commissioner of taxation (*Clyne v DCT (NSW) (No 5)* (1982)

13 ATR 677), Crown prosecutors (*Grimwade v Victoria* (1997) 90 A Crim R 526) and collectors of customs (*Baume v Commonwealth* (1906) 4 CLR 97). Varne Thesis (7) continues: '[a]lthough well established, this position has been criticised considerably both judicially and by commentators as arbitrary, having unfair consequences and based on outdated precedent. It has been over-ruled at common law in some jurisdictions, and there has also been a general legislative trend to reduce or eliminate the effects of the rule by either express legislative abolition or by deeming the police to be Crown-employees for specific matters.' (footnotes omitted). Also see Varne Thesis, 7 footnotes 34–8.

355 **'Martin Bennett told the media ...'**: S. Cowan and M. Lam, 'You owe us, say brothers', *West Australian*, 9 August 2004, 7.

356 **The Perth Mint's civil actions**: S. Cowan, 'Returned gold to fund legal campaign', *West Australian*, 14 August 2004, 3; P. Taylor, 'Mickelberg back in mint condition', *The Australian*, 14 August 2004, 3. The Perth Mint had also earlier in 1983 commenced civil proceedings against the Mickelberg brothers claiming damages for fraud or deceit as arising from the Mint swindle. Those proceedings were unsuccessful (see *Perth Mint v Peter Mickelberg and Raymond Mickelberg* [1984] WAR 230; *Perth Mint v Peter Mickelberg and Raymond Mickelberg* [1985] WAR 117). See also *Peter Mickelberg and Raymond Mickelberg v Director of Perth Mint* [1986] WAR 365. The 1986 *Mickelberg v Director of Perth Mint* case has become an important legal precedent in its own right as authority for the proposition that evidence of criminal convictions is admissible in civil proceedings as proof of the plaintiff's involvement in the criminal acts. This abolished the rule in *Hollington v Hewthorn* which previously prohibited this (*Hollington v F Hewthorn & Co Ltd* [1943] KB 587). See *Minh Dung Luu v Minister for Immigration and Multicultural Affairs* (1998) 86 FCR 304; *Roberts v Western Australia* (2005) 29 WAR 445; *Director of Public Prosecutions v Mansfield* (2006) 161 A Crim R 210. In fact, a report of the Law Reform Commission of Western Australia had recommended this change in 1972 but the proposed legislation abolishing the rule was no longer needed after the 1986 decision (Law Reform Commission of Western Australia, *Project No 20: Evidence of Criminal Convictions in Civil Proceedings* (April 1972)).

357 **'In late June 2007, Master Newnes of the Supreme Court of Western Australia struck out the Mickelbergs' civil action'**: *Raymond Mickelberg, Peter Mickelberg and (the estate of) Brian Mickelberg v The Queen* [2007] WASC 140 (Unreported, Supreme Court of Western Australia, Newnes J, 29 June 2007). Under Order 20 Rule 19 of the *Rules of the Supreme Court 1971* (WA), a party to a civil action can make an application to 'strike-out' aspects of a plaintiff's case before trial if, amongst other things, that particular aspect of the plaintiff's case 'discloses no reasonable cause of action' against the defendant. Here, as the law clearly states that the state is *not* legally liable for the damages sustained by the brothers, there was no 'cause of action' against the state and the claim against it was struck out.

358 **The compensation negotiations**: The primary source used here was correspondence between the Mickelberg brothers through Malcolm McCusker QC and the Attorney-General Jim McGinty.

359 **Vincent Narkle**: Narkle did claim he had been coerced into signing a con-

fession but this was disputed and the Court of Criminal Appeal did not accept the claim. For Narkle's unsuccessful appeal see *Narkle v R* (Unreported, Supreme Court Western Australia Court of Criminal Appeal, Ipp, Murray and Anderson JJ, 23 June 1993). For the 2006 quashing of Narkle's conviction see *Narkle v R* [2006] WASCA 113 (Unreported, Supreme Court Western Australia Court of Criminal Appeal, Steytler P, Wheeler and McLure JJA, 12 April 2006).

360 **The formula**: McGinty denied that such a formula or 'tariff' was in place and that the figures for Narkle and Button were arrived at due to the particular circumstances of each case and just happened to equate to $9,000 per month of gaol. Of course, based on what Martin Bennett had previously said, the thrust of the compensation claim was not to arrive at a value for time spent in prison but the value of assets the Mickelbergs lost due to their wrongful imprisonment.

361 **The police apologise**: G. Adshead and S. Cowan, 'We're sorry, police tell Mickelbergs', *West Australian*, 15 December 2007, 1–2. Also see B. Cowie, 'Mickelberg Brothers Entitled to Presumption of Innocence,' *Police Media Release*, 15 December 2007. The apology plus a cash payment brought the defamation action to an end.

362 **Negotiations continue:** G. Adshead, 'Mickelbergs win $1m comp payout', *West Australian*, 16 January 2008, 1, 14.

363 **'... Mick Dean, was also unhappy'**: G. Adshead, 'Union in threat to brothers' Mint deal', *West Australian*, 17 January 2008, 5.

364 **Ray's stealing charge:** See N. Prior, 'Mickelberg to fight Bunnings shoplifting charge', *West Australian*, 30 January 2009, 3.

365 **'Finally in May 2009 the WA Police Union agreed to settle the Mickelbergs' civil action by making a confidential monetary payout'**: See G. Adshead, 'Police union payout to Mickelberg brothers,' *West Australian*, 2 May 2009, 1. Adshead states that it was 'believed to be a six-figure deal.'

366 **Andrew Mallard's compensation:** For information about the ex gratia payment offer made to Mallard, see Western Australia, *Parliamentary Debates*, Legislative Assembly, 5 May 2009, 3279b–3280a, (Hon. Christian Porter). For Mallard's initial response, see A. Banks and R. Taylor, 'Mallard fears a return to court', *West Australian*, 8 May 2009, 19. For Mallard's conditional acceptance of the $3.25 million see P. Taylor, '$3m payout won't stop lawsuit, says Mallard', *The Australian*, 26 May 2009, 5; A. Banks, 'Mallard accepts $3.25m gift', *West Australian*, 25 May 2009, 3.

367 **Peter Mickelberg and John Button's reaction to the Mallard compensation:** G. Williams and T. Cardy, 'Wrongly jailed demand fair compo', *Sunday Times*, 14 June 2009, 4. Williams and Cardy note that Mallard received the equivalent of $741 per day of imprisonment compared to the $199 per day given to both Peter Mickelberg and John Button and the $167 per day given to Raymond. This also compares to the $250 per day given as compensation for those imprisoned for too long after defaulting on the payment of fines under the new s.108A of the *Fines, Penalties and Infringement Notices Enforcement Act 1994* (WA) (introduced by the *Fines, Penalties and Infringement Notices Enforcement Amendment (Compensation) Act 2009* (WA).

368 '**... ongoing disputes and concerns have led some to call for an independent body to be responsible for the making of ex gratia payments'**: See Malcolm McCusker QC's comments in D. Emerson, 'Change payout law for wrongful jailing: QC', *West Australian*, 22 October 2009, 13. In general terms ex gratia payments are made as an exercise of executive (or prerogative) power that is totally discretionary (T. Percy, 'Despised outsiders: compensation for wrongful convictions' (2007) 81 *Precedent* 20, 20; S. Arrowsmith, *Civil Liability and Public Authorities* (Winteringham: Earlsgate, 1992), 244–8), with no fixed rules operating (S. Major, 'Am I Special Enough? The Payment of Ex Gratia Compensation by the Commonwealth' (1995) 6 *Australian Institute of Administrative Law Forum* 14, 14, 16; Arrowsmith, *Civil Liability and Public Authorities* (Winteringham: Earlsgate, 1992), 247–8) and no judicial review available (S. Major, 'Am I Special Enough? The Payment of Ex Gratia Compensation by the Commonwealth' (1995) 6 *Australian Institute of Administrative Law Forum* 14, 14, 16; S. Arrowsmith, *Civil Liability and Public Authorities* (Winteringham: Earlsgate, 1992), 247–8.). The final Mickelberg payout also shows that these payments can be entirely confidential. Arbitrariness tends to emerge when considering the various discretionary decision making of the executive in this context or when comparing different decisions made at different times by different governments or ministers (T. Percy, 'Despised outsiders: compensation for wrongful convictions' (2007) 81 *Precedent* 20, 20–1). Payments are also often inadequate in quantum and generally far less than if judicially ascertained (G. Walsh, 'Injury by Justice: Inadequacy of Ex-Gratia Compensation for Wrongful Conviction' (1994) 32(5) *Law Society Journal* 32, 6; T. Percy, 'Despised outsiders: compensation for wrongful convictions' (2007) 81 *Precedent* 20, 20). Although there is some guidance provided for the provision of ex gratia payments under section 80 of the *Financial Management Act 2006* (WA), reg. 8 of the *Financial Management Regulations 2007* (WA) and Treasurer's Instruction 319 made pursuant to section 78 of the *Financial Management Act 2006* (WA), the problems of arbitrariness and an unbridled governmental discretion remain. This can be contrasted with the practice in the United Kingdom since 1988 where an independent commission is responsible for deciding whether any ex gratia payment is made and if so, the quantum of that payment. See section 133 of the *English Criminal Justice Act 1988* (UK) implementing article 14.6 of the *International Covenant on Civil and Political Rights* (*International Covenant on Civil and Political Rights*, opened for signature 16 December 1966, 999 UNTS 171 (entered into force 23 March 1976).

369 **Ray's cancer battle:** G. Adshead, 'Mickelberg faces cancer battle', *West Australian*, 9 May 2009, 5.

INDEX